INTIMATE ALIEN

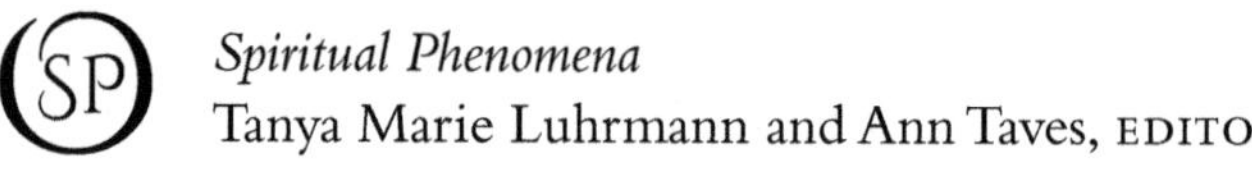

Spiritual Phenomena
Tanya Marie Luhrmann and Ann Taves, EDITORS

Intimate Alien

THE HIDDEN STORY OF THE UFO

David J. Halperin

STANFORD UNIVERSITY PRESS
Stanford, California

STANFORD UNIVERSITY PRESS
Stanford, California

Library of Congress Cataloging-in-Publication Data
Names: Halperin, David J. (David Joel), author.
Title: Intimate alien : the hidden story of the UFO / David J. Halperin.
Other titles: Spiritual phenomena.
Description: Stanford : Stanford University Press, 2020. |
Series: Spiritual phenomena | Includes bibliographical references and index.
Identifiers: LCCN 2019033546 (print) | LCCN 2019033547 (ebook) |
ISBN 9781503607088 (cloth) | ISBN 9781503612129 (epub)
Subjects: LCSH: Halperin, David J. (David Joel) | Unidentified flying objects—Mythology. | Unidentified flying objects—Psychological aspects. | Unidentified flying objects—Sightings and encounters—History. | Social psychology—United States. | Ufologists—United States—Biography.
Classification: LCC TL789 .H355 2020 (print) | LCC TL789 (ebook) |
DDC 001.942092 [B]—dc23
LC record available at https://lccn.loc.gov/2019033546
LC ebook record available at https://lccn.loc.gov/2019033547

Cover design: Rob Ehle

Cover photo: iStock

Text design: Kevin Barrett Kane

Typeset at Stanford University Press in 12/15 Bembo Std

To Rose

CONTENTS

FIGURES

INTIMATE ALIEN

INTRODUCTION

THIS IS A BOOK ABOUT UFOS. Most such books try to make a case for UFOs' physical existence as visitors from other planets or possibly other dimensions. A much smaller but still substantial chunk of the literature will argue that they're a sustained absurdity, a mishmash of honest human mistakes compounded by dishonest ones. Those are the two main currents of thought on the subject: that of the "believers" and that of the "debunkers."

I'm writing as someone with a particular investment in the topic. Back in the 1960s, I was a teenage "UFOlogist." I grew up to be a professor of religious studies whose main research interests have been religious traditions of heavenly ascents and otherworldly journeys. I've worked with the visions of the Biblical prophet Ezekiel, particularly the first and strangest of them: the vision of the "living creatures" and the wheels that sometimes rested on the ground, sometimes flew in the air. In other words, UFOs.

I don't believe, nor do I debunk. This book will advocate for a third way.

My starting point: *UFOs are a myth.* But in saying this, I don't mean what you might think I do.

A little over fifty years ago, two books appeared within a few years of each other bearing almost identical titles—and almost opposite messages. One was *The World of Flying Saucers: A Scientific Examination of a Major Myth of the Space Age*, by astrophysicist Donald Menzel. The other was *Flying Saucers: A Modern Myth of Things Seen in the Skies*, by psychologist Carl Jung. Menzel, the most vocal and prominent UFO skeptic of the era, used *myth* as people often do, to mean "bunk, nonsense," or at least something that isn't true. For Jung the word had nearly the opposite meaning: not falsehood, but the profoundest truth of all.

Jung's writings are notoriously dense and difficult. *Flying Saucers*, the last book he published before his death in 1961, is no exception. How valiantly I struggled through it as a budding UFOlogist, just past my thirteenth birthday! (It was one of three books on UFOs in our local library.) Of course I could make neither head nor tail of it. I hadn't a clue about the assumption on which it rests: that our ordinary awareness is an eggshell boat on the vast roiling sea of the unconscious, the deeper ("collective") levels of which we share with all other humans.

These depths, accessed through individual dreams and the collective dreams called myths, aren't always bright or benign. But they're holy, or "numinous," as Jung liked to say: uncanny, transcendent, timeless. When a myth takes visible form, when it's projected into the sky as a flying disk (or "mandala," as Jung would say), that's a major event, akin to what our ancestors might have called a vision of God.

All this is controversial, hardly less so than UFOs themselves. I find Jung's models just plausible enough that I'm prepared to use them as tools if they make sense of the otherwise unintelligible.

When other tools work, I also take them up gladly. The insights of twenty-first century cognitive psychologists into the evolutionary grounding of our disposition toward myth add depth and poignancy to our human inclination to trust what the Bible calls "the evidence of things not seen" (Hebrews 11:1). The timeworn Freudian dictum that "every memory returning from the forgotten past . . . puts forward an irresistible claim to be believed, against which all logical objections remain powerless" turns out to shed unexpected light on some of the thornier riddles of the UFO. None of these approaches can be ignored.

In his emphasis on the gravity of myth, on the force of its claim to our attention and respect, Jung marks out the path I've chosen to travel. As "myth," UFOs *aren't* nonsense. They're about the furthest thing from "bunk" that can be imagined. They're a creation of the space age and yet as real, as vital, as universal as any myth that has spoken from our unconscious since the dawn of prehistory. The central question that needs to be asked about them isn't, What are they? or Where do they come from? or, conversely, How can any sensible person believe such rubbish? The question is, *What do they mean?*

Should we care?

Grant that UFOs are a myth. Or even more: a full mythology, complex and ramified, stretching into areas of experience that seem far removed from objects in the sky, its true subject not space aliens but who we are as human beings. Yet there's a sharp difference between UFOlogy and the great mythical systems of the past, such as that of the Greeks. Those mythologies were the consensus beliefs of entire cultures. UFOs seem doomed to a shadow existence on the fringes of ours.

They may have "conquered the world," as the title of a recent book on UFOs puts it, but it's a hollow sort of conquest. More than seventy years after their emergence, they show no sign of going away, but neither do they show the smallest capacity to move into the mainstream. They remain the province of the eccentric, the discontented, and the deluded, if at times the wildly gifted. Can a mythology of losers and misfits be of any significance for the rest of us?

The following reply suggests itself: Who says the rest of us are nonmisfits, nonlosers? "Fitting" in this life is a painful, difficult, always inadequate process, and at the end each and every one of us loses that which our whole being strains most terribly to keep. We point a mocking finger at the "losers," the "kooks," the marginal. Beneath our laughter is an awareness that we're not really so different. What we see in those "losers" is here in all of us.

"The words of the prophets are written on the subway walls / And tenement halls," Simon and Garfunkel sang a generation and a half ago. As a scholar of religion, I've been well served by Freud's insight that it's often the jumbled and bizarre, the disreputable and seemingly senseless that's the pathway into our deepest secrets. A mythology of the fringe is not to be presumed negligible, especially when it's as plugged into the wider society as this one is. From the hinterlands, UFOs cast their shadows across our culture.

Ever hear of Roswell, New Mexico? Area 51? Chances are you have, even if you're not sure exactly what's supposed to have happened at Roswell or what Area 51, the top-secret tract of Nevada desert that's seen some of the Cold War's most horrific weapons tests, has to do with UFOs. When Barack Obama declared in 2013 that "when you first become president, one of the questions that people ask you is, 'What's really going on in Area 51?'" of course he was joking. But the joke would have fallen flat if there'd been no truth in it that his audience could understand and appreciate. Hillary Clinton may have been less than serious in promising a New Hampshire reporter that if elected in 2016 she'd "get to the bottom" of UFOs, sending a "task force" to Area 51. But would she have said such things if she hadn't calculated that "courting the UFO believer vote," as one web headline put it, would resonate with a substantial chunk of her constituency? And when some cartoon or advertisement depicts a creature with a face shaped like an old-fashioned light bulb and just as hairless, dominated by two enormous slanted, solid-black eyes, do you need to be told it's an alien?

"Thirty-six percent of Americans, about 80 million people, believe UFOs exist," ABC News announced in June 2012 on the basis of a study by the National Geographic Channel. Nearly four-fifths of those polled, moreover, thought the government was hiding something about UFOs. These figures, which can't have escaped the shrewd Ms. Clinton, were in line with earlier surveys that suggest that an even larger percentage of Americans—something like half—believe in UFOs. This is not exactly a "fringe." Not only are the UFOs embedded in our cultural awareness. In very considerable numbers, we seem to think they're real.

Yet not to be taken seriously. In our culture UFOs are funny; those who see them, funnier; and those "fringe" types for whom they're a significant part of reality, the funniest of all. This is a paradox, one of many to be explored in this book. Why does the UFO-themed *Close Encounters of the Third Kind* gross over $300 million and become a cinema classic, while organizations dedicated to UFO research languish for want of public interest? Why, in the words of folklorist Thomas Bullard, are UFOs "at once so popular and so despised?"

The resolution of the paradox lies in the slippery, elusive, "as-if" quality of UFO belief, which needs to be explored if we're to understand its significance. This is a peculiar sort of belief, not quite what it appears on the surface. I should know. I once held it myself.

When Donald Menzel's *The World of Flying Saucers* appeared in 1963, I was fifteen years old. I'd been a UFOlogist for two and a half of those years. I was not quite at the zenith of my UFO career, but I was approaching it. I'd known about Menzel's book for a couple of months before I got my hands on a copy, and I dreaded the encounter.

I'd been warned: Menzel was the most persuasive of the UFO skeptics. His explanations of UFO sightings were so convincing that even the committed UFOlogists with whom I exchanged ten- and twenty-page letters in those pre-internet days—they were mostly teenage boys like me—found their faith wavering. Would the same happen to me?

Then I read the book, and my fears were assuaged.

This was the same-old, same-old, I decided: a stuck-up, closed-minded scientific debunker parroting the line fed him by the Air Force debunkers. The UFOs were still flying as far as I was concerned, whether Professor Menzel liked it or not.

There's something wrong with this picture. My belief at the time, which I held *with complete sincerity*—I can't say this emphatically enough—was that UFOs were hostile. They'd come not as benevolent "space brothers" but as attackers, very likely as invaders. The newly discovered laser beams might be Earth's best hope for self-defense. So shouldn't I have been relieved to be convinced UFOs *didn't* exist, and not the reverse?

I'd read H. G. Wells's *The War of the Worlds*. I had a pretty good idea, or at least a scary fantasy, of what an invasion from space would be like. Surely I should have felt some trepidation at the prospect? Yet I know for a fact that I wasn't one hundredth as afraid of the looming invasion as I was of my father's rages, or of the possibility that if I were ever to ask a girl for a date, she'd say, "*Go out . . . with YOU???!!!*" and spread it all over the school.

An "as-if" belief: Something that's believed but not truly believed—the way I believe, say, that if I step in front of a moving vehicle, I'm apt to land in the hospital. A "let's-pretend" belief. Yet at the same time absolutely real.

I'm not the only person to have held such a belief. Again and again, invited to bet real money that we'd see mass UFO landings in the near future, prominent UFO advocates have squirmed away from the challenge. Were they insincere? No more than I was; I'd have responded the same way. "I say that such belief has no reality," George Orwell once wrote in a different but comparable context. "It is a sham currency." But my belief wasn't a sham. It did have reality. Just not the reality I thought it had.

My UFO belief was a stand-in for something left unexpressed, a representation of something indeed fearsome, indeed hostile, in my real, everyday life at the time. It needed to be acknowledged; it could not be acknowledged. It was a thing called *death*—specifically, my mother's impending death—and like Medusa's face in the ancient myth, it could be viewed only in a mirror.

Shatter that mirror, as Menzel threatened to do, and I'd have been left to face the unfaccable.

It's not only UFO belief that demands our scrutiny. UFO *disbelief* does as well.

At first sight this statement seems odd. Menzel was right: there are no spaceships hurtling around our skies. Isn't denying them a simple acknowledgment of reality? But it's not so simple. UFO debunkers sometimes betray an emotional engagement that suggests a motivation beyond the rational.

An example: When the American Association for the Advancement of Science scheduled a symposium on UFOs for December 1969, some in the association went so far as to send letters to members of Congress, even to then-Vice President Spiro Agnew, demanding that they force its cancellation. No wonder that two psychiatrists who spoke at the imperiled conference came away with the impression that believers and disbelievers alike are invested in UFOs, perhaps in parallel ways. At issue, the psychiatrists suggested, was an "unconscious concern with death and immortality." For believers, the UFO "symbolically represents a denial of the finite nature of life." On the other hand, "those who have a need to deny that there is any anxiety at all around the issues of death and immortality may be led to attack the hypothesis with considerable passion."

I won't insist that the psychiatrists' interpretation is correct, although for reasons that will soon become clear it resonates strongly for me, and evidence supporting it will accumulate in the course of the book. The essential point is that UFOs are capable of evoking visceral fury (or panic?) among those who don't believe in them, as well as spacy enthusiasm among those who do. Such is their power to override what we think of as normal rationality. To understand that power, to trace the ways in which it plays itself out in our society and others, at present and in the past, is what this book is about.

The UFO doesn't happen only, or even primarily, or even authentically in the sky. The witness is as much a part of the sighting as the object witnessed. So are those who hear the story, who believe it, who transmit it in speech or in writing, in the newspapers or on the internet. Those who debunk it, who ridicule it, who make the unfortunate witness's life a misery for daring to speak of it—they're part of the sighting too. The UFO mystery is the mystery of *them*, or more correctly the mystery of *us*.

Where does one begin to explore so protean an enigma? I begin with *me*.

I know the hold UFOs once had on me. I know also that they still do. To cite Orwell again, I believe the years have given me the perspective to "feel the emotional tug of such things, and yet see them dispassionately for what they are." So in following the trail of what I call the "hidden story of the UFO," I'll start with my own story. From there I'll branch off to the stories of others.

I won't offer an explanation for each and every UFO sighting. I freely admit that many remain unsolved. These include the Kenneth Arnold sighting with which the UFO era began; they include the 1964 physical-trace episode in Socorro, New Mexico, described in my first chapter. I've never seen a satisfying explanation of the latter incident, which has reasonably been called (albeit with a question mark attached) "the best UFO case ever?" A few other cases where UFOs are reported to have left marks of their presence behind them—never, let it be noted, an actual piece of hardware that can be analyzed and shown to be otherworldly[1]—continue to perplex.

In my UFOlogist days, I would have declared such cases the solid nucleus of the phenomenon, proof that something tangible and alien had penetrated our skies. Grant that 90 percent of the reports, say, could be explained; as long as 10 percent were unsolved, the reality of the UFO was established. I'm now more struck by how unlikely it is that we can have had alien visitors for over seventy years with only a handful of genuinely puzzling incidents to attest to their presence.

No, I can't explain the photos taken by an Oregon farmer in May 1950, which seem to show a solid disk-shaped object in the sky. (Did the farmer and his wife hoax them? They would have been acting out of character, but people sometimes do that.) But I'm more impressed by the challenge posed by present-day skeptics: Why haven't the twenty-first century's incomparably greater opportunities for on-the-spot photography produced a harvest of equally persuasive pictures? And the mysterious light that triggered the first of the UFO abduction reports (as described in chapter 3),

---

1 In December 2017, veteran *New York Times* correspondent Ralph Blumenthal revealed, on the basis of what seemed good authority, that certain buildings in Las Vegas had been modified to store "metal alloys and other materials . . . recovered from unidentified aerial phenomena." Interviewed on MSNBC, Blumenthal went yet further: "They have, as we reported in the paper, some material from these objects that is being studied so that scientists can try to figure out what accounts for their amazing properties . . . some kind of compound that they don't recognize." If this turns out to be true, it wouldn't be just "news that's fit to print" as the *Times* slogan has it. It would be just about the biggest news in human history. Nearly a year and a half has passed since Blumenthal's revelations; we've heard nothing more about these "alloys" and their "amazing properties." My inference: they don't exist. I'm similarly skeptical of the report in religion scholar D.W. Pasulka's intriguing and often insightful new book *American Cosmic: UFOs, Religion, Technology* of a metallic stuff found somewhere in the New Mexico desert, bearing no obvious signs of having been part of a UFO but which, analyzed by unnamed "research scientists," proved "so anomalous as to be incomprehensible." Of course, events could prove me wrong any day now. But I don't think they will.

identified more than forty years afterward thanks to a clue that's since disappeared, should be a caution to anyone who thinks that *unidentified* readily translates into *extraterrestrial*.

The case for the UFOs' physical reality is neither frivolous nor negligible. It's problematic enough, though, to encourage us to seek out an alternative. That's what I try to do in this book. My aim is to provide a different framework for understanding the UFO and to argue that this approach explains better than anything else why people see UFOs and believe—and disbelieve—in them, as well as what gives this despised phenomenon its enduring power of enchantment.

This trail of ours will be wandering and idiosyncratic. It will lead us on detours from the post–World War II UFO phenomenon to remote times, places, and events. The ships of the Atlantic slave trade . . . the moon over the Dardanelles one July evening in 1683 . . . back to Ezekiel in the Old Testament and Paul in the New . . . and far, far back to the prehistoric Balkans. It will take us all the way to 1947 in Roswell, New Mexico, the place where—symbolically speaking—UFOs have their beginning. Perhaps also their end.

PART I

Approaching the UFO

CHAPTER 1

Confessions of a Teenage UFOlogist

I BECAME A UFOLOGIST in October of 1960. I was twelve going on thirteen. I was in eighth grade; I'd just become interested in girls. Or rather, I had just become aware of my interest in girls, since I'd previously managed to persuade myself that my fascination with a beautiful, brown-eyed and brown-haired, prematurely voluptuous seventh-grade classmate was pure platonic friendship. (It helped that this girl was also a very nice person. Her name was Barbara.) Anything other than platonic friendship would have unsettled my mother, who was housebound with a heart condition and slowly dying, although I didn't know that. Or I didn't know I knew it.

The UFO mystery was at the time a full thirteen years old. It had begun in 1947, the same year I was born. On June 24 a private pilot named Kenneth Arnold was flying from Chehalis to Yakima, Washington, when he spotted nine silvery, glittering objects flying in formation over the Cascade Mountains. He described their motion as "like saucers skipping over water." The press turned this into "flying saucers" and thereby gave the impression that what Arnold had seen was nine disks, although there's some evidence that his objects were originally crescent-shaped. Whatever its details, Arnold's experience attracted enormous attention in what we now call "the media," and other people all over the United States soon reported flying disks as well. The first of the great "flaps," or sighting waves, of UFO history had begun.

About two weeks into the 1947 flap, debris from one of the newly named flying saucers came down on a ranch near Roswell, New Mexico. This was announced proudly by the public information officer at Roswell Army Air Field, who told local press and radio outlets that "the many rumors regarding the flying disc became a reality yesterday" when the base intelligence office "was fortunate enough to gain possession of a disc through the cooperation of one of the local ranchers and the sheriff's office of Chaves County." A few hours later the military higher-ups intervened, declaring the debris to be a weather balloon. The incident slid into obscurity, forgotten by nearly everyone.

When I started eighth grade, I'd never heard of Kenneth Arnold. I would not hear about Roswell until many years later. It was a lonely time. My close friends from seventh grade had mostly been assigned to other classes. This included Barbara, who was rumored to have a seventeen-year-old boyfriend whom she planned to marry when he graduated high school. I trudged alone from class to class, amid knots of joking, laughing junior high kids. I tried to hear the jokes and laugh at them too, and thereby incorporate myself into one of the groups. But the speakers were too far away, and I missed the punch lines. Back home my mother was growing steadily, almost imperceptibly weaker. My father, who'd been running on empty for years, grew angrier and more bitter at his lot in life, which I certainly wasn't making any easier for him. I had no brothers or sisters.

That was when the UFOs entered my life.

There was a science class. There was a boy I'll call Bryan, the closest I had to a friend in that eighth-grade class. I'd known him from elementary school. He wore glasses, though not quite as thick as mine, and like me had a quiet, reserved air. We gravitated toward each other, and in October 1960 we resolved to write a science paper together. Originally it was going to be on life on other planets, with a chapter on flying saucers and the different ways people tried to explain them. We bicycled to the public library of Levittown, Pennsylvania, and looked up "flying saucers" in the card catalog.

The library had three books on the subject. One of them, as I've said, was Jung's. But the one I read first, that changed my life permanently, was Gray Barker's *They Knew Too Much About Flying Saucers*, published in 1956 under the respectable-sounding imprint of "University Books." I took it home and began reading. Pretty soon I was so scared I wanted to hide under my bed.

"THREE MEN IN BLACK"

They Knew Too Much begins with a seven-foot monster "worse than Frankenstein" that was seen to land with a luminescent globe on a West Virginia hilltop one September evening in 1952. The sight of this thing—"from Moon or from Mars / Maybe from God and not from the stars," as a country ballad of the time had it—frightened the witnesses so badly that "they had to clean one of them like a baby."

Having thus primed us to expect something fearsome, Gray Barker takes us back to the seriously scary "Shaver Mystery" of the 1940s: the pulp-magazine revelations of the perverted creatures called "dero" who dwell in hidden caves deep within the earth. These dero, degenerate remnants of a race of prehistoric space colonists, get their pleasure from kidnapping and torturing us surface humans. They also "engage in interplanetary traffic with evil beings from other planets"—hence, the strange things seen in the sky. On the truth of these stories, Barker professes a sober agnosticism. They may all, he cautions, be products of the subconscious of Richard S. Shaver, the Pennsylvania man who learned of them from voices speaking through his welding machine. "But if that is so, Shaver has the most remarkable subconscious of any man living on this earth."[2]

All this is prelude, however, to the centerpiece of Barker's book: the "Bender mystery." Who were the three men dressed in black who paid an unwelcome visit to a Bridgeport, Connecticut, researcher named Albert K. Bender in the autumn of 1953?[3] And what had Bender learned about UFOs that the three men were so anxious he not reveal?

Here's how Barker envisions the scene, putting his eager, captivated reader—twelve-year-old me—into the middle of it:

> Three men in black suits with threatening expressions on their faces. Three men who walk in on you and make certain demands.
>
> Three men who know that *you* know what the saucers really are.
>
> They don't want you to tell anyone else what you know.
>
> The answer had hit you like a flash, one night when you had gone to bed after running all the theories through the hopper of your brain. You had sat up in bed, snapped your fingers, and said, "This is IT! I KNOW I have the ANSWER!"
>
> The next day . . . you wrote this down and sent it to someone. When the three men came into your house one of them had that very same piece of paper in his hand.
>
> They said that you, among the thousands working on the same thing, had hit pay dirt. *You* had the *answer*! Then they filled you in with the details.

---

2 On Shaver and the "mystery" to which his name is attached, see chapter 7.

3 And yes, the *Men in Black* movies of 1997, 2002, 2012, and 2019 ("Here come the Men in Black / The galaxy defenders; / Here come the Men in Black / They won't let you remember") are rooted in the mythos created forty years earlier by Gray Barker. We'll come back to this in chapter 6.

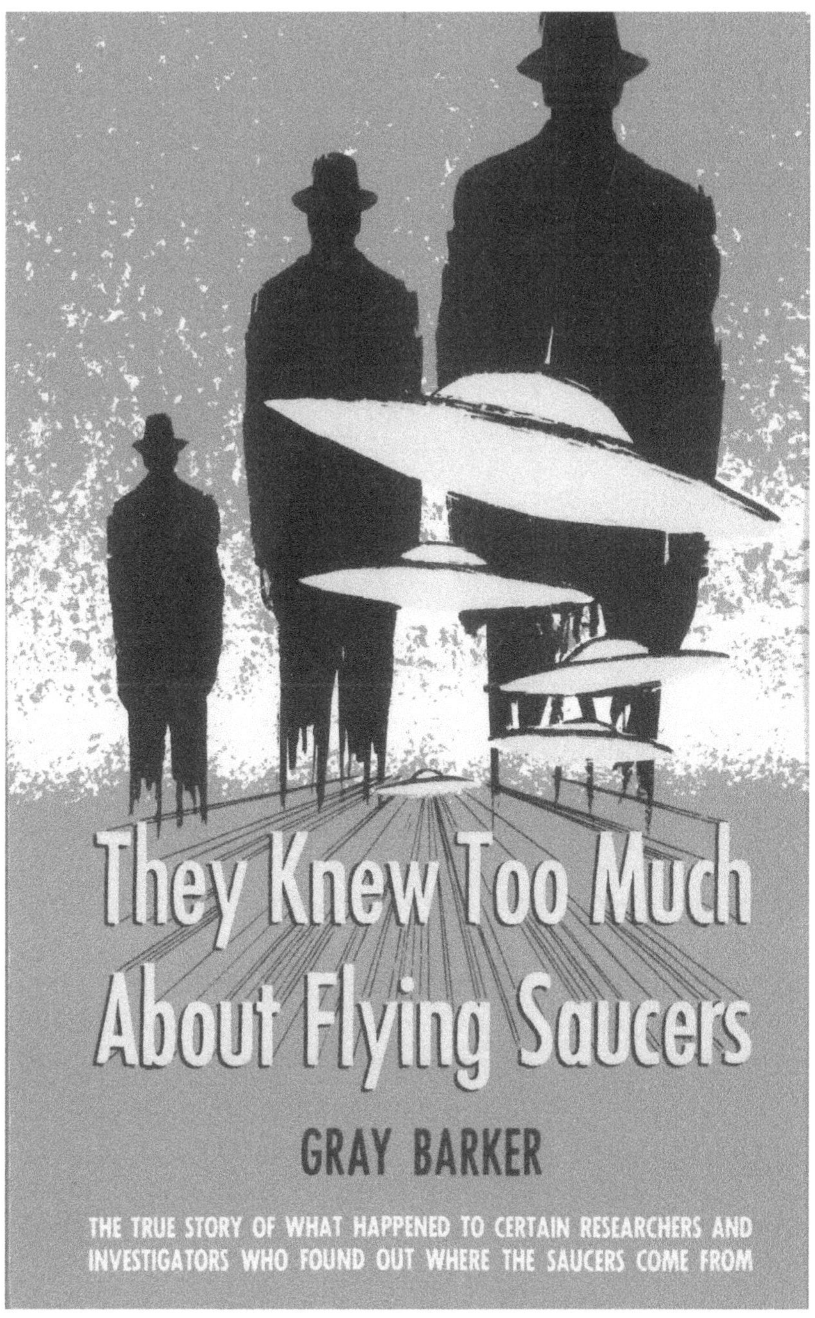

FIGURE 1. The cover of Gray Barker's *They Knew Too Much About Flying Saucers* (University Books, 1956).

> After they got through with you, you wished you'd have never heard of the word "saucer."
>
> You turned pale and got awfully sick.
>
> You couldn't get anything to stay on your stomach for three long days.

I finished the book scared but also thrilled, energized. I'd found my mission: to walk Bender's path, to discover the secret of what Barker called "the elusive disks." For the next five years I pursued that goal.

First through a school club called "the Flying Saucer Investigators," founded by Bryan and me. A few of our classmates, including two girls on whom he and I had crushes, joined the Investigators. Soon they drifted away—the girls, I suspect, because they were waiting for us to ask them out and we were too shy, or too crippled by circumstances we hadn't yet understood, to do that. Bryan also lost interest. I was left to "chase the saucers," as Gray Barker liked to call the activity, all alone.

Yet in another sense far from alone. Over the next couple of years I drifted into a correspondence network that stretched over the country and even overseas. These were people whom I'd never met face to face and about whose lives I knew next to nothing but who were in some ways my best friends. They might have impressive titles like "director" of this or that. But most of them were boys—hardly any girls—much like me. I didn't yet know the phrase "invisible college," coined by scientifically inclined esotericists in the seventeenth century and borrowed by UFOlogically inclined scientists in the 1970s. But that was exactly what I felt us to be: a select society of young people who'd turned away from conventional teenage excitements and pleasures to pursue a scorned and unrecognized truth. I lived for their letters.

My adult relatives, teachers, and acquaintances were baffled, often amused. My father was baffled and enraged. Why oh *why* did a bright kid like me believe in this crap? My reply was to reel off the evidence, the roster of unexplained sightings from Kenneth Arnold onward. So massive was this evidence, so circumstantial and convincing, that to disregard it had to be willful blindness. My arguments, however, made no impact. The blindness was impenetrable.

Looking back, I can see why. An odd thing in the sky that you can't account for is just that: an odd thing in the sky. It's not an interplanetary spaceship. I was indeed a bright kid—some might say very bright. I wasn't a "kook," unless that jeering, meaningless tag is to be fastened onto anyone out of the ordinary. Yet I was caught up in a delusional system, which I could not recognize as such and which I grew out of when the time was ripe but never explicitly discarded. The blindness was mine. In a smart boy who must have known better, it demands explanation.

"A PECULIAR DISEASE"

Let's run through the simple answers. I was twelve years old when I read—and was knocked off my feet by—*They Knew Too Much About Flying Saucers*. Suburban twelve-year-olds tend not to know very much about the world, and, as is sometimes the case with very bright kids, I knew less than most. Books were the mainstay of my childhood—my comfort, my school. I was naturally inclined to believe in books as kids now do in the internet: if it was between two covers, it had to be true.

Barker's book offered no obvious clues that it wasn't to be trusted. The light blue binding of the library copy seemed safe and sober. (It was years later that I saw the lurid dust jacket: a string of yellow disks spinning at you, against the ominous background of three black human silhouettes.) It had a bibliography and an index, the way any book I'd use for a school report might. Its chapter titles—"Flatwoods, West Virginia," "Brush Creek, California," "Jersey City, New Jersey"—seemed to root its story in consensus geography and thereby in reality. To my twelve-year-old mind, the imprint "University Books" promised academic respectability.

Then there was Barker's seductive invitation to the reader. "I have always felt," he wrote, "if I could organize these notes into some kind of readable whole and distribute these findings widely, somewhere there would be someone in whose mind they would sound an inspired tinkle. One little idea from a reader may be the final key to unlocking the entire mystery." And a few pages later: "My readers seemed to be more than subscribers; they considered themselves parts of a great team that eventually might make sense out of what seemed to be not simple confusion, but often *organized confusion*."

If you were invited to be on that team, would you say no?

You especially wouldn't if you were a boy who not long before had been obsessed with Sherlock Holmes, who'd looked to the great detective for instruction in how to solve crimes, how to have near-magical knowledge about everyone you met. Now here was a real-life mystery to be solved, more momentous than any dinky murder. Gray Barker had put forth an earnest call for help. What budding boy-detective could turn it down?

But there's more. There has to be. Bryan also read *They Knew Too Much About Flying Saucers*; UFOs didn't go on to dominate his adolescence. There must have been something about the book, and about me, that made me particularly vulnerable to its appeal.

A memory comes to me: Before I'd read more than a chapter or two, I flipped ahead through the book. My eyes fell upon the words

> died of a peculiar disease. They seemed to age quickly; girls of twenty soon appeared to be old women.

I remember the thrill I felt as I saw this, my eagerness to read ahead so I would know who these "girls" were, what the "peculiar disease" was that they'd died of. Was there some recognition involved in this excitement? Yes. Absolutely.

My mother: forty-two years old, but I could see her withering away before my eyes, arms and legs spindly, belly swollen like the victim of some African famine. "Could see"—but most of the time I didn't. I didn't allow myself to. I knew she'd had a heart attack when I was three. I knew she'd been in mortal danger, hadn't been expected to live. But that was all past. She was better now. A "semi-invalid," we called her; she had to rest after every meal, never left the house on her own, needed continual quiet. But she was better now, she told me and I repeated to myself. She would be fine.

Yet she grew worse, imperceptibly from day to day, measurably from year to year.

Now here at last was a book that would explain to me what was happening.

Explain in language that meant something to me. Sure, I knew the reasons: She'd had rheumatic fever as a girl. It had weakened her heart. My birth had strained it further—and this, of course, was why I had no brothers or sisters. She'd had a stroke and then a heart attack and we'd moved to one of those boxy little Levittown houses that sprang up after the war, a one-story house that didn't have any stairs she'd need to climb. But this was the language of the head, and it meant nothing.

They Knew Too Much About Flying Saucers spoke the language of myth, which is the language of the heart.

> Whoever or whatever visited Bender had deeply impressed him, and greatly frightened him. Later on, when I continued my investigations into similar avenues, I was to find that for some reason a man will not talk after one of these visitations. When such a person is approached, whoever tells the person to shut up does so in such a way or imparts such terrifying information that the man on the receiving end is scared almost out of his wits!

The dreadful vagueness of that "whoever or whatever"! We too had been "silenced" by a reality too terrifying for either me or my mother to face. I'm quite sure my father knew it. But he wouldn't speak of it either, at least not to us. The "cover-up" was real, but it had nothing to do with alien objects in the skies. Or everything to do with them. Our skies had been penetrated by the ultimate alien, death, and like the victims of the men in black, we could not talk about it.

Now, for the first time, I'd found a book that spoke the unspeakable.

UFOLOGY

So I believed in UFOs because I believed in the three men, and I believed in the three men because I knew the effects of their presence from personal experience. Outer space, life on other planets, had nothing originally to do with it. Initially I believed that the saucers might come from other planets but that this was improbable. Barker himself had left open the possibility, as per the "Shaver Mystery," that they'd emerged from some unknown place within this earth. My own feeling at the time was that they were likely to be secret U.S. devices. What counted for me was not their extraterrestrial origin. It was their mystery and their suppression.

Once I'd left the Flying Saucer Investigators behind me and had begun to make my way into the wider world of UFOlogy, I had no choice but to adopt the conventions of that world. I became persuaded: the UFOs couldn't be of human manufacture. Their aerial feats, like instant acceleration from hovering to zooming at thousands of miles per hour, were impossible by the standard of modern physics. It followed that they had to employ a physics more advanced than our own. Pretty soon I was speaking the party line. There was no doubt at all that our skies were host to visitors from other worlds.

This belief, let it be noted, was less irrational in the early 1960s than it is today. We, like the Russians, were beginning to expand into outer space. Space was the "new frontier," as President Kennedy called it, and most people assumed that explorations of other planets were about to follow. It made sense that beings from the other planets might be here exploring us. It was still just barely possible to imagine there might be intelligent life on the Earthlike planets Venus and Mars. The problem of how the UFOs managed to cross interstellar space wasn't quite as acute as it would become a few years later, when no corner of the solar system was left to be their home.

But why didn't our extraterrestrial visitors land and declare themselves, with the take-me-to-your-leader speech beloved by cartoon artists? Why had they spent the past fifteen years showboating in the sky, then zooming back to wherever they called home? We UFOlogists had our replies ready. These usually involved the prediction that there was bound to be some dramatic denouement—a public contact or, God forbid, a mass invasion—within the next year, or two, or three. The UFO books of the 1950s and 1960s are filled with such prophecies. We didn't yet have the burden of explaining why, after decades passed, nothing of the sort seemed to happen.

It was possible, too, that the UFOs had established local bases—on the far side of the moon, say, which until the mid-1960s had been largely hidden from human eyes. From there, going at or near the speed of light, they could travel in the blink of an eye to McMinnville, Oregon, or Farmington, New Mexico, or Tremonton, Utah, to name a few localities where they'd been seen or even photographed. But what would a spaceship be doing in such places? That was part of the mystery our "invisible college" had set itself to solve, through careful gathering of sighting data, plotting it on maps, studying the timing of the great UFO flaps. This was what "objective UFO research" was about, and if there was any reason a junior high or high school student couldn't do it as well as a university professor, I didn't see what that was.

I did find time for other, more conventional interests. I wrote for the junior high newspaper and afterward the high school literary magazine. I played on the chess team, which technically was a sport although not the kind that got you any great kudos in my high school environment. What I didn't do, and which made me increasingly an oddity among my classmates as the years passed and I moved from one grade to the next, was go out with girls.

The official reason for this was that there weren't any suitable girls for me to go out with. Our school was overwhelmingly non-Jewish, and the few Jewish girls weren't (supposedly) the kind who might be drawn to an eccentric intellectual like me. The real reason was that my mother's illness broadcast a continual unconscious SOS for me not to abandon her. True, I couldn't save her from the death she must deep down have known was coming. But I could at least stick by her and not shift my attachment to some younger female, while she told herself (and once or twice me) that although I was intellectually advanced way beyond my years, I was socially kind of retarded and hadn't yet gotten interested in girls. I nodded in agreement, although I knew how false this was, and I dressed in clothing that did not become me—checkered, dull-colored flannel shirts predominant—and told myself I was too ugly for any girl to like me. When an intelligent, warmhearted, strikingly attractive redhead announced before an entire class that she'd go out with me if I asked because I had "personality," I heard her words and afterwards remembered them. I understood their meaning in the English language. They made no emotional impact whatever.

Meanwhile there were the UFOs.

UFOlogy has been aptly called "the last great public investigative enterprise wherein the gifted amateur is not at any disadvantage." I was gifted, and I longed to make my mark. At the end of the summer of 1963, I got my chance. The director of an organization to which I belonged, the New Jersey Association on Aerial Phenomena (NJAAP), retired from the field, as many of the UFOlogists of the time did, to go to college. I was then a rising junior with two years of high school left to go. I stepped in to take his place.

At its height, NJAAP had a membership of about two dozen. They weren't just in New Jersey, however, but all over the country; we may even have had one or two members overseas. So at age fifteen I was director of a national, if not an international, scientific organization and, in my eyes, had come a long way from the Flying Saucer Investigators. In the course of my eleventh-grade year, I produced almost single-handedly three issues of the mimeographed *NJAAP Bulletin* and mailed them out to my subscribers. I'm proud to say they represented the highest standards of scientific UFOlogy, such as these were.

It was in the spring of 1964, when I'd already put out two issues of the bulletin and was beginning to plan the third, that the UFO world unexpectedly erupted.

On April 24 of that year, a New Mexico police officer named Lonnie Zamora claimed to have seen an egg-shaped metallic object resting at the bottom of a ravine near the town of Socorro, and beside it two figures looking like small boys in coveralls. The object took off with a "very loud" roar, leaving four imprints, asymmetrically placed, with one of the markings set off in good Jungian fashion from the other three.[4] It was hard to imagine any natural phenomenon that could have left those markings. Zamora could have made them, but that would mean he was a hoaxer and a liar, and nearly everyone who knew him thought him a solid citizen and an upright lawman.

Socorro's importance went far beyond the incident itself. For the first time in years the media took notice of UFOs, and soon another nationwide flap was underway. For us UFOlogists, it was a dream come true. Over the past three and a half years, whenever I'd tried to talk with people about UFOs, I'd have to field some remark like "It seems that a few years ago they were seeing a lot of those things, but now they don't see them anymore." I would assure the other person that it wasn't true, that the UFOs hadn't vanished, and I'd start reeling

---

4 We'll explore the Jungian concept of the quaternity, the 3 + 1, in the next chapter.

off recent sightings to prove the point, whereupon he or she would get bored and change the subject or just walk away. Now the UFOs, bless their hearts, had made my argument for me.

Not that I had the leisure to enjoy this vindication. I remember the spring of 1964 as a frantic nightmare, with nights spent at my typewriter pounding away obsessively at an English paper that had gotten out of hand and was more than three hundred pages long when I handed it in two months after the April deadline. When I wasn't doing that, I was winning a summer trip to Israel in a Bible contest but also twice failing my driver's exam—a double defeat that left me for years convinced I could never learn to drive. I pined for my old crush of the Flying Saucer Investigators days, whom I still adored but who was and would forever be unavailable to me—although in retrospect I can see I was the one who'd made myself unavailable to her. I kept up with my UFOlogy, telling myself that five hours of sleep were plenty for a night and that my mother, skeletal now apart from her swollen belly, wasn't any sicker than she'd ever been and probably was improving, even as it was plain that she had no strength left, that she couldn't go twenty feet into the backyard without assistance, that a minor fall would leave her with a garishly colored, hideous bruise that persisted for weeks, and in short that her life was a fragile thread about to be snapped. On July 5, I mailed out the third and as it turned out final edition of *The NJAAP Bulletin*, twenty-seven single-spaced pages long, its feature attraction "A Chronology of the 1964 Flap," listing ninety cases from April 24 through June 8. This "chronology" was later reprinted, with attribution but without permission, in a pulp magazine called *Flying Saucers*.[5] This was the high-water mark of the national attention gained by NJAAP, which has since vanished from the collective memory of UFOlogy without even a footnote to mark its existence. Two days after sending out the bulletin, exhausted, I boarded a post-midnight flight from the newly

---

5 See chapter 7 for more on *Flying Saucers* magazine and its place in the publishing activities of Raymond Palmer.

renamed Kennedy Airport to Tel Aviv. When I got home eight weeks later, my mother was dead.

AFTERMATH

In theory, nothing had changed with her gone. The UFOs were still zooming around up there, except on occasion, as in Socorro, when they touched down, presumably to gather soil samples or the like. One UFO, in fact, landed in September of that year in a clearing in the woods near Glassboro, New Jersey, reachable from Levittown by bus. As at Socorro, it left holes in the ground as a sign of its presence: three small ones arranged in a very rough triangle, plus a fourth, larger, central hole. A high school senior now, I conducted an investigation and prepared to write a monograph on the landing. It was too large and complex an issue to be covered in an article for *The NJAAP Bulletin*.

I never wrote that monograph, beyond a table of contents and a few pages. Nor did I produce any more *NJAAP Bulletins*. If my UFOlogy was an elaborate way of coping with and perhaps warding off my mother's impending death, it would make sense that the spirit would go out of it once she died, and that was precisely what happened. I still went through the motions, but I barely had the energy to sustain the correspondence network that had once been the joy and solace of my life. When, in January, a New Jersey college student came forward to announce that he and two friends had dug the holes at Glassboro, set off gunpowder in them, and scared a couple of local kids into thinking a UFO had landed, I didn't believe his confession. He just wanted attention, I argued, plus the money he thought he could extract for his story from some Philadelphia newspaper. But I couldn't convince anyone else, even my fellow UFOlogists, and eventually I let the subject drop.[6]

---

6 I couldn't have guessed that my Glassboro adventure would have a surprise sequel fifty years afterward that would help me understand the events, famous by then, in Roswell, New Mexico. See chapter 8.

Meanwhile my life was changing in ways I wouldn't have expected. My mother's death had been, in a sense, the end of my world. I grieved her and missed her terribly. But in some ways life was better now. My father and I grew, I wouldn't say closer, but more amicable. For years he'd carried on his back a sick wife, as well as a peculiar son whose obsessions he could make no sense of. The first burden, at least, he was now relieved of. And I'd become rather less peculiar, both in his eyes and perhaps also in reality. Early that winter I unburdened myself to a boy named Stephen, who was sort of a friend and who was soon to become a much better one, of my bitterness and sorrow that I was never invited to parties. The birthday parties of my childhood had long since petered out, replaced by teenage parties from which I was excluded. Stephen listened, and a few weeks later, lo and behold, I started getting invited to parties. Turned out I hadn't been excluded at all. It simply hadn't occurred to anyone that I might be interested.

So I began to catch up with the life I'd missed. At one of those parties I found myself on a couch with a girl and tried necking with her. She pulled away, but what the heck, I'd tried. A few months later I did find a girlfriend. She wasn't Jewish; my mother wouldn't have approved; my father didn't care. I faced the fact that no further issues of *The NJAAP Bulletin* would appear and refunded my subscribers, all twenty or so, the balance of their subscription money. One of them wrote to me, sending in appreciation of my honesty the gift of a cigarette lighter with my signature, "Sincerely, Dave Halperin," imprinted on the side. I never took up cigarette smoking, but I kept the lighter. I have it to this day.

My entry to UFOlogy was a sudden conversion. My exit was a process far more gradual. There wasn't any one morning when I woke up and realized it wasn't true; we aren't being visited by beings from outer space. Active interest faded long before belief.

I went off to college in the fall of 1965, a little over a year after my mother's death. The following summer I exchanged letters with one of my most valued UFO friends, a wonderful, peppery lady of about sixty named Isabel Davis, whom I would occasionally visit in New York City. In my letter I explained why I was retiring from UFOlogy. There was no question, I wrote, that UFOs were real and probably extraterrestrial. But how was it possible to discover anything about them? Whizzing through the skies or briefly landing, they were inaccessible to us, beyond our scrutiny. I'd long since outgrown Gray Barker, with his tales of hilltop monsters and men in black. His claim that Albert Bender had somehow solved the mystery and that any of us might hope to do the same—which was what had gotten me into UFOlogy in the first place—was, to say the least, improbable. There was no adequate method, I wrote Isabel. Research was hopeless. We would learn the truth about UFOs at the initiative of the UFO beings themselves. This might happen tomorrow, or it might take another thousand years. Meanwhile there were other things to do with one's time.

Isabel wasn't persuaded. Like me, she may have had her own unconscious motives for continuing not only to believe but to search. It would be futile and unseemly to speculate about her reasons now that this fine, intelligent woman has, like so many of the old-time UFOlogists, departed this life. Our correspondence ended amicably; I never saw her again. I immersed myself in the studies of classical and Semitic languages that would eventually lead me, by a crooked and wandering path, back to UFOs.

FAST-FORWARD

. . . to 1987. I'm nearly forty years old, a tenured professor of religious studies at the University of North Carolina, Chapel Hill. I'm in a bookstore on Franklin Street, across from the campus. Prominently displayed on one table are several stacks of a hardcover book called *Communion*, by one Whitley Strieber. A face stares up at me from the book jacket.

It's a face I've never seen before, though all of us will see it many times in the years to come. Shaped like a light bulb, as light bulbs used to be. Dominated by two slanted, enormous, anatomically impossible eyes: almond-shaped, black, without iris or pupil or any visible lids, each with a gleam of white amid the blackness and just the hint of a split running from end to end. I've never seen anything like this—not in *Close Encounters of the Third Kind* or *E.T.*, not in the UFO literature of my youth. I have no idea that this face and the being to which it's attached will become an icon, a cultural staple, instantly recognizable when used in cartoons and comic strips, taking its place in three-dimensional miniature on the dollar-store racks at Halloween time, alongside the plastic witches and ghosts and spiders that are the traditional, time-honored inhabitants of the boo-I-scared-you gallery.

I open the book; I flip through it. I can't make much of it. It's not a UFO book, at least not the way I've always known UFO books. And since when do UFO books get this kind of VIP treatment from bookstores? "That book started to sell," the publisher will recall a year or two afterward, "the minute it appeared on the bookshelves; no reviews, no appearances, nothing. And we had word from the bookstores that *Communion*, with this strange picture on the cover, was selling." I don't know that yet, of course. Nor do I know *Communion* will spend thirty weeks on the *New York Times* bestseller list, sometimes in the top nonfiction spot, or that Whitley Strieber was given a million-dollar advance for it. I, at any rate, am not one of the buyers. It doesn't fit into any of my categories of what books, even UFO books, ought to be. Anyway, I'm a busy professor and UFOs aren't my thing anymore. I snap the book shut and walk out of the store.

CHAPTER 2

Scenes from Magonia

IN JULY 1959, aviation hero Charles Lindbergh paid a visit to Carl Jung's home in Bollingen, Switzerland, to meet the grand old man of depth psychology. He and Jung fell to arguing about—what else?—UFOs.

We have the story only in Lindbergh's version. "I had expected," Lindbergh wrote afterward, "a fascinating discussion about psychological aspects of the numerous and recurring flying-saucer reports." But to Lindbergh's surprise, Jung seemed to have no interest in the psychological question. No, no, he insisted, the flying saucers were real. Lindbergh protested. Why, no less a personage than General Carl Spaatz, chief of the US Air Force, had assured him there weren't any such things! "Slim," Spaatz had told Lindbergh, "don't you suppose that if there was anything true about this flying-saucer business, you and I would have heard about it by this time?" To which Jung retorted: "There are a great many things going on around this earth that you and General Spaatz don't know about."

"More things in heaven and earth, Horatio, than dreamt of in your philosophy." That line from *Hamlet* had been a mantra for Jung's old teacher, Sigmund Freud; Jung himself certainly accepted its truth. Were UFOs, for him, among those undreamt-of things? The question has been debated since the 1950s, when Jung began issuing pronouncements on the subject of flying saucers. The pronouncements were always ambiguous; hence the controversy. Even the publication of Jung's *Flying Saucers: A Modern Myth of Things Seen in the Skies*—in the German original in 1958, in English translation the following year—did little to resolve the issue of what exactly its author believed or didn't believe.

This book proclaimed the essence of the UFOs to be something arising from within us, their physical existence a puzzling byway. In its final, very brief chapter, "UFOs Considered in a Non-Psychological Light," Jung acknowledged that any purely psychological explanation is bound to run into some inconvenient facts. UFOs have been photographed; they've been detected on radar. The archskeptic Donald Menzel, Jung declared, "has not succeeded, despite all his efforts, in offering a satisfying scientific explanation of even one authentic UFO report." He added, "It boils down to nothing less than this: that either psychic projections throw back a radar echo, or else the appearance of real objects affords an opportunity for mythological projections."

So which was it? Jung continued to waffle. On the one hand, UFOs behave as no physical, mechanical objects could possibly behave. To perform the aerial maneuvers typical of UFOs, a spacecraft would have to be without mass or weight, which is inconceivable. But if a weightless vehicle is "a hard hypothesis to swallow," the alternative notion of a "materialized psychism"—a mental projection that somehow takes on tangible reality in the physical realm—"opens a bottomless void under our feet."

I've already said how I read *Flying Saucers: A Modern Myth* at age thirteen and, unsurprisingly, got rather little from the experience. One thing, at least, I did manage to understand. Jung didn't turn everything into sex, as I'd imagined all psychologists did. As part of his long-running quarrel with his dead Papa Freud—about which, of course, I knew nothing—Jung dismissed the idea that might have been Freud's if he'd lived into the UFO era: that the flying saucer was "a sexual fantasy . . . a repressed uterus was coming down from the sky." But what *did* Jung think UFOs were? I couldn't make any sense of what he was trying to say, or the weird dreams and paintings he invoked in support.

Nearly ten years later, long after I'd dropped out of active UFOlogy, I met a man whose ideas seemed to dovetail neatly with Jung's, and the encounter prompted me to give Jung's book a second reading. The man was Jacques Vallee, and even those who've never heard his name probably know a version of him. The character Claude Lacombe, the French scientist and UFOlogist played by François Truffaut in Steven Spielberg's *Close Encounters of the Third Kind*, was modeled after Vallee.

In 1969, the year before I made his acquaintance, Vallee published a book that was perceived at the time as groundbreaking and that has reverberated through UFOlogy ever since. It was entitled *Passport to Magonia: From Folklore to Flying Saucers.* Its central point was that the reported sightings of diminutive UFO occupants, which by the late '60s had begun to pile up and to be taken seriously by even the stodgiest UFOlogists, bore an odd resemblance to traditional folktales of fairies and elves and leprechauns.

Vallee didn't conclude from this parallel, as he well might have, that UFOs and their pilots didn't exist any more than fairies and elves did. It was easy, after all, to explain away centuries-old stories of human encounters with the "wee folk." The human experiencers had probably never existed in the first place. Even if they were once real people, they'd surely never claimed to have seen or done the impossible things rumor fathered on them. But the witnesses in close-up UFO encounters certainly existed, and if you wanted to deny the encounters, you had to look those sober-seeming people in the eye and call them lunatics or liars. An oft-repeated story, almost certainly apocryphal, has Thomas Jefferson brushing off reports of a meteorite with the snide remark that it's easier to believe witnesses can lie than stones fall from the sky. The UFOlogists weren't about to repeat that mistake.

Vallee chose a more exciting if vaguer path. The folktales and the UFO reports both described actual events: visitations from some realm that wasn't outer space—that was a twentieth-century conventionalization—but an aspect of human existence on this earth, coterminous with our ordinary world yet somehow beyond it. His code name for this realm was Magonia.

The name derived from a medieval French folk belief in a place in the clouds called Magonia, "land of the magicians," from which sky-ships come to plunder the crops of honest farmers. (The belief was literal and concrete. On one occasion a peasant mob got hold of four people they thought had fallen from a "Magonian" ship and came close to lynching them.) As Vallee used the word *Magonia*, it wasn't quite identical with Jung's "collective unconscious." But both pointed in the same direction, toward something that's part of us yet at the same time beyond us, manifesting recognizably in the Middle Ages and in the twentieth century, with superficial alterations like the replacement of cloud-ships with spaceships.

Thus was born the "psychosocial" theory of UFO reality.

The idea caught on. How could it not? It had a seductive appeal to both imagination and common sense. It insisted on the reality and importance of the UFO phenomenon, if not the UFOs themselves, and at the same time recognized what could not be evaded: that UFOs seemed to mirror and to be rooted in the human conditions of their times. It was an advantage that you didn't have to be a UFO believer to appreciate its virtues. The debunkers, less squeamish than the UFOlogists about calling people liars or deluded, found they could put the psychosocial theory to excellent use.

Gradually the psychosocial advocates divided themselves into two branches. There were the skeptics who used the approach to reduce UFOs, insofar as they weren't simply errors in perception, to familiar manifestations of individual and group psychology. Then there were those, more faithful to Vallee, who insisted on some irreducible mystery, redefined now as an essentially human enigma. For answers they looked not to the spaceship but to the soul and the transcendent dimensions Jung had attributed to the human unconscious. Along these lines, they argued, the solution would be found.

But it wasn't. By the late 1980s the psychosocial hypothesis had lost its luster among UFO proponents. It had led nowhere except to implausible New Agey speculations about the power of the mind to shape the physical world. The reality represented by the name *Magonia* remained as vague and elusive as ever. If you said UFOs were spacecraft from some remote, hypothetical planetary system—Venus and Mars having dropped out of the running long ago—you still had the problem of all those light-years in between. But at least you were talking about our normal physical universe. You didn't have to mess around with "materialized psychisms" or enter some fairyland of Jungian archetypes. The old "extraterrestrial hypothesis," for all its implausibilities, seemed the safer way.

Now here I am, proposing to revisit that Jungian fairyland. How does one do such a thing?

The way two porcupines make love: very, very carefully.

In what remains of this chapter, I'll set forth four case studies, in thematic rather than chronological sequence. In each of them I'll construct, step by step, a psychological bridge between reported experience and postulated cause; I'll hope to persuade you to come with me across that bridge. Inevitably I'll turn to Jung. But as Jung himself did in his career as a psychologist, I'll begin with Freud.

The Jungians, after all, have never denied Freud's insights or that he was the pioneer without whom their psychology could not have existed. Freud was right, they say; his only significant mistake was to believe he'd discovered the whole truth, when in fact his sexual theories represented only a portion of it. And it appears that every so often a repressed uterus, or its male equivalent, does come down from the sky.

PHILADELPHIA, 1974

"It ain't a fit night out fer man nor beast" runs a recurrent line in a classic W.C. Fields movie. The weather in Philadelphia on the evening of January 15, 1974, suited that description. Philadelphia in January is not noted for the splendors of its climate. But that night was particularly unpleasant, and if UFOlogist Matt Graeber's phone hadn't rung just as he was sitting down to a late dinner, it's doubtful anything could have sent him racing out into the snowy, bitter darkness.

But ring it did.

A young man was on the line, and he sounded excited. "Is this the place where you report seeing a UFO?"

"That's right," Graeber said. Graeber was representative of a private organization called the UFO Report and Information Center, normally referred to by the whimsical acronym UFORIC. (Never say UFOlogists are without a sense of humor.) The young man had phoned Information asking where he could call to report a UFO sighting, and he'd been given Graeber's number.

Graeber asked when the sighting had taken place.

The man said it was happening then. He was calling from a public phone, watching the object as he spoke.

Graeber asked him where he was located.

Parked at the edge of a field on the property of the Byberry state mental hospital, the caller said. The UFO was flying low over the field, occasionally hovering. The man told Graeber he was waiting for his wife and her parents to get there so they could watch it with him.

If Graeber engaged in any snickering speculation over the sighting's locale, he doesn't mention it in his report. Most likely the thought never crossed his mind. He knew from long experience that most UFO witnesses are sane, rational people who've seen something they can't explain and report it in the hopes of getting an answer. He assumed, correctly as it turned out, that his caller was in that category. He told the man he was on his way.

That "way" was a thirty- to forty-minute drive from his home. Despite the snow and the icy roads, he managed to find the area the caller had indicated. But, though he circled repeatedly through the dark streets, he saw no sign of any UFO or four people standing by a car looking into the sky.

It occurred to him he'd been the victim of a nasty prank, sending him out on a wild goose chase on a miserable night. But when he got back home, his wife told him that the caller, whom Graeber refers to as Tim, had phoned several more times to describe what he and his in-laws were seeing. The UFO, Tim claimed, "was actually approaching his family as they were parked, and when he would turn his auto's headlights on, the object would retreat back into the darkness. There were also times when the UFO would playfully blink back at the auto's headlights as if in response."

Trying to communicate?

If this were a joke, why did Tim keep calling back? Why did he want report forms to use for the sighting? Why did he want Graeber to meet with him and his in-laws the next day? Surely a prankster would have pulled his trick and then vanished into the darkness.

So the following day Graeber did meet with the witnesses: Tim, his pregnant wife, "Sarah," and Sarah's parents, with whom the couple was living. Tim was twenty-three years old, one year older than Sarah, an auto mechanic by trade and a student pilot.

Graeber interviewed the four separately and together, at the family's home and at the scene of the sighting. They seemed sincere, surprised and baffled by what they'd seen the night before. None of them gave the impression of any prior interest in UFOs. Their stories meshed: "They all agreed a strange object was silently flying about very slowly and hovering in the area. They all told of how the object reacted to the auto's headlights, they even said they thought the UFO had struck the tops of the trees."

But then Graeber looked at the sketches the four of them had drawn, independently, of the UFO. It was as if they'd seen two different objects above that field.

Sarah and her parents drew a more or less conventional flying saucer: two soup bowls joined together at the rims, the upper one inverted on the lower, a Saturn-like ring at the point of juncture, and a raised dome on top. Whereas Tim had drawn . . .

"When I brought this discrepancy to the attention of the group," Graeber wrote in his subsequent report, "they seemed to be genuinely surprised and dismayed about the whole thing. Tim simply couldn't believe they thought the UFO looked as they had sketched it," while Sarah's father "shook his head in disbelief at what his son-in-law thought the object looked like." Graeber was as baffled as the rest:

> I had never encountered such a vast difference in a simultaneously observed multi-witnessed event. It seemed to me that if the incident were a hoax, the hoaxers probably would have been able to tell the same story about what the object supposedly looked like. One would think that would be one of the first things they would discuss and agree upon. Yet, here it was in black and white, three of four observers sketching a double-convex disk with a dome and revolving rim, and the fourth witness saying it was a cylindrical craft. Yet, all had observed the same UFO at relatively close range (50 yards being the closest estimate) with the aid of two automobiles' high-beam headlights.

A page or so later, Graeber adds what seems a throwaway detail. Tim and his pregnant young wife—well, they weren't exactly married.

Think back, if you're old enough, to the mid-1970s. Among wide and growing segments of our population, it was accepted as

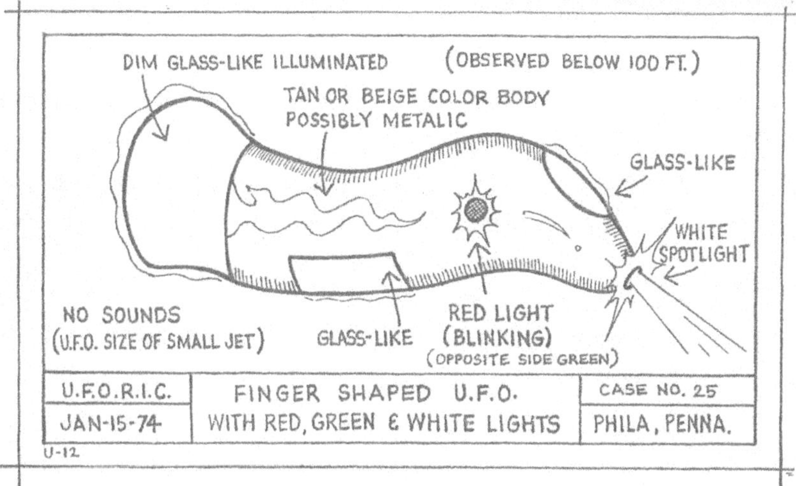

FIGURE 2. The Philadelphia UFO of January 1974, drawn by the late Matthew J. Graeber on the basis of the witness's sketch. Image provided through the kindness of Matthew J. Graeber, Jr.

natural and appropriate for unmarried couples to sleep together, live together. This was a big change from ten years earlier; the sexual revolution came in between. Unlike today, it was absolutely *not* accepted for unmarried couples to have children. If a couple were having sex, as they probably were, they made sure to use birth control. If that failed, there were big decisions to be made. Fast. Under pressure.

Now look at Tim's drawing. Ignore the labels. What do you see?

What I see is a detumescing penis shooting out sperm, sheathed in a condom that's ruptured precisely where it needs to stay intact.

At the beginning of 2013, I posted the drawing to my Facebook Fan Page and asked my readers to tell me what they saw in it. Not everyone saw the same thing I did. But I got enough support to reassure me this wasn't some figment of my own sex-addled brain. A woman, the first person to post a comment, wrote, "Looks like a worm," but added, less than a minute later, "Or maybe a condom." "Looks like a snake or maybe a dick," wrote one man. Another man: "It's the infamous condomous maximus Trojanus." Another posted a link to a ribald YouTube video featuring an outrageously phallic UFO, testicles and all.

One man made a comment that didn't answer the precise question I'd asked but was an eye-opener anyway: "I'm not sure what it looks like, but the obvious thing that sticks out is the fact, one side had a blinking green light, the other side a red one. This is a standard set by the FAA for all aircraft flying. I don't think UFO's have to follow FAA regulations."

There's the answer. What Tim saw, and presumably the others as well, was an airplane.

But airplanes don't hover, unless they're helicopters; and Graeber contacted a nearby airport and "found no helicopters were aloft the night of the 15th." (Besides, a low-flying helicopter would have made an unmistakable racket.) An airplane doesn't hang around the same spot for a half hour or an hour, which must have been the duration of the sighting. It doesn't come within fifty yards of people on the ground. It certainly doesn't withdraw when those people turn on their automobile headlights or "playfully blink back at the auto's headlights as if in response."

So what are our choices? *Do* UFOs obey FAA regulations, at least while they're within our airspace? Was it pure coincidence that this space vehicle sported green and red lights like any earthly aircraft? Or was there some truly astounding gap, which we'd be tempted to call unbelievable, between the physical stimulus for the sighting and the sighting as the witnesses experienced it? This last option doesn't seem any more appetizing than the first two—until we recall that there had to have been such a gap. Otherwise, how to explain the divergence between Tim's drawing and the other three?[7]

---

7 The UFO annals attest to perceptual and memory gaps of this sort. On the night of March 3, 1968, fragments of the Soviet moon probe Zond IV came streaking through the upper atmosphere. Some of the people who witnessed the dramatic reentry accurately described meteor-like lights moving along straight paths. But others saw an object "shaped like a fat cigar" with "square-shaped windows" and "a metallic look about the fuselage," which was "constructed of many pieces of flat sheets of metal-like material with a 'riveted together look.'" Or it was reported, "The object flew at about tree-top level and was seen very clearly since it was

It's in this gap, between stimulus and perception, that the real UFO mystery lies.

The essential point is this: Tim's UFO was a vehicle for meaning. Interplanetary spacecraft, if by some chance they exist, don't *mean* anything, any more than an airplane *means* something. They just *are*. But for Tim, the thing in the sky was a graphic representation of the agonizing dilemma into which he'd been plunged. His seeing it as he did doesn't indicate anything abnormal about him beyond the emotional turmoil that anyone in his position would experience. It's precisely because he comes across as so sane, so normal, that his experience can serve as an entry point to understand what happens when other sane, normal, honest people see inexplicable things in the sky.

When a young lady is pregnant, and she and her young man are living with her parents (who presumably aren't thrilled at the situation), and the young man looks into the sky and sees a ruptured condom—really, there has to be a connection. But did the heavenly apparition bear other meanings as well? Did the three-against-one split in perception mirror a conflict of Tim versus Sarah and her parents over what ought to be done about her pregnancy? Did the sighting's taking place over a notorious insane asylum reflect a perception, shared by all four, that their lives had turned into a madhouse?

Here our bridge grows shaky. The psychological information is too sparse to tell us all we want to know. Shrewdly, Graeber

---

just a few yards away. All of the observers saw a long jet airplane, looking like a vehicle without wings. It was on fire both in front and behind. All the observers observed many windows. . . . My cousin said 'If there had been anybody in the UFO near the windows, I would have seen them.'" On November 17, 1975, two college students near Cedar Rapids, Iowa, watched what seem to have been the lights of airplanes landing at a nearby airport. One student preserved a more or less accurate memory of what he'd seen, though he was at a loss to explain it. But within two days his friend had begun to remember "a domed disk that had a glassed-in cockpit. And just days after that, she was telling people that she had seen humanoid shapes behind the lights." The investigator who reported the case found no reason to doubt the young woman's sincerity. The mundane stimulus had been transformed within her; or, as I would put it, *the UFO had come from inside.*

intuited this and tried to elicit more. At first Tim and Sarah were willing to talk. Then they clammed up. Almost as if they'd had a visit from three men in black . . . Or, to translate from mythical to psychological terms, as if they'd become aware there was something concealed within the UFO that, if brought to light, would be too unbearable to be faced.

Says Graeber:

> Generally speaking, UFO witnesses would be cooperative with our investigators . . . but, when the subject of psychology came up many terminated their participation. I think they felt their personal life was not part of a random encounter with a UFO, and to imply it might have been was often felt to be an insult of some kind.

But a UFO encounter is not random. The witness's psychic life is an essential part of it. That's what this book is about.

BELGIUM, 1989–1990

The UFOs invaded on November 29, 1989. From then through the following spring, the skies of Belgium—oddly, not those of neighboring countries—were filled with them. By the time the wave subsided, more than twelve hundred sightings had been recorded.

Some of the incidents were dramatic, like the aerial chase of UFOs by F-16 jets one night in March 1990, which the Belgian military declared in its report to be beyond their power to explain. Radar as well as visual observations were involved in that incident, recalling Jung's puzzlement as to how it can be that "psychic projections throw back a radar echo." There were photographs taken by witnesses of what they saw; none showed anything of the smallest interest. The one exception turned out to be a fake.

The first really impressive sighting happened at about 5:20 p.m. on November 29, when two police officers east of Liège "saw a luminous patch about 120 feet in diameter in a field. Then, they saw a flat object in the shape of an elongated triangle with three large lights underneath in a triangular position. They estimated it to be about 90 to 100 feet across at the base, 70 feet in length, and 6 feet thick. The object was at about 375 feet up in the air. It was silent. There was a red rotating light in the middle of the white lights."

I'm quoting the description of the officers' experience given by Canadian sociologist Eric Ouellet, based on the documentation assembled in two dense five-hundred-page volumes by a UFO group called the Belgian Society for the Study of Space Phenomena (*Société belge d'étude des phénomènes spatiaux*, SOBEPS for short), which provide the definitive history of the Belgian wave. Ouellet notes that what the two policemen saw was the single most characteristic shape reported in the wave: a triangular object with a very bright white light in each corner and a weaker red light in the middle. The UFOs of 1989–1990 came in all different shapes, but Ouellet estimates that about half of them were triangular.

The systematic history of the triangular UFO has only recently been undertaken. Such things were unheard of in my teenage UFOlogy days. The two classic shapes we had to reckon with were the disk and the cigar-shaped UFO, which was normally bigger than the disk and which we assumed to be the "mother ship" sending out the smaller disklike craft. That was back in the sixties. Gradually, through the next two decades, reports of triangular objects began to trickle in, assuming some prominence among the Hudson Valley sightings of the mid-1980s. But it was in Belgium that they claimed their full share of the UFO stage.

Multiple witnesses, their sincerity beyond question, saw the flying triangles, often at low altitudes and very close range. Some were able to photograph them. Developed, the photos showed vague blobs of light or else nothing at all. In April 1990, a young man known as "Patrick M." supposedly took a photo that clearly showed the now-classic Belgian UFO: a triangle, white lights at the points, red light at the center. Twenty-one years later, Patrick confessed he'd hoaxed the picture and explained how he'd done it. But he was a minority of one. All through Belgium, honest and sane people were seeing things in the sky, sometimes several people seeing the same thing. Yet what they saw corresponded, as far as we can tell, to nothing that was there. As in Philadelphia in 1974: the gap between stimulus and perception. And as in Philadelphia, the key question that needs to be asked about the Belgian UFOs is, *What did they mean?*

November 1989 was not exactly an uneventful time in European history. On November 9, twenty days before the UFOs showed up en masse, the Berlin Wall had come down. What no one could have anticipated—the fall of Communism in central and eastern Europe, for the most part without bloodshed—was happening before the world's amazed eyes. The process didn't begin with the demise of the wall. But that event accelerated it, and over the coming months the "evil empire," as President Reagan had called the Soviet Union and its satellites, was visibly crumbling. Those were the months during which Belgium, whose capital, Brussels, houses NATO's headquarters, experienced its great UFO wave.

Can this be coincidence?

Of course it can. Wilder coincidences happen every day. But Ouellet has called attention to a symbolic link that brilliantly answers the question of the meaning of the Belgian UFOs and makes the idea of random coincidence entirely unappealing.

Think about what people were seeing in the skies: *three brilliant white lights, surrounding and enclosing a dimmer red light.* Aha, Jung would have said: that's the "quaternity," the archetype that manifests as a group of four, of which the fourth is in some way different from the other three. (We'll soon take a closer look at the quaternity and its role in Jungian thought.) But substitute *star* for *light*, and a more concrete historical symbolism begins to emerge. The red star, as Ouellet points out, was a symbol for Communism. The white star was and remains the symbol of NATO.

This all feels very archaic, very medieval. In the Middle Ages into the early modern era, and indeed back in Roman antiquity, men and women saw "signs and wonders" in the skies that crystallized in visual form what they knew to be happening around them. Was war about to break out? They looked upward and saw marching men, or flying shields or stars or "large black balls" battling amid the clouds. We might properly speak of their experiences as "visions," and it's an apt word for the UFOs of 1989–1990. The people of Belgium felt themselves in a world transforming itself, the once-triumphant and menacing red star fading away, hemmed in by the brilliant, shining power of the West. *They projected that intuitive awareness into the sky*, in symbols organized through Jungian archetypes and given nuts-and-bolts detail by the machinery of the Space Age.[8]

So were those UFOs "real"? Or were they not?

I'll be the last to claim that Ouellet's insight accounts for everything that happened in Belgium that winter and spring. The aerial chase of the night of March 30–31, with its radar as well as visual observations of unidentified things in the sky, remains baffling. We UFOlogists had grown used to thinking of "radar-visual" sightings as our best evidence, proof that solid, unknown machines were flying around up there. Yet radar is not infallible—"anomalous radar propagation," in which unusual atmospheric conditions cause blips to appear on the screen without anything physical corresponding to them, is a documented phenomenon—and we preferred to ignore the instances where radar and visual observations fail to jibe. The fact is that the Belgian pilots who went up after the UFOs never saw the lights they were supposed to be chasing. They got brief radar locks on objects doing the most extraordinary things—like shooting off at speeds that would have broken the sound barrier, without creating any sonic waves. (Proof, by itself, that they can't

8 This machinery included the American F-117 jet, unveiled earlier in the 1980s, whose near-triangular shape is likely to have had some influence on the Belgian "visionaries."

have been solid objects.) But where their radar said the objects were supposed to be, the pilots saw nothing at all.

So plenty of questions remain, yet the balance of the evidence is that the Belgian UFOs had no physical reality. If I were a debunker, I would declare victory, case closed. But my conviction, which dominates this book, is that *psychic realities are every bit as significant, every bit as "real," as physical ones.* What the Belgian people saw in the sky may in some cases, possibly most cases, have been triggered by something physically there. But this "something" was not the UFO. *The UFOs came from within*, and they were seen, not because they were there—they weren't—but because they came bearing meaning.

In Philadelphia in 1974, the "meaning" borne by the UFO was the personal dilemma of one family. In Belgium in 1989, it was a world made new.

ON SEEING WHAT ISN'T THERE

Are we speaking, then, of hallucinations? Probably. But I don't want to use that word unless we can first cleanse it of its pejorative connotations, the images it evokes of falling-down drunks seeing pink elephants or six-foot rabbits. Since such purification seems unlikely, I prefer to find a different term.

Several years ago I met a charming, intelligent, obviously sane librarian in western North Carolina—she was in her fifties but looked much younger—who told me of the UFO aliens she'd seen standing outside her home as a child looking out through her bedroom windows. "I know they weren't really there," she said. "But I did see them." I believe both parts of her statement, and part of my project as a UFOlogist is to understand how they are both true—how, without benefit of drink or drugs or sensory deprivation, far less insanity, we genuinely see things that aren't physically there.

Perhaps we'll call them apparitions, following Morton Schatzman, an American psychiatrist resident in London who treated a young American woman he calls "Ruth." She came to him for relief from the apparition of her father, a monumentally nasty man who'd abused her as a girl and now was sending his shape across the Atlantic to continue the torment. The apparition was real in every meaningful sense, apart from the fact that when it appeared in Schatzman's office, he couldn't see it any more than Hamlet's mother could see the ghost of her late husband.[9]

Not only did Ruth's father's shape appear, but when it passed before a portion of Schatzman's wall or a piece of his furniture, these things vanished from her sight—just as though blocked from view by a physical entity. Nor was sight the only sense through which the apparition manifested itself. She could put her hand to its beard, compare it with the touch of Schatzman's beard and judge them equally prickly.

Schatzman chose to treat Ruth's apparitions not as pathological symptoms but as marks of an extraordinary talent, perhaps more widespread than we know but seldom so fully developed. He taught her to control the apparitions, banishing her abusive father and evoking others more to her liking. Once, when her husband was away on a business trip, she summoned an apparition of him in their bedroom, wearing undershorts, which he then removed. The apparition and she went on to have blowout sex.[10]

Or maybe Ruth's talent wasn't so extraordinary after all. Historian Ronald Hutton has recorded his conviction, based on his experiences researching the witch religion in modern Britain, that "there is a significant minority of people within British society

---

9 HAMLET: "Do you see nothing there?" QUEEN: "Nothing at all; yet all that is I see" (*Hamlet*, act 3, scene 4). Schatzman quotes this passage and wonders how she knew that "all that is I see."

10 An experience known to more than one UFO abductee. A single mother in her thirties, in California in 1992, went to bed after watching mysterious golden globes dancing around the night sky. She "felt a warm sexual tingle between her legs" which "grew to waves of orgasmic passion as she felt something hard penetrating her in a way that could not be mistaken for anything other than raw sex." She awoke with her thighs scratched and red. Challenged as to whether she might have been dreaming, she retorted, "I know the smell of sex."

(and doubtless in many—perhaps all—others) who regularly see, hear, or feel phenomena which most others do not perceive to be present, but which are very real to them." He adds:

> Let no readers of these paragraphs feel that their personal belief systems are being challenged; the experiences concerned may be the products of chemicals in the brain, or of communications from God Almighty, the Goddess, angels, the spirits of the dear departed, or a range of other entities. The only limitation that I myself would place upon interpretation of them is that the empirical evidence causes me to reject the notions that they are caused by mere overactive imaginations, or by general mental imbalance. I also find it highly significant that modern Western society is apparently unique in the human record in that it provides no generally accepted frame of reference for them and no system of explanation within which they may be sustained or discussed.

I wouldn't be surprised if some of the witnesses to the "Miracle of the Sun" on October 13, 1917, suffered from "overactive imaginations" or "general mental imbalance." A crowd of seventy thousand (according to some estimates) had gathered at Fátima, Portugal, to watch the climax of a series of appearances of a diminutive female humanoid whom the Church had declared to be the Virgin Mary. Put that many people in one place, and you're bound to have some whose ties to reality are less than secure. But the vast majority of the observers at Fátima were sane, normal human beings, and all saw much the same thing that October afternoon. The sun danced in the sky, changed colors, appeared to some as "a metallic disk as if of silver." Then it fell to the earth.

Can we agree that, remarkable as our sun may be in many ways, there are some things it can't possibly do and falling to the ground is one of them? Yet tens of thousands of men and women saw it do just that.

The UFO books I knew as a teenager often had an obligatory chapter titled "Flying Saucers of Other Days" or something like that. The aim was to show that UFOs are nothing new, that our ancestors saw mysterious objects in the sky which they called by different names, not realizing they were interplanetary spaceships.

I don't think any of the books I read mentioned the Miracle of the Sun. Possibly the authors sensed it might antagonize religious Catholics to see one of the Blessed Virgin's most extraordinary miracles dismissed as "just" a flying saucer. Yet religion scholar Jeffrey Kripal, following the suggestions of Jacques Vallee and drawing on archival research by Portuguese UFOlogists, has pointed to intriguing resemblances between the appearance and behavior of the sun that day in 1917 and the UFO phenomenon thirty years later. The "small, pretty lady" from the sky who had appeared five months earlier to the three young shepherds of Fátima, her eyes black and her dress white and her height a little over one meter, would have been at home in an "occupant" report of the 1950s or '60s. The three children were eventually persuaded by their elders, who of course knew better than they, to believe that the lady they met was none other than Our Lady. But at first they made no such identification.

The UFO writers of my youth might have declared the lady of Fátima to have "really" been a spacewoman.[11] Kripal does no such thing. To label her an extraterrestrial, he argues, is no less a conventionalization than to call her Mary. Rather, treat Fátima and the UFO as manifestations of the same phenomenon, the one Hutton kept running up against. It's a *human* phenomenon, and since the human animal remains much the same from one century to the next, premodern experiences of it are bound to be relevant to understanding the modern ones.

---

11 A spacewoman such as Aura Rhanes, a petite, stunning five-hundred-year-old brunette from the planet "Clarion," who shared enlightenment and rides in her flying saucer with American contactee Truman Bethurum in the 1950s. Bethurum's wife, suing for divorce, named Aura Rhanes as co-respondent.

And so we come to one very special premodern "sighting" that you won't find in any UFO book. I wasn't looking for UFOs when I discovered it. I was trying to understand an extraordinary man of the seventeenth century, in the process of translating a sample of his writings from their original Hebrew. But a UFO, manifesting as a moon as uncanny as the sun at Fátima, was what I found.

ÇANAKKALE, 1683

On the evening of July 5, 1683, the Jewish magus, theologian, and cult leader Abraham Cardozo stepped outside his house and looked at the moon. What he saw there triggered a series of visions that lasted for weeks, nearly destroyed his health along with his faith, and would haunt him for the rest of his life.

Cardozo was then living in Çanakkale by the Dardanelles, where Turkey thrusts itself into the Aegean, about two hundred miles east-southeast of Istanbul. He was in exile, banned and excommunicated as a heretic. Eighteen years earlier he'd been caught up in the disastrous enthusiasm stirred up by the would-be Messiah Sabbatai Zevi. When Sabbatai converted to Islam and the mass movement grown up around him fell apart, Cardozo kept on believing. And preaching. And writing. And making himself generally obnoxious to the rabbis of his time, who paid him back by harassing him every way they could.

I've never been to Çanakkale, but they tell me the moon there on a summer night is a sight to inspire awe. It was approaching fullness on the evening of July 5, when Cardozo noticed it didn't look quite as usual. He turned to his wife, his son, a serving boy, and two houseguests who were with him at the time. He said, "I see what appear to be shapes on the moon."

The others saw them too. They recognized them. There on the moon were Sabbatai Zevi, the man who'd been Sabbatai's prophet, and a sixteenth-century mystic named Isaac Luria. All three had been dead for years. Also "a fourth shape that looks to be a woman," Cardozo's companions told him.

He could see them clearly now. He wasn't yet ready to make contact. The company must first eat, then say the evening prayer. Only afterward, "about a half hour past nightfall," did they hear the mysterious entities "speaking with us from the moon, loudly, in human voices . . . as distinctly as though they were conversing with us in the garden." Cardozo invited them down into the garden, suggesting they might stand on the trees. And they came.

So travel from the moon to the Dardanelles happens instantaneously, and you can hear the voices of lunar beings from your garden. Cardozo must have known better. People in his time may not have been able to calculate the precise distance of the moon from the earth, but they knew it was many thousands of miles. (Fifty thousand, the pioneer astronomer Johannes Kepler had calculated.) Carried by wild swans flying at propeller-plane velocity, like the hero of a science-fiction bestseller of 1638, you'd need "Eleven or Twelve daies" to get there. Cardozo's "moon," which like the UFO in Philadelphia and many in Belgium seemed only a few hundred yards away, was a psychic construction of his own, bearer of meaning within his symbolic universe. That moon-apparition superimposed itself on the real moon, the two fusing together.

The moon-people stayed two hours in Cardozo's garden, discussing religious subjects with him and his friends. The next night they reappeared in his bedroom—only three of them, however. The fourth "shape," the one like a woman, seems never to have left the moon. It was during this second visit that things began to turn ugly.

Cross-examined, the visitors admitted they weren't the blessed ghosts they'd at first appeared to be. They'd come to reveal a dreadful truth: Cardozo's God has been dethroned, stripped of power. The Devil now rules the world. They proved their point by spewing out blasphemies, taunting Cardozo to call on his God to "send fire to burn us up."

Cardozo realized he was dealing with demons. It was too late; he couldn't get them out of his bedroom. Horribly, it wasn't they who burned in fire but Cardozo himself. He took to his bed with *fiebre ardiente*, "burning fever," while the three men stood gloating beside the bed, "all dressed in black." *Three men in black*: here they are in Çanakkale, 270 years before coming to visit Albert Bender in Bridgeport, Connecticut, and we realize Bender was lucky to come out of his encounter with three days of an upset stomach. Cardozo almost died.

Was that *fiebre ardiente*, perhaps, the only part of Cardozo's story that belonged to the real world? Was the rest a fever-hallucination, projected back into the time before the onset of the disease? Maybe. But it's also possible that he and his five companions really did experience a shared vision on the evening of July 5, perhaps triggered by some irregularity in the moon's appearance, some odd contours that atmospheric conditions had lent to the lunar markings. Either way it's a weird encounter, with beings at once earthly and extraterrestrial. It yields its meaning on two levels. And the enigmatic Fourth—the woman on the moon, who appears at the beginning of the story and then vanishes—is key to both.

For Abraham Cardozo hadn't always been Jewish. He had been born in Spain in 1627 to a family that had converted to Catholicism in 1492, when all Jews were expelled from Spain. He had been christened Miguel and brought up a Catholic—in a country awash in paintings and sculptures of the Virgin of the Immaculate Conception *standing on the moon*.

In this artwork the Virgin is usually accompanied by cherubs, often three of them—winged, so they might be imagined to fly down to earth while she stays on the moon. She's very beautiful. We can almost see little Miguel staring, openmouthed with awe, at some portrait of the tender, mysterious Lady who rules the night sky. He'll grow up to convert to Judaism, spurn his childhood faith and damn its "Blessed Virgin" as a supreme she-devil. The powerful, seductive images will stay lodged in his brain. They'll erupt one summer night many years later, in a compelling, devastating vision.

That's one level of interpretation, and it will explain much of Cardozo's experience. But something else is operating here also, more archaic and universal than Cardozo and the culture from which he came. Like the symbolism of Communism and NATO in the Belgian UFO wave, the seventeenth-century art of the Immaculate Conception came flowing through channels hewn out thousands, perhaps many thousands, of years earlier. Dr. Jung, please call your office.

WHAT JUNG WAS TRYING TO SAY

We humans, according to Jung, are hard-wired to organize our perceptions into a number of fixed and universal patterns. These patterns, these matrixes as it were, are called *archetypes*. They're fixed within the *collective unconscious* of our species and will crop up spontaneously, independently, and without any influence from one culture to another in the art and religion, the myth and the literature and the folkways, of societies in all ages and everywhere on the globe. Archetypes also turn up, just as prominently and just as spontaneously, in the dreams of individuals. Properly analyzed, they serve as benign guides to the unfolding of our spiritual lives.

One of these archetypes is the *quaternity*. This is a group of four—doesn't matter four what; the content of the archetype will vary but the organizing pattern remains stable—organized as a 3 + 1. In other words, three of the four are alike, while the fourth is in some way different. Again, it doesn't matter how it is different. But that difference is always of immense importance for understanding how the archetype functions.

Take, for example, the New Testament Gospels. Three of them, Matthew, Mark, and Luke, are called the Synoptic Gospels because they see eye to eye ("syn-optic"). They tell, with variations to be sure, essentially the same story of Jesus's life, teachings, miracles, death, and resurrection. The Fourth Gospel, John, is different.

For the early Church, at least as far back as the second century, there could be four Gospels and only four. Their fourness was something embedded in the fabric of reality. It was prefigured in the four "living creatures," one human and three with animal faces, in the Book of Revelation. Also farther back, in the Old Testament, Ezekiel sees four "living creatures," each of which has four faces, three animal and one human. 3 + 1 once more.

The Christian Trinity, Jung thought, is a mutilated quaternity. In that mutilation, the suppression of the Fourth, lies the basic flaw of the Christian religion. What is that Fourth? Jung wavered between two alternatives, which, from a psychological perspective, can be seen as complementing one another: The Fourth is Satan. Christianity had suppressed its dark side, forcing its "shadow" (to use the Jungian term) into the unconscious. From there, unrecognized, it could work havoc that would have been impossible if it had been acknowledged and properly integrated (as, according to Jungian psychology, we all need to do with our "shadows" if we're to become whole human beings). Or the Fourth is Mary, the feminine aspect of God, expelled into the darkness by historical Christianity's one-sided insistence on masculinity.

"One, two, three—but where is the Fourth?"[12] This is the question that, for Jung, must be asked whenever we come across a Three—in our dreams and also in our myths, which Jung understands as a kind of shared, communal dreaming.[13]

The method has its dangers. After reading Freud, you see sexual symbols wherever you look. Once in the Jungian mindset, you find archetypes everywhere. Quaternities turn up in places like the ancient rabbinic literature, where Jung himself never thought to look for them, dramatically confirming his ideas. That's the danger. Pretty much everything can serve as confirmation for the system, while there's hardly anything that can *disconfirm* it—a sign

---

12 Quoted by Jung from the beginning of Plato's *Timaeus*.

13 Or in the communal rituals we call sports? It's possible to see the baseball diamond, with its three identical bases + home plate, as a material embodiment of the quaternity.

that, while the theory may be true, it also can give the illusion of truth because its own rules make it impossible to argue against. A cigar, Freud is famously though improbably reported to have said, is sometimes just a cigar. Does every threesome in this world have to be a Trinity? Every foursome a Quaternity?

Well, but a cigar in a dream is never just a cigar. It's not necessarily a penis, but it's something beyond itself. Otherwise it's meaningless. When three dead men and an unknown woman appear together on a visionary moon, it's a fair guess their number is not accidental.

It's still less likely to be accidental, in that a parallel quaternity crops up in a different corner of Cardozo's psychic life. Four Messiahs, he says, are destined to come into the world, three of them male. The fourth is a woman, a mysterious lady without any precedent in Jewish tradition, whom Cardozo never tries to explain. Like the woman on the moon, he leaves her an enigma.

The two quaternities mirror each other. One is divine, the other demonic. Both are divided by gender, 3 + 1; a cryptic female is the pivot of both. It's likely that Cardozo doesn't try to identify his woman Messiah because he himself has no idea who she is. She springs unbidden from his unconscious.

The same can be said of all four of the entities Cardozo and the other witnesses saw on the moon that July night in 1683. Only these manifested not as a theological hypothesis, but as an observed phenomenon within the physical world. That's what makes them UFOs.

PAPUA NEW GUINEA, 1959

We're now equipped to understand what was seen in the sky at Boianai, on the coast at the southeastern tip of Papua New Guinea, on the nights of Friday, June 26 and Saturday, June 27, 1959. It's referred to in the UFO annals as the "Gill sighting"; researchers have hailed it, for good reason, as one of the best and most baffling "close-encounter" cases ever recorded, indeed as "history's best case." To this day it's never been satisfactorily explained.[14]

Like many of the Belgian UFOs, like Cardozo's sighting of the people on the moon, the event was multiply witnessed. Again, as in Cardozo's sighting, the primary witness was a figure of some religious authority, in this case a young Anglican priest in charge of the mission at Boianai. "Presumably a reliable witness," we UFOlogists used to say smugly of any clergyman reporting a UFO, in those innocent days when it was taken for granted that people of the cloth were upstanding folk who would never tell a lie. This presumption has been a bone in the throats of the UFO debunkers, who've had to find some way to explain how the priest didn't really see the amazing things he said he saw. Even the caustic Menzel felt bound to declare that "there is no question, of course, of the integrity of Father Gill," while hinting not too subtly that he didn't entirely believe that. But Philip Klass, Menzel's successor as archskeptic, belonged to a younger, more openly cynical generation. Klass was less circumspect in saying what he thought of the Reverend William Booth Gill.

The incident for which Gill became famous began at 6:45 on the evening of Friday, June 26. "Sighted bright white light from front direction N.W.," runs the first of the jottings in Gill's notebook, into which he recorded his impressions of the strange events as they happened. Then: "Coming closer, not so bright. Coming down 500 ft?, orange?, deep yellow?"

Gill sent one of his assistants "to call people." Soon a crowd of thirty-eight had gathered. Later that evening, twenty-five of them would sign their names to a series of sketches made independently by Gill and two of the Papuan teachers at the mission school, attesting

---

14 The primary source for the Gill case is a typewritten report prepared in November 1959 by the Victorian Flying Saucer Research Society (VFSRS, of Victoria, Australia) and incorporating an earlier report by Gill, dated July 15. I am more grateful than I can say to Martin Kottmeyer for having shared with me his copy of this report. All quotations from Gill, unless stated otherwise, are taken from it.

that they too had seen the object depicted in those drawings. "One object on top, move—man?" Gill wrote in his notebook. "Now three men—moving, glowing, doing something on deck. Gone."

First one man, then three, self-luminous ("glowing"), as one might expect angels to be. Soon they were four, apparently distinct from each other and recognizable as individuals, like Cardozo's foursome on the moon. "Men 1, 3, 4, 2 (appeared in that order). Thin elct. [electric] blue spot light. Men gone, spot light still there." (To judge from the sketches, the "spot light" was shining at a 45-degree angle up into the sky.) The "men" returned to the UFO's deck, or at least two of them did, until at 7:20 the "spot light" went off and the "men go," and the "UFO goes through cloud" and could no longer be seen.

The disjointed quality of these notes speaks for their genuineness. If Gill were fabricating a story, surely he'd have come up with something more coherent. He'd have made up his mind, for example, whether the UFO's color was orange or yellow. As an honest, baffled observer, scribbling down his impressions of something beyond his ken, his wavering on this point makes sense.

Over an hour after disappearing in the clouds, the UFO was back. By 8:50 there were four of them, the original "mother ship," or "Mother," as Gill calls it, and three "satellites" "coming and going through clouds." Here's the 3 + 1 quaternity—once again, shades of Cardozo.[15] (The woman Cardozo saw on the moon, if indeed the Virgin Mary, was the Mother par excellence.) One or more of the UFOs remained intermittently visible until past 10:30. The four luminescent humanoids, however, didn't show themselves again until the following evening.

At about 6:00 p.m. on Saturday, June 27, a Papuan woman who worked as Gill's medical assistant noticed a "large U.F.O." in the same

---

15 Adding one more "four" to the mix, the sketches by Gill and the Papuans show four legs—functionless, since the UFOs never landed—on the "mother ship" and each of the three "satellites."

spot in the sky where the mother ship had been the evening before. A few minutes later Gill saw it too. "I called Ananias [Rarata, a teacher at the mission school] and several others," Gill wrote two and a half weeks later in his report, "and we stood in the open to watch it. . . . We watched figures appear on top—four of them—no doubt that they are human. Possibly the same object I took to be the 'Mother' ship last night." *No doubt that they are human.* Yet their luminosity points to something more, and Gill would remember years later, "I thought they were angels." The paradox, that the visitors were human and also beyond human, must be allowed to stand intact.

Two smaller UFOs, stationary, could also be seen in the darkening sky.

> On the large one two of the figures seemed to be doing something near the centre of the deck—were occasionally bending over and raising their arms as though adjusting or "setting up" something (not visible). One figure seemed to be standing looking down at us (a group of about a dozen). I stretched my arm above my head and waved, to our surprise the figure did the same. Ananias waved both arms over his head then the two outside figures did the same. Ananias and self began waving our arms and all four now seemed to wave back. There *seemed* to be no doubt that our movements were answered. All mission boys made audible gasps (of either joy or surprise perhaps both).

As in Philadelphia in 1974, the UFO responded to, even mirrored, the actions of the observers.

> As dark was beginning to close in, I sent Eric Kodawara for a torch [flashlight] and directed a series of long dashes towards the U.F.O. After a minute or two of this, the U.F.O. apparently acknowledged by making several wavering motions back and forth. Waving by us was repeated and this followed by more flashes of torch, then the U.F.O. began slowly to become bigger, apparently coming in our direction. It ceased after perhaps half a minute and came no further. After a further two or three minutes the figures

> apparently lost interest in us for they disappeared "below" deck. At 6:25 p.m. two figures re-appeared to carry on with whatever they were doing before the interruption (?). The blue spot light came on for a few seconds, twice in succession.

Five minutes later Gill went inside to dinner.

So, apparently, did everyone else. At 7:00, when Gill checked back, "No. 1 U.F.O. still present, but appeared somewhat smaller—observers go to church for Evensong." Forty-five minutes later, the service over, Gill found the sky covered with cloud, the visibility very poor, and the UFOs gone.

Gill's self-reported behavior seems odd by any standard. As far as Philip Klass was concerned, it gave the lie to Gill's whole story. How could anyone, on the brink of the first human contact with extraterrestrials, have interrupted the thrilling event to eat dinner and lead a church service? To this criticism Gill offered a string of rejoinders. He didn't realize at the time there was anything "eerie or otherworldly" about what he was seeing; he imagined it was probably some kind of American or possibly Australian "hovercraft." Anyway, he and the Papuans weren't getting anywhere with their efforts to persuade the pilots to land and have dinner with them. So why not go eat?

This all has the feel of after-the-fact rationalization. For me, what's important is that nearly three centuries earlier Cardozo and his friends, faced with a similar circumstance, reacted in *precisely the same way.* "After our meal," Cardozo told his fellow witnesses, "we shall say the evening prayer"—and only afterward return to communicate with the moon-beings. It sounds very much as if this impulse, to eat and then to worship, is not a distraction from the experience but part and parcel of it.

What were the UFOs, really? To which I'll respond: what do we mean by *really*? Reading the report, I come away with the same impression as Menzel: heavenly bodies seen under unusual atmospheric conditions. This would explain why the objects came and went as the clouds parted or thickened—a detail that also has deeper resonances of the Magonian sky-ships of medieval France, which were said to "come in the clouds." Nearly twenty years after the sighting, Gill visited the United States and met with two UFOlogists, who had him point out the positions his UFOs had occupied in the sky. Their conclusion was that the "satellite" UFOs, but not the "mother ship," could be explained as bright stars and planets. But this is too modest. Skeptic Martin Kottmeyer's close analysis of Gill's diagram of the positions of the Friday evening UFOs, done in 2007, shows convincingly that Friday's "mother ship" (and therefore Saturday's also) was the planet Jupiter, its three "satellites" the planet Saturn and the stars Spica and Rigel Kentaurus.

Of course the witnesses' perceptions underwent a distortion that borders on the incredible. So what else is new? We saw the same thing in Philadelphia in 1974, where an airplane was transmogrified into a low-flying, hovering object that blinked or retreated in response to the witnesses' auto headlights. We saw it at Fátima, where a crowd of many thousands—not a mere twenty-five as at Boianai—collectively saw the sun do things it couldn't have done. The process will seem less fantastic when we recall that *the external stimulus for the UFO sighting is only a trigger. The "real" UFO, the bearer of significance, comes from inside.*

Menzel, more reluctant than Klass to call Gill a liar, made another supposition almost as insulting. He conjectured that "the priest, perhaps unknown to himself, has considerable myopia and astigmatism in his eye." As for the Papuan witnesses, Menzel dismissed them as docile, impressionable primitives eager to please their "great white leader" and echo whatever he said. Gill, who wore glasses and would have noticed if they were missing, scoffed at both ideas. His parishioners were educated, strong-minded men and women who'd been doing all their schoolwork in English since third grade. When they attached their names to his report, they knew perfectly well what they were signing. They saw the UFO too.

Yet they didn't see it independent of Gill, or of each other. There must have been cries—mutually intelligible, in whatever language uttered—of "Do you see that?" and "Yes, yes, I do!" (just as Cardozo didn't know quite what he was seeing on the moon until his friends told him). Nonverbal cues and inflections of tone must have played their part. We humans are capable of conveying extraordinary amounts of information to one another in the most extraordinarily subtle ways, much of the time unaware we're doing it. The construction of the disk-shaped craft with its four luminescent beings—or better, its displacement from the psyche into the sky—was a joint activity of all the witnesses, Gill included. Or, more accurately, of those twenty-five who signed their names to the drawings. The thirteen who didn't sign were presumably those who, despite their best efforts, couldn't quite manage to see what the majority saw.

Menzel's and Klass's assumptions to the contrary, it's not at all obvious that Gill was the sole or even the principal architect of that process. An indigenous belief, widespread in the Highlands of Papua New Guinea, held the sky to be inhabited by humanlike ghosts or spirits who sometimes take full human form and descend to earth. This was the land of the cargo cults, religious movements aimed at manipulating the ancestral sky beings into disgorging plentiful "cargo" for their children on earth, as the Japanese and Americans did for their soldiers in World War II. In 1981, a Papuan university student who "was trying to be very respectful of the traditions of his people" told his Australian professor how he had once seen "the heavens open and a group of angels in white clothing high in the sky. I saw it with my own eyes." Subtract the "white clothing," add the up-to-date hovercraft machinery, and we have an experience akin to the collective vision at Boianai.

"That 'great white leader' business," said Gill—referring back to Menzel—"might happen in Hollywood movies about African missionaries, but certainly not where I was." (In 1959 Papua New Guinea was a "territory" governed by Australia. It wouldn't get its independence for another sixteen years.) "I was sent to Boianai to sort things out," Gill explained, "because there were certain problems caused by a growing anti-European feeling. They didn't want a European there at all, really, and they wanted me least of all because I was a stranger to the district. . . . We had some real difficulties." Those difficulties, whatever they were, evidently proved intractable. Three months after the sighting, in September 1959, Gill was no longer in Boianai.

And I'm left wondering whether the visions shared by Gill and the Papuans those June evenings represent a joint psychic effort to transcend their difficulties, to integrate their tensions. For Jung the "mandala"—the circle, the wheel, the sphere—is one of the most widespread and powerful of the archetypes, a representation of "totality whose simple round form portrays the archetype of the self . . . uniting apparently irreconcilable opposites." It's a profoundly religious manifestation, for is not God "a circle whose centre is everywhere and the circumference nowhere"? No wonder that when Jung heard about flying saucers in the sky, his thoughts went to mandalas.

So the mandala-disk and its quaternity of riders complement each other, like Cardozo's "moon" and the quaternity he saw standing on it. Confronted with this vision, what does Gill do? He goes to dinner.

Alone? Or with the others, his Papuan congregants with whom he must have shared deep feelings of affection, along with the tensions that soon were to drive him away? The evidence is ambiguous. "At 6:30 p.m. I went to dinner," Gill wrote in his notebook—*I*, not *we*. On the other hand, he spoke afterward of his hope that "if we got them to land we would find the pilots to be ordinary earthmen in military uniforms and we would have dinner with them." *We*, not *I*. I'll guess that the second version conveys the truer picture, and that the "dinner" was to be a shared communion at which the four shining visitors were anticipated and honored guests, like the angelic trio to whom Abraham offered his hospitality in Genesis chapter 18 (and whom the Bible story, like Gill, calls simply "men"). The meal was followed, appropriately, by a communal act of worship.

Seen from this perspective, Gill's and the Papuans' response to the UFO's numinous presence wasn't at all odd or unsuitable. Vision and rite worked in tandem toward a goal of reconciliation and unity. If the rifts proved too deep to be healed, that wasn't the fault of the UFO.

And maybe Gill was lucky the UFO couldn't be persuaded to land. Cardozo tells what might have happened if it did.

In this chapter I've offered a fair number of conjectures. I can't expect the reader to accept them all. But I hope I've established the following main points:

First, *the external stimulus for the UFO sighting is apt to undergo major and seemingly fantastic distortion* in the course of its transformation into the UFO. This doesn't always happen—which is why many UFO sightings are easy to explain—but it's a common feature of the phenomenon.

Second, the distortion is not random or meaningless, but *rooted in and explicable through the psyche of the observers.* The stimulus is mundane. The distortion—or better, the transformation—is *the true UFO*, and the real object of inquiry.

Third, the psychological roots of the transformation may be relatively shallow—as in Philadelphia, where they reflected a transient crisis over a young woman's pregnancy. They may go deeper, into collective awareness of a decisive historical moment, as in Belgium. Or they can plunge very deep, into *layers of the human psyche that transcend centuries and cultures.* Call this the "collective unconscious," "Magonia," or whatever you will. It's something real—and no less alien, no less mysterious, than any planet in the depths of interstellar space.

It's a realm we'll need to explore if we're to understand one of the most baffling aspects of the UFO enigma: the alien abduction.

PART II

Inside the UFO

CHAPTER 3

The Abductions Begin

AT ABOUT 8:00 A.M. ON SATURDAY, December 14, 1963, a New Hampshire couple named Betty and Barney Hill arrived at the office of Boston psychiatrist Benjamin Simon for their first scheduled appointment. They'd come for treatment of Betty's nightmares, apprehension, persistent anxiety and of Barney's anxiety and insomnia, ulcers and high blood pressure. Along with these worrisome symptoms, Barney had one other that was trivial but distinctly weird. A ring of warts had appeared in a perfect circle around his groin and needed to be surgically removed.

In all but two respects, the Hills were ordinary middle-class New Englanders in early middle age. Betty was a social worker for the State of New Hampshire. Barney worked night shift in a Boston post office; these hours, and a sixty-mile commute, took a further toll on his already shaky health. The couple was active in their Unitarian Universalist church in Portsmouth, New

Hampshire. They were also active in the civil rights movement, at a time when Martin Luther King's "I Have a Dream" speech was in the very recent past and civil rights were less than respectable in many quarters. Their life together was an embodiment of King's dream. Betty was white; Barney was black.

That was one unusual thing about the Hills. The other was that they came into Simon's office with a vague but emphatic sense that their troubles were rooted in an encounter with a UFO on a lonely mountain road more than two years earlier. What they remembered of the encounter was dramatic enough. But for the past two years Betty, in particular, had had the nagging conviction there was more to it than could be recalled, which surfaced only in strange dreams. That amnesia, they suspected, was at the root of all their other symptoms. They'd been told that hypnosis could help retrieve lost memories. Dr. Benjamin Simon was an acknowledged expert in therapeutic hypnosis; he'd used it extensively to treat military psychiatric disorders during World War II, when he was chief of neuropsychiatry and executive officer at Mason General Hospital on Long Island. That was why the Hills turned to him.

Dr. Benjamin Simon didn't believe in UFOs, didn't care about UFOs. He had only one commitment: to help his patients. He must at some time or other have read Freud's *Interpretation of Dreams*, where the principle is laid down that "in analysing a dream I insist that the whole scale of estimates of certainty shall be abandoned and that the faintest possibility that something of this or that sort may have occurred in the dream shall be treated as complete certainty." For the therapist, doubt is the enemy, the agent of resistance. Doubt must be cast aside.

Simon spent his first few sessions with the Hills bringing them in and out of trance, familiarizing them with the process. Then, on February 22, 1964, he brought Barney into his office while Betty stayed in the waiting room. He loaded the tape cartridges into his recording machine, and he and Barney set to work.

It's not often in the study of mythology that you can pinpoint a specific date when this or that mythic theme sprang into existence. Still more rarely can you name the person or persons who brought it into being. Normally myth is an anonymous, collective creation. By the time it's noticed, it's been part of people's awareness so long it seems to have been around forever. It becomes what in the collective unconscious it's always been: timeless, ahistorical.

The UFO mythology breaks this mold. Again and again, the birthing of a mythic theme related to UFOs can be traced back to a specific time, a specific place, a specific person. The theme spreads, diffuses, hidden and silent at first like the mustard seed of the parable. The creation of one person's psyche—or of two or three persons, acting in unwitting collusion—it evokes resonances in thousands, then millions of others. Decades after its initial emergence, the theme has become a common cultural property. Allusions to it are instantly intelligible, even to people who know little or nothing of its details. Alien abduction is one of those UFO mythic themes—and in Dr. Simon's office on Bay State Road in Boston, on that Saturday morning in February 1964, it was about to be born.

UFO INCIDENT

Over two years earlier, in mid-September 1961, the Hills had made a spur-of-the-moment decision to take a short driving vacation. They'd see Niagara Falls, circle through Canada to Montreal, and then head back home to Portsmouth. In their spontaneous enthusiasm they didn't plan as carefully as they might. By September 19, the last day of their trip, money had run low. They couldn't afford one more night in a motel. They decided to drive all night until they reached home.

Sometime in the middle of that night, as they drove south from Colebrook through the White Mountains of New Hampshire on the nearly deserted Route 3, they became aware of a light in the sky that seemed to be following them.

It couldn't be a star; it couldn't be a planet. It was moving against the background of the heavenly bodies. Barney insisted it had to be a plane, even though it made no sound that they could hear. Betty thought it was something more unusual.

"We stopped our car and got out to observe it more closely with our binoculars," Betty wrote a week later to Major Donald E. Keyhoe. Retired from the Marine Corps, Keyhoe was director of a private organization called the National Investigations Committee on Aerial Phenomena (NICAP), which was at the time the gold standard for "objective" UFOlogy. For a while the Hills drove and stopped, drove and stopped, Betty wrote Keyhoe. Then the object seemed to approach their car.

> We stopped again. As it hovered in the air in front of us, it appeared to be pancake in shape, ringed with windows in the front through which we could see bright blue-white lights. Suddenly, two red lights appeared on each side. By this time my husband was standing in the road, watching closely. He saw wings protrude on each side and the red lights were on the wing tips.
>
> As it glided closer he was able to see inside the object, but not too closely. [Barney was using his binoculars at the time.] He did see several figures scurrying about as though they were making some hurried type of preparation. One figure was observing us from the windows. From the distance this was seen, the figures appeared to be about the size of a pencil, and seemed to be dressed in some type of shiny black uniform.
>
> At this point, my husband became shocked and got back in the car, in a hysterical condition, laughing and repeating they were going to capture us. He started driving the car—the motor had been left running. As we started to move, we heard several buzzing or beeping sounds which seemed to be striking the trunk of our car.

The Hills remembered little of what happened next. There was a second series of beeps and a vague impression of something like the moon sitting in the road. They reached their home a little after 5:00 a.m., a couple of hours later than anticipated. Peculiar shiny circles, which Betty was convinced were radioactive, had appeared on the trunk of their car. Ten days later Betty began having strange dreams in which she and Barney were stopped at a roadblock and taken aboard an alien craft. The dreams went on for five nights, then stopped.

Barney pooh-poohed it all. There were no such things as flying saucers; end of discussion. Yet as 1961 passed into 1962, he went along with Betty on a string of compulsive, futile trips back to Route 3, hunting for the site of their experience, hoping somehow to find the key to whatever was troubling them. His ulcers worsened; the warts appeared in his groin. Conventional psychotherapy didn't help. At last they turned to Benjamin Simon.

HYPNOTIC REGRESSION

> DOCTOR: I want you to tell me in full detail *all* your experiences, *all* of your thoughts, and *all* of your feelings, beginning with the time you left your hotel.

This was Dr. Simon's charge to Barney on the morning of February 22, 1964. Transcripts of the tape-recorded hypnotic sessions were published two years later by John G. Fuller in his book *The Interrupted Journey: Two Lost Hours "Aboard a Flying Saucer"* and in a two-part article in the October 4 and 18, 1966, issues of *Look* magazine. Those two issues set new sales records for the magazine.

> BARNEY: We arrived at night [September 18, the night before the sighting] at this motel, and I did not notice any name in the motel. . . . The thoughts that were going through my mind were: Would they accept me? Because they might say they were filled up, and I wondered if they were going to do this, because I was prejudiced. . . .
>
> DOCTOR: Because *you* were prejudiced?

BARNEY: . . . because *they* were prejudiced.

DOCTOR: Because you were a Negro?

BARNEY: Because I am a Negro.

Again and again Barney returns to his fear of prejudice, of rejection, and we're reminded that for Barney and Betty daily life was a continual exercise in courage. The motel, in any event, did not turn them away. They spent the night there and drove all the next day, crossing from Canada into the United States. Late that night, they stopped at a restaurant in Colebrook, near the northern border of New Hampshire.

> I park—and we go in. There is a dark-skinned woman in there, I think, dark by Caucasian standards, and I wonder—is she a light-skinned Negro, or is she Indian, or is she white?—and she waits on us, and she is not very friendly, and I notice this, and others are there and they are looking at me and Betty, and they seem to be friendly or pleased, but this dark-skinned woman doesn't. I wonder then more so—is she Negro and wonder if I—if she is wondering if I know she is Negro and is passing for white.

It's now 10:05 p.m. on September 19; the Hills are about to begin their drive south down Route 3. But before he continues his story, Barney's thoughts go back to a restaurant they'd earlier visited in Canada. As he and Betty walk to it, "everybody on the street passing us by is looking. And we go in to this restaurant, and all eyes are upon us. And I see what I call the stereotype of the 'hoodlum.' The ducktail haircut. And I immediately go on guard against any hostility."

Barney begins to rebuke himself: "I should get hold of myself, and not think everyone was hostile, or rather suspect hostility, when there was no hostility there. . . . The people were friendly . . . why was I ready to be defensive—just because these boys were wearing this style of haircut." He holds himself to very high standards not just of conduct but of thought. Why was he so ready to be defensive? In August 1955, a little over six years before the Hills took their drive into Canada, a black teenager from Chicago named Emmett Till had been lynched in Mississippi for supposedly making suggestive remarks to a white woman. Granted, New Hampshire was not Mississippi. But the message of what this country still could do to a black man who took his liberty too seriously had been delivered.

Barney relives for the doctor his and Betty's experience as they drove southward through the darkness. The light appears. At first he thinks it's a star, then a satellite. Then he's sure it's an airplane. But why won't it go away?

"Betty!" he exclaims in his trance. "This is *not* a flying saucer. What are you doing this for? You want to believe in this thing, and I don't."

Suddenly he cries out: "I want to wake up!" The doctor reassures him: he's safe, he can go on. And he does: "It's right over my right! God! What is it? . . . And I try to maintain control, so Betty cannot tell I am *scared. God*, I'm scared!"

(Later that morning, after the Hills leave his office, Simon will dictate into his tape recorder that the patient "showed very marked emotional discharge" at this point in his story. "Tears rolled down his cheeks, he would clutch his face, his head, and writhe in considerable agony." Nearly three years later, Simon will tell UFO debunker Philip Klass that "he had never had a patient become so excited under hypnosis"—so much so that "he feared that Barney might try to jump out of the office window." He will play for Klass the tape of Barney reliving his UFO experience, and even the skeptical Klass will "agree completely with the doctor that Barney had indeed seen 'something,' and it had been a terrifying experience.")

Barney remembers more: going into the trunk for the tire wrench, which he'll use to defend himself if he has to. "I'm *not* afraid. I'm *not* afraid," he insists. "I'll fight it off. I'm not *afraid!*"

He remembers crossing the road toward the thing. He still has his binoculars. He can see the object, now less than a thousand feet away; it's shaped like a big pancake, with rows of windows. Through a window, a face looks out at him. It's not the face of an intergalactic alien, however, but something that puts him in mind of "a red-headed Irishman."

A red-headed Irishman? Barney explains:

> I think I know why. Because Irish are usually hostile to Negroes. And when I see a friendly Irish person, I react to him by thinking—*I* will be friendly. And I think this one that is looking over his shoulder is friendly.

The perpetual tightrope walk that was Barney Hill's life: be on guard against hostility, but where there's friendliness, be prepared to reciprocate. This Irishman is smiling, friendly.

But then he's gone, and suddenly the face is "evil . . . He looks like a German Nazi. He's a Nazi. . . . He had a black scarf around his neck, dangling over his left shoulder"—and, it later comes out, a "black, black shiny jacket," which naturally makes Dr. Simon think of the ducktailed teenagers back in the Canadian restaurant. He asks if they had been wearing black shiny coats, as such boys often do, and Barney replies that no, they hadn't.

How, then, did a "German Nazi" get aboard the UFO? This detail goes back at least to October 1961, when NICAP investigator Walter Webb interviewed the Hills and reported that the figures inside the UFO "reminded the observer [Barney] of the cold precision of German officers." But now it's taken on fresh emotional power, and I think we can guess why. Later Barney will note that "somehow, Dr. Simon had become sort of a close friend. He had become more than a close friend. He had become someone I loved, and I didn't want any harm to come to." To judge from his name, Benjamin Simon was Jewish. The well-read Barney certainly knew what sort of "harm" a Jew, or a black man for that matter, might expect to experience from a "German Nazi."

Abruptly Barney exclaims: "I feel like a rabbit. I feel like a rabbit." "What do you mean by that?" the doctor asks, and Barney thinks back to a scene from his distant past:

> I was hunting for rabbits in Virginia. And this cute little bunny went into a bush that was not very big. And my cousin Marge was on one side of the bush, and I was on the other—with a hat. And the poor little bunny thought he was safe. And it tickled me, because he was just hiding behind a little stalk, which meant security to him—when I pounced on him, and threw my hat on him, and captured the poor little bunny who thought he was safe.

Is he also remembering, unconsciously, a scene from a past even more distant?

AFRICAN INTERLUDE

The year: 1763. The place: a fishing village at the mouth of the Formosa River on what's now the coast of Nigeria, about one hundred miles east-southeast of Lagos, where the river flows into the Gulf of Benin.

An old man, a young man, and a young woman, strangers to the region, are paddling past the village in their canoe. Surely they've spotted the alien craft that sits motionless out in the Gulf. They may have made efforts, as futile as Betty's and Barney's two hundred years later, to assimilate this unknown phenomenon to their categories of the real and familiar. By the time they realize they've been seen as well, that war canoes from the great ship's vicinity are headed in their direction, it's too late.

Perhaps they try to resist, to fight back. But whatever weapons they have are as ineffectual as Barney's tire wrench. Soon they're prisoners of an African bandit chief and professional kidnapper who prospers by doing business with the white men from across the sea. Brought onto the deck of the slave ship, they're offered to the captain for sale. The old man is refused and beheaded. The young man and woman are purchased and carried away for resale in the far-off colony of Virginia.

Episodes of this sort were legion in the heyday of the Atlantic slave trade. You were abducted, perhaps in a night raid on your village, accompanied by the burning of your and your neighbors' homes. (Was the thing like the moon, which Betty and Barney remembered sitting in the road, a reminiscence of such fires?) Or you were taken prisoner in war—which, since war in eighteenth-century West Africa tended to be a mechanism for getting human merchandise to sell to the strangers, amounted to the same thing. You were marched to the coast, your destination an alien craft to which, since it had to anchor some distance out, you were carried the last leg by canoe. As you drew near the craft, you might see, in the words of historian Marcus Rediker, "dark faces, framed by small holes in the side of the ship above the waterline, staring intently" at you, while above you "dozens of black women and children and a few red-faced men peered over the rail."

To the Africans in first contact with them, the slave ships were something altogether fantastic: "houses with wings upon them" that could "walk upon the water" through a technology beyond imagining. How was it possible, the Africans wondered, "by any sort of contrivance, to make so large a body move forwards by the common force of the wind"? In a long epic poem published in 1789 as an exposé of the slave trade, a British ex-slaver described the typical captive's response to the "vast machine" that was his or her entry to an alien and horrific world:

> Torn as his bosom is, still wonder grows,
> As o'er the vast machine the victim goes,
> Wonder, commix'd with anguish, shakes his frame
> At the strange sight his language cannot name.

REENACTMENT

It's an eye-opener to read the transcripts of Barney's and afterward Betty's hypnotic regressions with the historical slave experience in mind.

As their memories surface of the portions of the UFO experience to which they've had no conscious access, they speak of being taken prisoner, brought aboard the alien craft. Barney speaks repeatedly of being conveyed onto it by "floating"—an accurate reflex of the captive's being rowed on a canoe out to the slave ship. He finds himself having to step over what he calls a "bulkhead." Once on the UFO, he and Betty are separated—as the slaves were, divided by sexes for the duration of the voyage.

They're subjected to intrusive physical examinations, the details grotesque.[16] Betty remembers the UFO beings reaching into her mouth, trying to pull out her teeth. Her captors are surprised: why do Barney's teeth come out but hers don't? She has to explain that Barney wears dentures, nearly everybody does as they age. They ask, seemingly baffled, "What's 'aging' "? When she says it is something that happens to people with time, they ask, "What's 'time' "? This dialogue seems incongruous, so nearly comical that we're tempted to laugh. Really!—a species advanced enough to conquer space, yet perplexed as children by the mysteries of human dentition. Our laughter will fade when we recall it was standard operating procedure for the slave dealers to give the closest attention to their potential purchases' teeth.[17] These served as a reliable index to whether the merchandise was young enough to be worth paying for.

---

16 Given the central importance that the physical examination was to take on in the UFO abduction tradition, it's worth quoting one slave-trade historian's description of what such an examination might have involved in the eighteenth century:

> "They are thoroughly examined, even to the smallest Member, and that naked too both Men and Women, without the least Distinction or Modesty." . . . In order to avoid purchasing older slaves, captains were advised to check their teeth, examine their hair, and test the firmness of women's breasts. . . . The Portuguese were especially picky in their examinations of slaves, spending as much as four hours inspecting each African, smelling their throats, making them laugh and sing, and finally licking the chins of the men to find out whether they had beards and thereby gauge their age. . . . "Every joint was made to crack; hips, armpits, and groins were also examined. The mouth was duly inspected, and when a tooth fell short it was noted down as a deduction. The eyesight was minutely observed, the voice and speech was called into request. Nothing was forgotten; even the fingers and toes had to undergo similar inspection."

17 "My mouth was opened," Barney remembered under hypnosis, "and I could feel two fingers pulling it back." His ancestors must have felt exactly the same thing.

At one point in Betty's regression, she describes being shown a star chart, which she's told is a map of "trade routes." Trade routes in interstellar space? Shift the context to the eighteenth-century Atlantic and it makes perfect sense.

"There were two dreams, really," Dr. Simon remarks to Barney about Betty's abduction dreams in the weeks after the UFO encounter. "One of them was sort of like a moonbeam down on a lake, something like that, or over a body of water." Barney responds: "Yes, she told me about that." Barney can't make anything of that "body of water"—it's completely out of place in New Hampshire's White Mountains, in the vicinity of the UFO. He decides to forget about it. But the "body of water" would have been pivotal in the slave's experience of abduction.

Barney has his binoculars with him, worn on a leather strap around his neck, when he leaves the car to take a closer look at the UFO. At one point he tears them off with such force—he speaks of "the violent thrust of my arms breaking the binocular strap"—that his neck is left bruised. Why should he have tried so desperately to free himself from that strap? Remember that African captives were marched to the coast in "coffles," lines of men, women and children fastened together at the neck by ropes or chains or lengths of wood—and it falls into place.

Barney Hill was a well-read man. He might have learned from books the details of what his ancestors underwent at the slavers' hands. But there's another option. Psychologists and psychotherapists working with the children and grandchildren of Holocaust survivors have repeatedly run into the phenomenon of *unspoken transmission of trauma from one generation to the next.* "The second generation absorbs the unvocalized deep memory from the parent," Israeli therapist Dina Wardi told an interviewer. "The real stuff is never transmitted through words. . . . I believe that some of the survivors' children's nightmares are the result of absorbing the parents' deep memory." In Barney's case, the "deep memory" had at least half a dozen generations to cross before manifesting in

FIGURE 3. A slave coffle. From David and Charles Livingstone, *Narrative of an Expedition to the Zambesi and Its Tributaries* (Harper & Brothers, 1866).

his nightmare of UFO abduction. Yet for a trauma as massive and malignant as the slave experience, its wounds refreshed in each generation by a new set of injustices and outrages, is that resurfacing of memory really beyond belief?[18]

By April 1964, Dr. Simon judged the therapeutic process was advanced enough that the Hills could be allowed to hear the tapes

18 Could biological, epigenetic processes also have played a role in the echoing of the slave experience down the generations? In October 2007, PBS viewers learned from a NOVA program, appropriately entitled "Ghost in Your Genes," about an isolated, famine-prone village in northern Sweden named Överkalix. Sifting through the village archive, researchers found clear evidence that experiences of feast or famine in the grandparents' generation might shape the life expectancy of grandchildren who'd never known a hungry day. Could the trauma of slavery have been epigenetically heritable, like the trauma of hunger? And if so, how long might its effects have persisted? For now, at least, these questions have to lie open and unanswered.

of themselves reliving their experience. After he listened to those tapes, Barney said,

> I would look over at Betty. And she has a way of looking at me and being reassuring. It's sort of a look that she can give, almost to say 'I'm in love with you, Barney.' And I felt this reassurance. And it helped. . . . And then, as the tapes went deeper and deeper into the part I had never remembered, there was the feeling as if heavy chains were lifted off my shoulders. I felt that I need no longer suffer the anxieties of wondering what happened.

"Heavy chains lifted off my shoulders." No accident, that choice of words. Barney, with the woman who loved him, had relived the historic crime in which his ancestors and hers had joined hands—his as victims, hers as perpetrators. (Betty's family had lived in New England since the seventeenth century, and although there were Quakers and abolitionists among them, it's a fair guess there were also those who turned a profit off the trade in human flesh.)

Both relived that trauma. The UFO abduction emerged from his psyche and hers, working together in a hidden tandem of which we're only starting to get an inkling. Their emotional responses weren't quite the same. Philip Klass, listening to Dr. Simon's tapes of the hypnotic regressions, was struck by the calmness of Betty's voice while she spoke of the most harrowing events ("as if she had been describing a trip to the supermarket") in contrast to Barney's almost hysterical fear. This impression is contradicted by the doctor's notes to himself, which speak of considerable agitation on Betty's part as well as Barney's. Yet Klass may have hit upon something of the truth.

Betty, child of slavery's perpetrators, couldn't enter fully into the abject dread that its victims experienced. She dreamed of the abduction from the first days after the trip through the White Mountains. In giving it the mythic shape it acquired in the course of the hypnotic sessions, she did her share and perhaps more than her share. Her love for Barney gave her the empathy to reexperience with him the ancestral trauma that had defined his life. But empathy could go only so far. The abduction's raw terror was Barney's, and his alone.

WHAT WAS THAT LIGHT?

In 2007, some forty-six years after the Hills' drive south along Route 3, another New Hampshire family—Jim and Doyle Macdonald and their daughter Pip—tried the experiment of retracing, again late at night, the path Betty and Barney had taken. Pip read to her parents from Fuller's *The Interrupted Journey* as they drove.

Just south of Lancaster, New Hampshire, the Macdonalds were joined, as the Hills had been, by a mysterious light that seemed to follow them through the mountains. They had some advantages that Betty and Barney didn't. They'd traveled this route in daylight; they knew what to expect. They knew exactly what that light was.

It wasn't a star or a satellite or an airplane. It was an electric light on the roof of a thirty-five-foot observation tower at the top of Cannon Mountain (aka Profile Mountain). Naturally it had seemed to the Hills to accompany them, moving against the fixed lights of the starry sky. When the road dipped down, and the Hills (and Macdonalds) with it, it shot upward. As the road twisted through the mountains, it leaped from the right to the left of their car. Then back again, disappearing and reappearing. "Even if you know what it is, it's weird to watch," Macdonald later wrote. "It vanishes over here, it reappears over there . . . spooky."

There were some discrepancies. The tower light didn't have rows of windows with faces peering out from behind them. This is a recurrent feature of the now-familiar gap between stimulus and perception in UFO sightings—recall the "many windows" seen by witnesses to the Zond IV fragments burning up in the Earth's atmosphere, as described in chapter 2—and it doesn't bother me. I'm more troubled by the two red lights that the Hills saw on either side of the UFO. These can't have been a product of the hypnotic regressions, since Betty mentioned them in the letter she wrote to Major Keyhoe a week after the sighting. I don't know what about the tower light might have given rise to them. So there remain some loose ends.[19] But on the whole, Macdonald's identification is compelling.

The Macdonalds were lucky they performed their experiment when they did. By the fall of 2008 the observation tower had been torn down, its light with it. It was apparently replaced sometime before the fall of 2011. But the new light was far less intense, and it's doubtful whether the Macdonalds (or the Hills) would have been struck by it. The clue to the identity of the Hills' mystery light would have been lost. Those who aren't UFO believers would have had no choice but to stick, for want of anything better, with the standard debunking explanation that they saw the planet Jupiter—which never made much sense, since the light moved against the star field. Let this be a warning to those inclined to think UFOs must be unknown, physically real objects, just because there are cases that remain unsolved. They may be unsolved for precisely this reason: the clue is lost, and there isn't any way to guess at it.

So far we've identified two components of the Hills' UFO encounter: the *stimulus*, the light on Cannon Mountain, and the *deep collective experience* of African enslavement. There are others.

In the hypnotic regression of February 22, Barney described the eyes of one of the UFO beings as "slanted . . . but not like a Chinese." In a sketch he made under hypnosis, the eyes look indefinably sinister, malevolent: the irises and pupils, not distinguished

---

19 Nor do I have the slightest idea what the shiny circles were that appeared on the trunk of the Hills' car. (I haven't been able to find out whether they eventually faded, and if so how long this took, or whether anyone but the Hills ever saw them.) These are small mysteries connected with the Hills' experience, which are unlikely ever to be cleared up. By contrast, Macdonald has shown that the Hills' "missing time" was no mystery at all. Driving sleep-deprived down a narrow, winding, unfamiliar mountain road in pitch darkness, Barney naturally went a great deal more slowly than he imagined.

from each other, are close together, while the whites of the eyes trail away upward, toward the sides of the being's head. Barney later told John Fuller that "the eyes continued around to the sides of their heads, so that it appeared that they could see several degrees beyond the lateral extent of our vision."

In 1994, UFO skeptic and pop-culture expert Martin Kottmeyer announced a startling discovery. These "wraparound eyes," as they'd come to be known in UFO parlance, had been shown to the nation's television viewers on February 10, 1964—twelve days before Barney's hypnotic session—in an episode of the science fiction series *The Outer Limits*. The alien in "The Bellero Shield," as the episode was called, had eyes of precisely this sort. In other respects as well, the TV alien seemed to resemble the UFO pilots as Barney described them. Then there was the clincher:

> DOCTOR: There are men standing in the road?
>
> BARNEY: Yes. They won't talk to me. Only the eyes are talking to me. I—I—I—I don't understand that. Oh—the eyes don't have a body. They're just eyes.

We'll see in the next two chapters that the uncanny, terrifying, occasionally disembodied eyes that occur in this and other abduction stories are primal, archaic, long antedating "The Bellero Shield" and the Atlantic slave trade alike. Yet Kottmeyer is on target when he connects their property of *speech* with what the alien is made to say in "The Bellero Shield": "In all the universes, in all the unities beyond the universes, all who have eyes have eyes that speak."

Through most of Betty and Barney's hypnotic sessions, the UFO pilots come across as men. Their appearance is unfamiliar and frightening, but they're essentially male human beings. (Only near the end of therapy do they begin to shrink in size, as befits flying saucer entities.) This is precisely how the captive Africans perceived the people to whom they'd been sold: "white men with horrible looks, red faces, and loose hair." How to conceptualize,

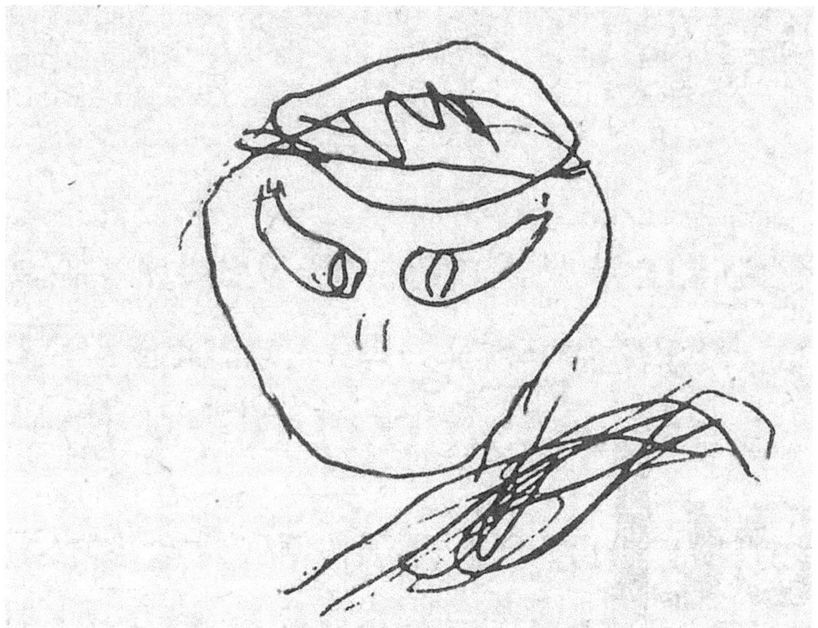

FIGURE 4. Drawing of alien head by Barney Hill, done under hypnosis. University of New Hampshire. Used with permission.

give concrete reality to those "horrible looks," that appalling alienness? The space alien of "The Bellero Shield" gave Barney a working model.

More recent African American experience also played a part in shaping his recollections. It influenced Betty's as well. Of all her hypnotically evoked memories, the most powerful and grisly is of the UFO beings laying her on their examination table and pushing a long needle deep into her navel. They told her it wouldn't hurt; it was in fact agonizingly painful. A procedure, in other words, that might be imagined to kill the fetus the black man might have implanted within her.

Barney underwent a corresponding ordeal. "I don't want to be operated on," he tells the doctor in his second hypnotic regression (February 29) as he describes being brought aboard the UFO. Then a few minutes later: "My groin feels cold." Later, when the doctor reminds him of this, he says: "I was lying on a table, and I thought someone was putting a cup around my groin. . . . If I keep real quiet and real still, I won't be harmed. And it will be over."

Eventually it was over. He and Betty were released; they arrived home in the early light of dawn. Without knowing why, Barney checked his groin, looking for a mark. There was none. That took four more months to appear, in the form of a circle of warts around his groin, the exact same spot where the UFO beings had placed the cup.

It takes no great leap of the imagination to realize what's going on. He's been castrated, the time-honored punishment for a black man who's allowed himself too much liberty with a white woman. Again, think Emmett Till. Although it doesn't seem that Till actually was castrated before his murder, this became part of the popular version of the story. The killing of the young black man inevitably evoked memories of the gruesome lynchings that became a feature of Southern life after the Civil War, in which genital mutilation played a major role. These memories found their place in the abduction of Betty and Barney Hill.

The warts remained to testify. If, as I've stressed over and over, the Hills' UFO came from deep within, Barney's warts demonstrate the corollary: the UFO was something real. Psychically rather than physically, yes; but Jung has taught us that psychic reality, though different from the physical, is by no means inferior to it. This particular "psychism," as Jung would have called it, was solid and tangible enough to leave material evidence of its presence, in an eerily perfect circle on the victim's skin.

AFTERMATH

Barney Hill died on February 25, 1969, five years almost to the day after hypnotic regression brought him face to face with the enormity of what he'd endured. Cause of death: cerebral hemorrhage resulting from stroke. He was forty-six years old.

Betty Hill, a few years older than her husband, survived him by more than thirty-five years. A few years after her death in October

2004, her niece Kathleen Marden began lobbying for an official commemoration of the heroic pair whose love had transcended, however briefly, the shame and pain of their past. Marden's efforts paid off. In 2011, shortly before the fiftieth anniversary of the abduction, a historical highway marker was set up near the spot where it was believed to have happened, under the seal of the State of New Hampshire:

> *BETTY AND BARNEY HILL*
> *INCIDENT*
>
> ---
>
> On the night of September 19–20, 1961, Portsmouth, NH couple Betty and Barney Hill experienced a close encounter with an unidentified flying object and two hours of "lost" time while driving south on Rte 3 near Lincoln. They filed an official Air Force Project Blue Book report of a brightly-lit cigar-shaped craft the next day, but were not public with their story until it was leaked in the Boston Traveler in 1965. This was the first widely-reported UFO abduction report in the United States.

Jointly they'd shaped a modern myth that, like all true myths, was also primordial and timeless. They planted it, seedlike, in the collective psyche of their nation. For years it quietly germinated. Near the end of the century it burst into fantastic bloom.

CHAPTER 4

The Lure of the Unremembered

DR. RIMA LAIBOW didn't know what to make of it. In 1988, the psychiatrist recalled a few years afterward, a patient had come to her "in a state of anxiety and panic" triggered by a book she'd glimpsed out of the corner of her eye. The patient, a forty-three-year-old cardiologist, had never read the book, yet the eerie face that gazed from its cover seemed to her something already known. She herself, she told Laibow, had encountered creatures like the one portrayed. She'd forgotten but now, seeing that cover, she remembered—and was terrified.

"Such notions had always struck me as psychotic," Laibow said, "but this patient taught me otherwise."

The book was Whitley Strieber's *Communion: A True Story*, published in January 1987 to stellar sales and no critical acclaim whatsoever. A work of purported nonfiction by a man who'd made his name as a novelist, it told of Strieber's unwilled, traumatic encounters with uncanny beings who might but need not have been UFO aliens. The face on the cover was painted at Strieber's direction by a master artist named Ted Jacobs. Even those who've never seen the book know that face: its light-bulb shape, its huge slanted eyes of impenetrable black, its cryptic, not quite Mona Lisa–like smile. That face is so much a part of our culture that it's hard to conceive that before 1987 it was unknown. At least to our conscious minds.

The reaction of Laibow's patient—"I've seen it! I'd forgotten but now I remember"—was far from unique. To pathologize it, to dismiss it as weird or abnormal, would bend the meaning of normalcy out of all usefulness. In the months and years that followed *Communion*'s appearance, Strieber was flooded with letters telling him, "Yes, I've lived it too." By 1997 he'd received nearly two hundred thousand such letters.

"Sitting right there on the kitchen stove," one man wrote to Strieber, describing something he remembered from 1958 when he was four years old,

> in front of God and all my family and relatives, was this creature that I had never seen before. I remember pointing to the creature on the stove, and by now I had everyone's attention. Obviously I was the only one who could see it, which only added to the terror. . . . I never again saw that face staring at me, that is, until I was browsing in a bookstore a few years ago and saw the book *Communion*, and right there on the cover was that all too familiar face almost laughing at me.

"Staring at me . . . laughing at me." Others, who never contacted Strieber, had also felt that stare. One man recalled (in 1992) a close-range sighting he'd experienced at age nineteen of a face in the UFO "looking down at me." When he saw the cover of *Communion* many years afterward, he was shocked, for here was the same face that "I imagined was looking down at me."

By all odds the strangest story, chilling yet bizarrely comical, was told by biochemist Kary Mullis—the same Kary Mullis who

FIGURE 5. Cover of Whitley Strieber, *Communion* (paperback; Avon Books, 1987).

won a Nobel Prize in 1993 for his discovery of the polymerase chain reaction, which made possible the forensic use of DNA testing that we now take for granted. In 1985, not yet a Nobelist, Mullis was spending the weekend at his cabin on a tract of wooded mountain country in Mendocino County, California. Shortly after midnight, en route to the outhouse, Mullis spotted something glowing alongside the path. He pointed his flashlight at it. It was a raccoon.

The raccoon said: "Good evening, doctor."

The next thing Mullis knew, it was early morning and he was walking on a road uphill from his cabin. His clothes, which if he'd slept outdoors should have been wet with the night dew, were dry and clean. The lights in his cabin were still on, as he'd left them. He tried to go into his woods but, overwhelmed by a panic he didn't understand, he turned and fled.

A year and a half or two years later Mullis, browsing in a bookstore in La Jolla, came upon Strieber's *Communion*. "On the cover was a drawing that captured my attention. An oval-shaped head with large inky eyes staring straight ahead." There was something vaguely, unsettlingly familiar about that face. Mullis bought the book, took it home, and immediately began reading. The phone rang. It was his adult daughter calling from Oregon.

Later she would tell him her own story of the mountain cabin. She'd gone there with her fiancé to spend the night, then vanished not long after they arrived. For three hours her fiancé, at his wit's end, hunted for her and called her name. Afterward she had no notion where she'd been. The first words she spoke when Mullis picked up the phone: "Dad, there's a book I want you to read. It's called *Communion*."

It's an odd sort of book. More than once I've had the disconcerting experience of picking up my paperback copy, finding it filled with marginal notes in what has to be my handwriting, yet realizing I have little or no recollection of what the book contains. I've explained to myself why I've found it so unmemorable: plowing through the long string of bizarre, inexplicable events that Strieber claims to have befallen him, my mind scrabbles for some interpretative key, some pattern of meaning. Finding none, it retreats in frustration.

Yet in a sense this forgettability is not a flaw, but the essence of what *Communion* is about: the unremembered.

Easy to make fun of this book. Incoherencies and absurdities abound; Strieber's experiences can be chalked up to temporal lobe epilepsy or brushed off with a wave of the hand and "Aah, he's nuts!" But the monumental fact about *Communion* remains unshakable and undeniable: the extraordinary recognition response it's evoked, not in a few people but in many tens of thousands.

To call them its "readers" would not be quite accurate. They didn't have to read the book to recognize that, in some way beyond their comprehending, it was part of their own experience. Just seeing the cover—unlike the contents, impossible to forget—might summon that awareness from inside them.

If the abduction myth was born in 1964, with the hypnotic regressions of Barney and Betty Hill, the appearance of *Communion* in 1987 marks its watershed moment—the date when a compelling image, etched permanently (as far as we can tell thirty years later) into the public imagination, came to represent it. The year 1964 was the start of the myth's *history*, with Barney Hill's recovery and reenactment of his ancestral trauma. The year 1987 opened a window into its *prehistory*, carrying us back, as we'll see in this and the next chapter, through antiquity into truly prehistoric times. Each is an aspect of the myth. It can't be understood without calling on both.

Let's start with Strieber's book.

THE ENTITY AND THE OWL

At *Communion*'s heart is something that happened, or allegedly happened, to Whitley Strieber on the night of December 26, 1985. His bedroom in his cabin in upstate New York was invaded by a small being, or possibly more than one. Naked, paralyzed, his arms and legs extended, he felt himself carried out to "a small sort of depression in the woods," which transformed itself into a "small, circular chamber" that seemed to rise above the treetops. There he was subjected to a range of weird, unsettling experiences, including an anal rape performed by a narrow "gray and scaly" object. He also seems to have encountered the female entity, uncanny and inhuman in her appearance, whom he would describe thirty years afterward as "the most essentially and powerfully feminine presence I have ever known." It was her portrait that appeared on *Communion*'s cover.

Strieber remembered nothing of this when he awoke in the morning. He had only an implausible but compelling recollection of a barn owl staring at him through his bedroom window sometime during the night. The details of his experience came back to him about a week later, spontaneously, without the aid of hypnotic regression.

Hypnosis would come later. By 1985 it was practically de rigueur in cases of abduction or suspected abduction. These had crystallized into more or less recognizable, more or less predictable dramas that called for the participation of a therapist/hypnotist, as important a figure in the story as the abductee himself or herself. Benjamin Simon's work with the Hills had provided the template. But Simon was a trained psychiatrist with special expertise in therapeutic hypnosis and no interest in UFOs; it was accident that assigned him his pivotal role in the birth of the tradition. Amateurs, eager UFOlogists, tended more and more to step into the role of therapist/hypnotist as time went on. They brought with them their own agendas, investigative rather than therapeutic.

Dr. Donald F. Klein, at any rate, was no amateur. He was professor of psychiatry at Columbia University, medical director of the New York State Psychiatric Institute. He was also a friend of Budd Hopkins—a New York City artist and UFO researcher, just beginning to emerge as the nation's foremost authority on alien abductions, to whom Strieber turned for guidance. Klein hypnotized Strieber on at least four occasions in the spring of 1986, with Hopkins present and occasionally chiming in with his own questions. Later Klein would author a statement, printed as Appendix I in *Communion*, attesting that Strieber wasn't psychotic, hallucinating, or afflicted with "an anxiety state, mood disorder, or personality disorder."

The goal of the regressions was the usual one in cases of alien abduction: to elicit details, presumed to have been experienced but afterward repressed, that would put into an intelligible context the strange dreams, baffling memory fragments, or peculiar symptoms or aversions (to a particular stretch of highway, for example) that the abduction had left behind. The transcripts of the Klein-Strieber-Hopkins sessions, quoted in *Communion*, are cryptic and perplexing. If clarity was their aim, they failed in their purpose. But their jumbled quality creates a sense of emotional authenticity, and one thing at least is perfectly clear. Gross sexual abuse practically cries out to the reader from the printed page.

Strieber speaks of being sodomized by a "big, gray thing" with "a little cage" at its end, wielded by an unspecified "they." Meanwhile the "woman" (or the "bug"—Strieber isn't sure) demands, "Can you be harder?" which he remembers as referring to his penis. At the same time he's told, "You are our chosen one." "That was a long time ago," he says. Klein asks how old he was. "Twelve," he answers; and it's hard to avoid thinking that he must have endured horrific abuse at human hands, quite possibly when he was twelve years old. The memories, emotionally overwhelming but distorted almost beyond recognition, took hallucinatory form. They came to him disguised as something contemporary—he was forty years old at the end of 1985—and with the perpetrators metamorphosed into fantastic beings of his imagination.[20]

---

20 As we'll see, Strieber himself was keenly aware of this possibility.

As imaginations go, Strieber's was extraordinarily powerful. Prior to the events that catapulted him to fame, he'd been a moderately successful writer of horror fiction: *The Wolfen* (1978), *The Hunger* (1981). The weird, grotesque, and ghastly had a pull on him, and on more than one occasion he could not tell what he remembered from what he imagined. Had he really been on the campus of the University of Texas at Austin, for example, on the dreadful day (August 1, 1966) when Charles Whitman began shooting from the university tower, killing sixteen people? He had a clear memory of being there. He also knew that the memory made no sense, and he could never decide whether it was true or not.

In the days after December 26, after his experience but before he could remember anything about it except the owl's face at the window, Strieber wrote a short story called "Pain." The narrator, a middle-aged writer named Alex who's doing research for a novel, hooks up with a pretty and deceptively wholesome-looking young prostitute named Janet O'Reilly. "I do pain," she tells Alex, and "pain" for her isn't just sadomasochism but something close to a philosophy of life, which she enacts on those who seek her out. Alex finds himself in her basement lair, locked in a telephone booth–like box, tortured by her with a blowtorch. "I was now at the threshold: she had taught me what is essentially needed to be well prepared for death."

In the end Alex is released. After his ordeal, he finds sex with his wife better than it ever was. So is his career. ("My reviews are excellent, there's talk of awards.") Yet somewhere out in the cold, Janet waits. "One day, she will come for me . . . she will tear my heart from my chest like the priests once did to their anointed victims on the altars of the Aztecs." Of course we know who she is: death incarnate. We can guess that for her author and creator, she and the "powerfully feminine presence" who engineered his torment on the night of December 26—and whose likeness on *Communion*'s cover propelled the book's sales into the stratosphere—were one and the same.

UFO ALIENS: A BRIEF HISTORY

Strieber never said that his "visitors," as he called them, were extraterrestrials. That was a lazy assumption often made by his critics, usually in a context of disparagement. He preferred to look inward, comparing his obsidian-eyed female to the Jungian "anima,"[21] to "someone I saw staring back at me from the depths of my unconscious." *Like* the anima, *like* the unconscious—yet not the same. Strieber's visitors, for all their internal presence, were something other than Strieber himself. They were a force, he wrote at the end of his preface, that "seeks the very depth of the soul; it seeks communion."

Nor did Strieber claim ever to have seen a UFO. The "small circular chamber" that lifted itself above the trees was as close as he came to that.[22] Yet the "visitors" plainly belong with the humanoid beings that have been part of UFO lore ever since there has been UFO lore. If we're to understand them as something more than extensions of Strieber's individual psyche—reenactments of his childhood traumas, perhaps—we need to fix them within the tradition of UFO occupants as these were envisioned or encountered during the forty preceding years.

No "little green men" among them. These belong to a dimension of the phenomenon that's purely folkloric, untethered to the reported experiencing of it; no UFO witness has ever described seeing "little green men." The occupants of the flying saucers said to have crashed in 1948 in the Southwestern deserts were indeed

---

21 In Jungian psychology, an "anima" is the female "self" that every man has within him, just as every woman has a male "animus." To bring the anima (or animus) into conscious awareness, to integrate it with one's maleness (or femaleness), is a key aim of Jungian psychotherapy.

22 And perhaps his hazy memory, which he dates to age two, of "a terrifying round object hanging in some forgotten babyhood sky, and seeing a crowd of big, gray monkeys coming up across the hillside."

"little men," ranging in height from three to three and a half feet. They weren't green, however. Apart from their diminutive size, they looked just like us.

Frank Scully told the story in his 1950 bestseller *Behind the Flying Saucers*. Scientists had examined the craft and the corpses, according to Scully, and suspected that they came from the planet Venus. Two years later it came out that the "crash" was a hoax. Scully had been duped by a pair of con men laying the groundwork for an oil-detection scam. His tale slid into oblivion, only to return at the end of the 1970s in the vastly more powerful and authentic form that we know as "Roswell."

Meanwhile other small humanoids, weirder in physiognomy and nastier in character, were making their appearances. On the night of August 21, 1955, small luminous beings, apparently from a flying saucer, swarmed around and over a Kentucky farmhouse. The creatures were three and a half feet tall and had large floppy ears, talons at the end of their fingers, and "large eyes, glowing yellow . . . set between the front and the side of the head." The people in the farmhouse shot at the invaders, and when the bullets knocked them over but couldn't kill or stop them, the people fled to the nearby town of Hopkinsville "in a state of near-hysteria."

Another hoax? It seems not. Whatever the people experienced or thought they experienced, it scared them badly. They came back with the police, who found nothing but sensed "a weird feeling" pervading the area. "It was partly uneasiness, but not entirely," the police chief later recalled. "Everyone had it. There were men there that I'd call brave men, men I've been in dangerous situations with. They felt it, too."

Not all the small-humanoid reports of the 1950s were from the United States. They figured prominently in the French UFO wave of the autumn of 1954. A few particularly disturbing reports filtered in from Venezuela near the end of that year. Witnesses claimed to have been attacked, sometimes mauled, by hairy, repellent dwarflike creatures who seemed to have emerged from landed UFOs. On one occasion a young boy, out rabbit hunting with a friend, was set upon by four of these beings and dragged toward their flying saucer. His friend rescued him by smashing a shotgun on the small monster's head.

The first successful kidnap was reported by a young Brazilian farmer named Antonio Villas-Boas. The date was October 16, 1957. Villas-Boas told of being taken forcibly aboard a landed UFO, then released more or less unharmed a few hours later. In the interval he was stripped naked and kept in a small room aboard the craft to await the arrival of a female alien as naked as himself. She was much shorter than Villas-Boas and slim, with "high and well-separated" breasts, large thighs, and "big blue eyes, rather longer than round, for they slanted outward, like those pencil-drawn girls made to look like Arabian princesses, that look as if they were slit." (Also freckled arms—a touching, unexpected detail.) Disconcertingly, her pubic hair was "bright red, nearly the color of blood," perhaps hinting at grisly mutilations enacted there.[23]

She had her way with Villas-Boas twice, making animal-like growls during the sex act but not otherwise speaking. She wouldn't kiss him but she did bite him once, softly, on the chin. Before letting him go, she smiled at him and pointed to her belly and then to the sky, which he took as a promise she'd come back for him. To his relief—or possibly regret or possibly both—she never did.

As a real event transpiring in the physical world, the episode makes no sense. (If attractive, raunchy space females are at the UFOs' controls, why do other occupant reports never mention

---

23 In 1967, Coral and Jim Lorenzen published the first full English translation of Villas-Boas's testimony in their book *Flying Saucer Occupants*. Arbitrarily, and without any indication of what they'd done, they shifted the blood-red hair from the alien's crotch to her armpits—proof that something about this detail made them squeamish. This is an example of what the Freudians call "displacement upward." We'll see other examples before long.

them?) It makes excellent sense as the fantasy of a lonely farm boy. Yet everyone to whom Villas-Boas told his tale was impressed by the sincerity with which he appeared to believe it. In his later years he left the farm and opened a law practice, married, and had four children. He never recanted his story. Neither did he ever try to make any money from it.

Then the abductions began. In retrospect, the Villas-Boas case appears as a prelude to the phenomenon, a transitional stage from the old-fashioned "close encounters of the third kind"—as reports of UFO occupants were coming to be called[24]—to the new genre that emerged in the wake of Betty and Barney Hill. This was a "fourth kind" of close encounter, characterized by memories repressed and later retrieved, usually with a therapist/hypnotist on hand to aid in their recovery. It suited a culture in which the therapist's office, once viewed with some derision (classically parodied by Lucy in the *Peanuts* comic strip, with her PSYCHIATRIC HELP—5¢ lemonade stand) was coming to be seen as a healing space where "ye shall know the truth, and the truth shall make you free."[25]

In his monumental two-volume *UFO Abductions: The Measure of a Mystery*, published in 1987 by the Fund for UFO Research, folklorist Thomas E. Bullard collected and analyzed 270 abduction reports involving 312 distinct incidents from the beginning of the phenomenon

---

24 The nomenclature was devised by J. Allen Hynek, professor of astronomy at Northwestern University and for many years the Air Force's scientific advisor on UFOs, and set forth in his classic, *The UFO Experience* (1972). "Close encounters of the first kind" are where the UFO "is seen at close range but there is no interaction with the environment," while in the "second kind" it does something like cause a car engine to stall or leaves some trace on the ground or vegetation. Hynek's taxonomy inspired the title and much of the content of the 1977 Steven Spielberg blockbuster *Close Encounters of the Third Kind* and earned Hynek a six-second cameo at the movie's climax.

25 A perception powerfully conveyed and reinforced in the popular 1980 film *Ordinary People*. I remember a *Dear Abby* column, whose date I can't recall but which must have appeared sometime in the 1970s, quoting John 8:32 to persuade a reluctant reader to go into therapy.

to the middle of 1985. He found that abducting aliens come in different shapes and sizes. They include giants and dwarfs, "humanoids" who couldn't walk down a city street without creating a sensation as well as beings who look entirely human, with a few stranger, more grotesque entities mixed in. Amid the variety, there were patterns. The humanoids accounted for two-thirds of the abductors and tended toward the small end of the height scale, commonly measuring between four and five feet. Their heads were often disproportionately large, with a shape described as being like a "light bulb" or a "pear."

"The large, compelling eyes of humanoids capture attention like no other bodily feature," Bullard wrote—we know we're in *Communion* territory. (The close-encounter reports of preabduction times laid no particular stress on the beings' eyes, even when they were unusually large, as at the Kentucky farmhouse.) They're "elongated," "slanted," "almond or walnut shaped," or to use the term introduced in connection with the Hill case, "wraparound," meaning that they extend from the face around to the sides of the head. There were exceptions. In the much-publicized abduction at Pascagoula, Mississippi, in October 1973, the UFO entities were wrinkled gray beings like mummies wrapped up in bandages, with no visible eyes at all. As if in compensation, a huge disembodied eye like a football floated around the two abductees, examining them.

Bullard's data didn't allow him to compare the number of cases in which the eyes had an iris and pupil, like those of terrestrial creatures, with those in which, as on the *Communion* cover, they were solid black. The most he could say was that "the supposition that the eyes are usually dark and uniform in coloration, or possessed of extensive pupils filling most or all of the eye, is reinforced by the poverty of alternatives." He cited several reports that speak of them as unblinking. This point is important because it drives a wedge between the aliens of the abduction reports and those in Steven Spielberg's box-office smash *Close Encounters of the Third Kind* (1977), sometimes proposed as a model that the abductees unwittingly followed.

Yes, the *Close Encounters* extraterrestrials have small spindly bodies topped by large oval heads. Yes, their eyes are larger than human eyes in proportion to their faces, though not by much. But they have an iris and a pupil, and they blink. So frequently and demonstratively do they blink that it's hard to believe Spielberg wasn't making a point with their blinking: See, however odd these beings may look, they aren't so alien after all. Their eyes are windows to a soul much like yours.[26]

The eyes on the *Communion* cover, by contrast, are windows to nothing. Smooth and featureless, impenetrable as the masklike face in which they're embedded, they stare but allow the object of their stare no clue to what's behind them. "Wells of darkness," Strieber calls them; "limitless" and "eternal," "the huge staring eyes of the old gods." They have no visible eyelids. How could they blink, much less close?

Yet on one occasion they did close. Strieber was sitting with Ted Jacobs, whom he and the ever-helpful Budd Hopkins had selected as the artist to render an image of his "visitor." "I was sitting with my eyes closed, describing this face as carefully as I could. I could see it in amazing detail"—and it moved as he observed it. Like Morton Schatzman's Ruth,[27] though perhaps in lesser degree, he had a gift for creating apparitions.

> Ted asked me many questions about the eyes. When he asked me how they looked closed, I got another shock: The image closed its eyes. I saw the huge, glassy structures recede and loosen, becoming wrinkled, and the lids come down and up at the same time, to close just below the middle of the eyeball.

If these closed eyes are tilted fully to the vertical, they'll suggest another part of the anatomy: the vulva, "displaced upward" as the

---

26 A message conveyed in a similar way in Spielberg's 1982 *E.T.*, when the boy and the extraterrestrial have flinch reactions to each other at precisely the same moment.

27 See "On Seeing What Isn't There" in chapter 2.

Freudians would have it. We've already noticed how Strieber's encounters with the "visitors" are drenched in sex, and not very pleasurable sex. Now we find him describing eyes that sound like something more than eyes. We'll see that he wasn't the only one.

ABDUCTIONS' HEYDAY: THE 1990s

It's a matter for debate whether *Communion*'s commercial success was the cause of what came afterward or a symptom of a process that would have unfolded even if there'd been no *Communion*. What's not debatable is that the ten or twelve years that followed were the heyday of UFO abductions. A story circulated that a pair of huge-eyed aliens had been seen poring over *Communion* in a Lexington Avenue bookstore in Manhattan, and although the tale may have started out as an advertising gimmick, what it conveyed was real and true. With the appearance of the book and its cover, something new—or perhaps ancient and unremembered—had established its presence in American life.

The number of abductions multiplied fantastically. For the period up to the middle of 1985, Bullard had needed to comb through the literature of more than two decades to find 270 cases. By the early 1990s that number had leaped into the thousands, and more were being uncovered every day. There was reason, though not very good reason, to suspect the true figure might be in the millions.

Not that all those millions of people reported or even remembered having been abducted. Failure of memory, whether caused by the aliens in pursuit of their agenda or the mind protecting itself against reliving the trauma, was becoming a recognized part of the phenomenon.[28] But a Roper poll of doubtful methodology, conducted in 1991 under the direction of three leading abduction researchers, found that 2 percent of the sample—which,

---

28 Parodied in a 1992 sequence of the comic strip *Guy Stuff*: "This TV show made it all clear, Sam—I was kidnapped by space aliens. . . . 9 out of 10 aimless lives are caused by post-alien abduction trauma!! And I've got the number one symptom!" "Which is . . . ," says Sam, who gets the reply: "No memory of being kidnapped by space aliens."

extrapolated, came to 3.7 million Americans—had experienced a combination of odd events such as "missing time" or seeing a strange figure in the bedroom. Any of these, taken by itself, might be given a mundane explanation. Taken together, they pointed (allegedly) toward abduction.

The dark, oppressive sexuality that had always been part of the abduction tradition now proclaimed itself, lurid and unabashed. Both men and women—now about equally represented in the abductee population[29]—remembered forced sex with the aliens or with other abductees. They experienced strange, pleasureless orgasms. Men were compelled on the "examination" tables to yield their sperm to bizarre machines; women, their ova. The women might be impregnated, then the babies mysteriously taken from their wombs weeks or months afterward. They or other abductees would report seeing what must have been the vanished children aboard some spaceship: rows upon rows of fetuses floating in tanks of liquid, or wan, sickly boys and girls craving human touch.

The "large, compelling" alien eyes became more prominent than ever, their sexual overtones sometimes very blatant. One woman recalled having been abducted as a fifteen-year-old girl and made to have intercourse with an older man while an alien came and stared into her eyes. "He's in my eyes. He's flooding my eyes. He's completely penetrating me, every bit of me is in my eyes." Others remembered *falling into* the alien eyes, sometimes having orgasm as they did so. A male abductee spoke of connecting with the aliens by "going in" their eyes. He had a vision of himself seeing inside a "giant vaginal hairball" which "clarified into the hair of a goddess being born . . . flowing from the vaginal lips"; and the two images were linked by his childhood nightmare of a witch forcing him to look into her "huge eyes," at which point "I was all hers and she would whisk me away."

---

29 In the pre-1985 cases collected by Bullard, men had outnumbered women by about two to one.

"Screen memories," a century-old Freudian concept given a new twist by the abduction theorists, found their way into the discussion. For Freud, a screen memory was a memory of some fragmentary scene from childhood, accurate in its detail but meaningless or trivial. It was remembered not for itself, but for its association with something vitally important that had been repressed. For the UFOlogists, the screen memory was a mask for something other than itself, a hint allowed into consciousness of an experience too unearthly, too frightening to be remembered for what it really was. Often the abducting aliens would be disguised in memory as animals, behaving in ways no animal ought: the owl at Whitley Strieber's window, the raccoon that said "Good evening, doctor" to Kary Mullis. It's no accident that both owl and raccoon are creatures with prominent, staring eyes; no wonder that Mullis, looking into the "large inky eyes" that gazed from the cover of *Communion*, had the sense that he'd seen this before.

Seen it before: that might be the watchword of the abductions. Abductees often recalled under hypnosis that their abductors had been familiar to them since childhood. No matter how far back they were regressed, there would always be something before that—if not a full-dress abduction, then some encounter with alien beings or strange animals, which only took on meaning in the light of the adult abduction experience.

THE EXPOSITORS

A phenomenon so elusive and complex, yet so rich with possibility for penetrating to the heart of the UFO mystery, called for a new class of specialists—ones who were expert in UFOlogy, trained or self-taught in hypnotic technique. Three men emerged in the 1990s as leaders in the field.

Foremost among the three was Budd Hopkins, Whitley Strieber's one-time friend and mentor. (The friendship soured after *Communion* ate into the sales of Hopkins's latest book on abductions, which came out the same year.) Then there was David Jacobs, professor of history at Temple University in Philadelphia—no relation to Ted Jacobs, as far as I know. Jacobs had appeared on the UFO scene in 1975 with his scholarly and dispassionate *The UFO Controversy in America*, which had the distinction of being the first book on UFOs to be published by a university press. But he was not only a historian of the UFO idea but a believer in it, and in time his interest shifted to abductions. Not only were they real in his opinion, not only were they widespread, but they were portents of grave danger to the human race.

Hopkins held a dim view of the character and intentions of the abducting aliens; Jacobs went far beyond him into the grim and foreboding. Behind the abductions, Jacobs thought, lay a scheme of mass hybridization, its goal the takeover of the Earth and the replacement of humanity by a half-human, half-alien species. "We now know the alarming dimensions of the alien agenda and its goals," he wrote at the end of his 1998 book, *The Threat*. "I could never have imagined it would turn out this way. I desperately wish it not to be true."

The most extraordinary, fascinating, and tragic of the trio was John Mack, professor of psychiatry at Harvard Medical School and the author of a Pulitzer Prize–winning biography of T. E. Lawrence ("Lawrence of Arabia"). Handsome and charismatic, Mack had been raised in a secular Jewish household where the only reality was the material, and religious faith was antiquated mumbo-jumbo. He spent his life in quest of the spirituality of which he'd been starved. On the meaning and purpose of the abduction phenomenon, he differed sharply from Hopkins and Jacobs. His vision was optimistic. The abductors, severe and heartless as their methods might occasionally seem, were heralds of a new spiritual dawn that would rescue humanity from the blind science-worship that was hustling us to our doom.

The thread running through Mack's endeavors was what Jung called the "uniting of opposites," represented in the archetype of the mandala wheel. The opposition that most resonated for him was Jews versus Arabs. Of the "experiencers" profiled in his 1994 book *Abduction: Human Encounters with Aliens*, his hands-down favorite was an Israeli woman who, under hypnosis, remembered a former life as a thirteenth-century Arab merchant renowned for his justice and benevolence.[30] In Beirut in 1980, Mack had been one of the first of a string of American Jewish intellectuals to make peace overtures to the Palestinian leader Yassir Arafat, contacts that helped pave the way for the 1993 Oslo Accords between Israel and the Palestinians. Mack's hero T. E. Lawrence was the godfather of Arab national liberation. He was also a pro-Zionist who poured his energy into bringing Zionist and Arab leaders together, dreaming of a Jewish-Arab confederation that would arise in the Middle East to "become a formidable element of world power." No wonder Mack was captivated by him.

In 1990, when Hopkins led Mack into the ranks of the abduction researchers, Lawrence's dream was long dead, bombed and machine-gunned into extinction. Mack would live just long enough to see the Oslo peace process toward which he'd labored disintegrate into blood and terror. But in the sky were the UFO mandalas, bearers of the magic that—in Schiller's words, which Beethoven put to music in his Ninth Symphony—could "bind together / That which custom has strictly divided."

Mack's faith in that magic proved his undoing on at least one occasion. A would-be writer named Donna Bassett, for motives that remain unclear, came to him pretending to be an abductee. In hypnotic trance, or what Mack thought was hypnotic trance, she told him how during the Cuban missile crisis of 1962 she'd been aboard the flying saucer to which President Kennedy and Soviet premier Nikita Khrushchev had also been abducted. Khrushchev

30 In the hypnotic regression of UFO abductees, there normally proves to be "something before that." When Mack had led his subjects back to earliest childhood and still found something before that, he had no choice but to extend his investigation into their past lives.

was crying, and Bassett sat on his lap, put her arms around his neck, and told him everything would be OK. She'd zeroed in on Mack's vulnerability; he swallowed the ridiculous story. It got him so excited "he leaned on the bed too heavily"—the sessions, according to Bassett, were held in a darkened bedroom in Mack's home—"and it collapsed."

Bassett proclaimed her coup, first to *Time* magazine, then at the 1994 conference of the Committee for the Scientific Investigation of Claims of the Paranormal (CSICOP) to which she and Mack were invited speakers. Conveniently, the CSICOP organizers had neglected to notify Mack that he and Bassett would be sharing a platform. "I faked it," she crowed to her appreciative audience while Mack sat nearby, blindsided and humiliated. "Women," she added, "have been doing it for centuries."

THE OPPONENTS

For skeptics in the CSICOP mold, Mack's folly was emblematic of the whole alien-abduction nonsense. All the rapidly accumulating data, as far as they were concerned, was a great pile of nothing. The consistencies among the abduction narratives, which advocates pointed to as evidence of their reality, had a simple if distressing explanation. They were creations of the so-called researchers, who'd brought their preconceived scenarios with them into the hypnotic sessions. Using leading questions, they coaxed out of their subjects the tales they expected to hear, convincing them in the process that those tales must be real. As for the abductees, they were troubled men and women who needed treatment by bona fide therapists, not exploitation by shamanic witch doctors with an eye on the next book contract.

How was it, Philip Klass wondered rhetorically, that the people hypnotized by Leo Sprinkle[31] remembered being abducted by aliens

---

31 A psychology professor at the University of Wyoming, one of the first of the UFOlogist/hypnotists to follow in Benjamin Simon's footsteps.

who were gentle and kindly like Sprinkle himself, while those hypnotized by Hopkins seemed to have fallen into the clutches of a harsher, crueler sort of ET? Wasn't it obvious that their "memories" were shaped by whoever had them on his couch? In the process, they were being done perhaps irreversible psychological harm. Klass dedicated his book *UFO Abductions: A Dangerous Game* (1989) to "those who will needlessly bear mental scars for the rest of their lives because of the foolish fantasies of a few."

The skeptics had a point. Even with the best of intentions, the hypnotists couldn't have avoided conveying hints of the answers they were looking for; the people they'd put into trance would do their best to comply. The techniques of leading might be extremely subtle, and presumably unconscious. Hopkins, for example, seems to have been in the habit of using the words "I bet" to introduce suggestions to which he wanted a negative response. His abductees were thus cued to create a response *opposite* to the one proposed, and Hopkins could point to their apparent resistance as proof they were immune to his influence.

But the skeptics went too far. They underestimated the desire of the hypnotizers to learn from their "experiencers," which put a brake on any impulse to control or influence them. They likewise underestimated the genuine resistance of the hypnotized, their ability to insist on what they thought they remembered even if it didn't make sense within the abduction scenario.

"Underground!" one of Hopkins' subjects cried out in her trance, as described by a more or less unbiased observer (the writer C. D. B. Bryan) whom Hopkins had invited to be present. "We're underground! Oh, I don't like being down here! This is terrible! . . . It's cold as *hell* down here!"

"How'd you get there, underground?" Hopkins asked, evidently puzzled. If you're abducted into a UFO, surely you ought to be going in the other direction.

"I don't know! I don't know. We're down underground," was the only answer the woman could give.

The friend who'd shared this woman's experience spoke similarly, also in a Hopkins-induced trance, of tumbling *down* into the UFO—not being caught up into it, as we might expect. The descent seems to be part of a pattern, larger than the conventional scenario and perhaps transcending it in time. Whitley Strieber, we recall, was conveyed by his captors into a "small sort of depression in the woods." And in the early centuries of the Common Era, Jewish mystics called *yordei merkavah*, "descenders to the chariot," struggled to reexperience the chariot vision of Ezekiel chapter 1 by going *down* to it and not up. More on these ancient mystics in the next chapter.

For now, my point is that some genuine experience seems to have asserted itself in the hypnotic regressions in the teeth of, rather than in obedience to, Hopkins's expectations. He and his fellow researchers were bringing a real phenomenon to light, and if it wasn't what they thought it was, that didn't make it any less real. The psychiatrist James S. Gordon, a sympathetic skeptic who'd taken the trouble to get to know several abductees and attend their hypnotic sessions, came away with precisely that impression: that "clearly *something* had happened to these people, something powerful, strange, and transformative."

Gordon was unusual. The skeptics normally preferred to criticize from a distance. Perhaps they intuited that if they allowed themselves to witness any of the hypnotic sessions—hearing the abductees' voices, watching their gestures and facial expressions and the contortions of their bodies—they might come face to face with something they preferred not to see. They kept themselves away.

For a time it seemed that Carl Sagan, Cornell astrophysicist and media superstar, might be another exception. Encountering Hopkins by accident in a Boston TV station where they'd been interviewed separately, Sagan told him: "Budd, the next really good abduction case you have, let me know, and I'll look into it with you." Hopkins was elated. But when Sagan's chance came the following year, he pulled back.

In the spring of 1988, Hopkins received a letter from a Cornell student who suspected he'd been abducted. Hopkins wrote Sagan: he would fly to Ithaca at Sagan's convenience so the two of them could investigate the case together. If hypnotic regression seemed warranted, it could be done by Hopkins or by a psychologist of Sagan's choice. If Sagan wanted to speak with the boy in advance, Hopkins had no objection; if he was worried about possible fallout, Hopkins promised confidentiality. Sagan waited nearly a month before replying. Then he sent a six-line note: the evidence in the case was "anecdotal," therefore of no interest. And that was that.

DECLINE AND FALL

By the end of the 1990s, abductions were losing steam. A second Roper poll, conducted in 1998, yielded far fewer encouraging results than its 1991 predecessor. The number of those who said yes to having had the peculiar experiences that were supposed to be abduction indicators had fallen by one-third to one-half. It wasn't that people were no longer being abducted; they plainly were. But if these polls could be trusted, average Americans were no longer as ready as they'd been seven years earlier to ascribe significance to things like a few hours having passed without their having any recollection of them ("missing time"). As a cultural phenomenon, alien abduction was in decline.

Part of the problem was that the research had hit a dead end. Hypnotic regressions had stopped yielding new information on who these beings were, what they wanted from us, why they seemed so endlessly fascinated by our reproductive organs. What we were discovering was what we'd already known, and when all was said and done we didn't know much more about the UFOs than we'd known before. External confirmation of what the abductees had experienced so intensely remained elusive. The "implants" that their captors had supposedly left in their bodies—the ET equivalents of the tracking devices biologists used with animals, some supposed—turned out, whenever they could be retrieved and examined, to be ordinary substances.

But something deeper was at work. Abduction research was not the era's only expedition back into the mists of the unremembered. The 1980s and early '90s were the age of the therapeutic quest to bring repressed memories of childhood sexual abuse into the light.

"Ye shall know the truth" of what befell you, of what you were compelled to endure and then to forget, and that truth shall bring you healing. That could have been Budd Hopkins's mission statement. It was also the mission of Ellen Bass and Laura Davis's best-selling self-help book *The Courage to Heal* (1988): "You may have no conscious memory of being abused. You may have forgotten large chunks of your childhood." Yet "the knowledge that you were abused starts with a tiny feeling, an intuition. It's important to trust that inner voice and work from there. . . . If you think you were abused and your life shows the symptoms, then you were."

I can imagine Hopkins nodding his approval. More important, I can imagine millions of Americans—instructed on the workings of memory by writers like Bass and Davis and the talk shows and newspaper columns parroting them—being prepared to give Hopkins and his colleagues the benefit of the doubt. These UFO tales are fantastic, yes, but also plausible. Don't we know that people recover long-forgotten memories of childhood abuse? So maybe these too . . . ?

The recovered-memory advocates had an advantage over the abduction researchers. The events they supposed to be lurking in the dark of the unconscious were events that did happen in the everyday world. Even the bitterest of their critics had to concede that sexual abuse of children was a reality, even if it hadn't taken place in every instance. But this advantage, and the power it gave them, made them targets of attack. In contrast, UFO aliens were beyond the reach of human justice. Rail at their misdeeds all you wanted; no one was harmed. But memories of sexual exploitation, once retrieved or imagined, tore families apart and sent people to prison. There was bound to be a backlash.

The backlash, when it came in the early to mid-1990s, was ferocious, as excessive and undiscriminating as the recovered-memory crusaders had been at their worst. It was also triumphant. Within a very few years the accepted wisdom had shifted 180 degrees. Repressed memories were "junk science"; genuine trauma, far from being forced out of consciousness, was remembered all too well. The substantial evidence that memories of sexual abuse sometimes *were* repressed, to return many years later with or without therapeutic involvement, was brushed off or ignored.[32] Most of this evidence was "anecdotal"; it had to be. Trauma didn't lend itself to laboratory experiment.

Bessel van der Kolk, professor of psychiatry at the Boston University School of Medicine and past president of the International Society for Traumatic Stress Studies, tells of being interviewed about traumatic memory by a London periodical. He patiently led his interviewer through the research that had been done in England for over a century on traumatic memory loss; he "suggested they

---

32 In its November 29, 1993, issue, *U.S. News & World Report* published a compelling eight-page article by Miriam Horn, entitled "Memories Lost and Found." It told the story of a Brown University political science professor named Ross Cheit, who in the spring of 1992 sank into a prolonged and inexplicable depression after his sister phoned him with the "happy news" that his nephew was going to sing in a boys' chorus, just as Cheit had in his early teen years. Cheit felt his marriage to be at risk and went into therapy. On vacation that summer, he awoke "with the baffling sense that a man he had not seen or thought of in 25 years was powerfully present in the room." It was the administrator of the boys' chorus summer camp, and over the course of the day, memories returned to Cheit of what the man had done to him: he had sat on Cheit's bed night after night as he was going to sleep, stroked his chest and stomach while telling him to relax, and "slowly [brought] his hand into my pants." Over the coming months Cheit tracked down others from the summer camp who had similar stories. He tracked down the administrator, kept him on the phone with a tape recorder while the man admitted what he'd done. He sued the man and won; he sued the boys' chorus and got an apology. His story does not stand alone. In his blog *Recovered Memory Project: Case Archive, Commentary, and Scholarly Resources* (blogs.brown.edu/recoveredmemory), Cheit currently maintains an archive of 110 corroborated cases of recovered memories of abuse.

look at an article published in *The Lancet* in 1944, which described the aftermath of the rescue of the entire British army from the beaches of Dunkirk in 1940. More than 10 percent of the soldiers who were studied had suffered from major memory loss after the evacuation." The result? "The following week the magazine told its readers that there was no evidence whatsoever that people sometimes lose some or all memory for traumatic events."

For UFO-abduction researchers, the belief in repressed memories of sexual abuse was a mixed blessing. On the one hand, it lent respectability to their claims and methods. On the other hand, it suggested a wholly terrestrial alternative to their conclusions. What if the outrages on the abductees' bodies that the hypnotic regressions were turning up were indeed something real, but perpetrated not by aliens but by trusted adults on helpless children? The UFOlogists' appeal to "screen memories" could be flipped on its head. The otherworldly spaceship scenario was not what was being "screened" by memory's disguises, but was itself the "screen"—for events that were mundane, yet too awful to be remembered in their sickening reality.

I've already suggested something of the sort with regard to Whitley Strieber. With characteristic self-awareness, Strieber has suggested it with regard to himself. What if something happened to him at age twelve, he mused thirty years after his life-changing 1985 encounter, "part of a pattern so shocking that I cannot face it directly even now and have transferred it into this strange memory in order to protect myself from what my unconscious mind regards as an unbearable truth? . . . A brutal rape by a beloved parent might become a brutal alien abduction, as the mind seizes on the most believable and acceptable alternative in order to avoid facing what it cannot bear to see."

By the 1990s, the apparent link between "the prevalence of childhood sexual abuse, and the sexually violating nature of many of the alien abduction stories," as one psychologist put it, had become hard to overlook. "One possible explanation is that the abduction/contact narratives are screen memories for early childhood trauma such as sexual abuse." The UFOlogists protested: "neither researchers nor therapists," David Jacobs wrote in 1992, "have found a single abduction case that is unequivocally generated from sexual or physical abuse." But what does it take for such a connection to be "unequivocal"?

In November 1992, Hopkins did a hypnotic regression on the woman who, in a subsequent session, would remember tumbling down into a UFO. This woman had long carried a memory of a fishing trip she'd taken with her father when she was twelve, from which she'd returned unwilling to speak to him and with blood in her underpants. She suspected he'd raped her, but couldn't recall the actual rape. Under hypnosis, however, she remembered it well. It wasn't her father who'd perpetrated it, but the aliens. Her father had stood by, watching helplessly.

"I feel *hatred* for him!" the woman cried out, still in trance. Why hadn't he intervened to protect her? Hopkins stepped in to explain: there was nothing the man could have done; the aliens had "paralyzed" him; instead of hating her father, she should hate the Beings who had abused her so cruelly. By the next morning, however, her doubts had returned. Maybe her father had been the rapist after all.

If this won't qualify as "unequivocal," what will?

The new millennium began. The Twin Towers fell. The notion of recovered memories, which had created such a stir at the end of the old century, was remembered mostly with shame, as an occasion for the harassment and prosecution of innocent people; the Salem witch trials were invoked in comparison. In the wake of that idea's discrediting, alien abductions faded as well. How could they have thrived in an atmosphere turned so hostile to the unremembered?

John Mack, visiting London in 2004 for a conference on his beloved Lawrence, was killed by a drunken driver. (His family pleaded for clemency for the driver, saying, no doubt correctly, that that was what John would have wanted.) Budd Hopkins died in 2011. David Jacobs soldiered on. But his "threat" from outer space seemed nebulous and distant compared to more immediate menaces: medieval religious war freshly reignited, a planet's climate spinning out of control.

Abductions were still reported and remembered, but as a cultural phenomenon, they'd had their day. From the vantage point of nearly twenty years, we can look back on them and ask, What were they? *What did they mean*?

COMMUNION AND PREDIONICA

At the end of 2013, I received an email from my old friend Professor Marc Bregman, then teaching at the University of North Carolina at Greensboro (UNC-G). "I have a vague recollection," he wrote, "of seeing via you a drawing of what someone thought an 'alien' face looked like—very big eyes, etc. Did you or I or we mention that this image is remarkably similar to some of the prehistoric (Neolithic) 'masks' thought to be of ancient gods?"

The alien face Marc remembered was from the cover of *Communion*. In March 2011 I'd given a PowerPoint lecture on UFOs at UNC-G, and one of the pictures I'd shown was Ted Jacobs's rendering of Strieber's "visitor." Writing in *Communion*, Strieber had likened that countenance to the "huge staring eyes of the old gods." But here was a god not just old but truly prehistoric: the Predionica mask—actually, a sculpted ceramic head wearing a mask, about seven inches high and six inches wide—found in the 1950s at Predionica, near Pristina, now the capital of Kosovo in the Balkans. Marc had come upon a photograph of it in Marija Gimbutas's *The Gods and Goddesses of Old Europe*. More than two and a half years after seeing the *Communion* cover projected onto a screen, he experienced a flash of recognition.

One more case of the "recognition response," this time in reverse. (First Marc saw the face on the cover, then, long afterward, something else that evoked the feeling he'd seen it before.) I could agree: the resemblance was remarkable. True, the nose of the Predionica sculpture was more prominent than on the *Communion* painting. The being depicted by the mask had hair, represented with lines etched into the clay, and seemingly ears as well; the *Communion* entity had neither. But as skeptical UFOlogist Martin Kottmeyer put it in an email to me, "The nature of the eyes and face lines generates a strong emotional resonance that overrides one's awareness of the disparities."

Marc wasn't the first to notice the resemblance. Kottmeyer directed me toward Michael Hesemann's *UFOs: The Secret History* (1998), which printed a drawing based on the *Communion* cover side by side with the Predionica mask, with the remark that Strieber's alien "has a very ancient double." Hesemann didn't say what the significance of that "double" might be. But it's clear enough what he was implying: that aliens like the one Strieber experienced had visited the Kosovo region thousands of years ago.

This is improbable, to put it very mildly. The Predionica mask is securely embedded within the art of the prehistoric Vinča culture of the central Balkans, the culmination of an evolutionary sequence of mask sculptures from pre-Vinča times to the late Vinča period (4500–3500 BCE). It's not an interloper, as it would be if the sculptor were depicting something he and his people had never seen before.

That leaves three possible explanations:

1. The resemblance is coincidental, without any significance.
2. Ted Jacobs had seen the Predionica mask or a photograph of it sometime before painting the "visitor" at Strieber's direction and was influenced by it as he translated Strieber's words into a visual image.
3. Or the face he painted and the face fashioned in clay by a forgotten but stunningly talented artist in prehistoric Kosovo were archetypal, hardwired into the human brain, occurring spontaneously and independently 6,000 years ago and now.

The second option seems the most economical and satisfying. I know of no evidence that Jacobs ever saw the mask, but there's

FIGURE 6. The Predionica mask. From Marija Gimbutas, *The Gods and Goddesses of Old Europe: 7000 to 3500 BC* (University of California Press, 1974).

no reason he couldn't have. A photo of the mask was published in 1959; the first edition of Gimbutas's book came out in 1974, the second in 1982. Jacobs was not only an accomplished artist but also a highly regarded teacher, first in New York City and later (from 1987 onward) at his own art school in France. He must have had a rich knowledge of art history and a curiosity that might well set him to poring over books like Gimbutas's. It's true that the mask's light brown color, one of the most striking features linking it with the *Communion* cover, doesn't come across in Gimbutas's photos, black and white in both editions. But perhaps color reproductions, on picture postcards, say, were also available to him?

I wouldn't rule out the first possibility either. Random coincidences, some of them fantastic, are part of our daily lives. The human imagination, through the generations, must have created thousands of facial images of uncanny and otherworldly beings. If we could comb through them all, we'd surely find at least a few "doubles" among them.[33]

Marc's recognition experience, though, makes me hesitate to adopt this explanation. I've known him for more than forty years; he's never shown any interest in UFOs except as a by-product of our friendship. Yet the sight of the Predionica mask triggered a recollection, admittedly "vague," of a similar face he'd seen *once*, more than two and a half years earlier. This suggests a genuine and significant link between the two.

Perhaps the problem belongs in a wider context. The massively documented recognition response to the *Communion* cover after its publication, with which this chapter began, points to something in the human psyche that responds to the Strieber/Jacobs face as a thing already seen, already known. This points us toward the third

---

33 A proposition testable in some measure through an update to the Google Arts & Culture app, introduced in December 2017. Users can find their "fine art doppelgänger" by sending in a selfie, which Google will match to its vast collection of paintings and sculpture from the world's museums. Most of these doppelgängers, to judge from the examples posted to the web, have not looked much like the people they're supposed to twin.

option, whether we choose to use the Jungian word *archetype* for it or go in search of some more appropriate terminology.

Indeed, it's possible that the second and third options combined will yield the best explanation of all. Jacobs's memory, conscious or unconscious, of the Predionica mask came to him as he listened to Strieber describe the "visitors," particularly the one who was "the most essentially and powerfully feminine presence" Strieber had ever known. He felt intuitively, without ever having seen that "visitor," that this was the right model to use in depicting her. Why? Because he knew that when the human mind gazes into darkness, this is the face it's apt to see staring back.

It's a female face, both for Strieber and for the nameless genius of ancient Kosovo. (Gimbutas infers the gender from the arrangement of its hair.) It shades into the animal, as do the aliens of the abduction tradition. "Was it the sculptor's intention to portray on the mask an animal or half-animal, half-human creature?" Gimbutas asks. "Though we cannot know for certain, we feel that the creature is endowed with an awe-inspiring power, the very essence of the significance of the mask."

Strieber must have felt the same when Jacobs showed him the painting. So did many thousands of bookstore browsers at the beginning of 1987. "That book started to sell the minute it appeared on the bookshelves," its publisher recalled a year or so later; "no reviews, no appearances, nothing. And we had word from the bookstores that *Communion, with this strange picture on the cover,* was selling." The italics are mine; the point is made even without them. It was that "strange," "awe-inspiring" picture—archaic and numinous, with the "huge staring eyes of the old gods"—that sold the book.

And that will lead us back into the tangled prehistory of alien abduction.

CHAPTER 5

Ancient Abductees

LET'S PAUSE TO TAKE STOCK.

I led off chapter 3 with the bold claim that the abduction phenomenon of the late twentieth century can be traced back, like humanity in the Bible story, to a single pair. These were the New Englanders Barney and Betty Hill, a black man and a white woman, together channeling a collective memory of his ancestral trauma, her ancestral crime.

A paradox: it was her people and not his who were destined to reenact his trauma over and over in the coming decades. The overwhelming majority of the abductees since the Hills have been white. It's as if the UFOs took on the role assigned to the Mother Wheel, their counterpart in the apocalyptic doctrine of the Nation of Islam (the so-called Black Muslims), of inflicting measure-for-measure retribution on white America for its atrocities against its blacks.[34] Psychologically, this makes perfect sense. In a vast historic crime, like the slave trade in the eighteenth century or the Holocaust in the twentieth, perpetrators and victims become entwined, enmeshed, bonded. Both carry for generations the wounds of the atrocities they suffered or inflicted.[35]

As the abduction tradition grew—from a trickle of reports in the late 1960s and early '70s, turning into a stream in the late '70s and a torrent at the end of the '80s—it accumulated additional baggage of personal trauma, mostly of a sexual nature. Yet these factors together still won't account for the abduction phenomenon, and for its meaning to those who've experienced it. The staring, compelling eyes of the Predionica head bear witness: *there was something before that.*

Beyond the abused children of the twentieth century, beyond the European American mass atrocity of the eighteenth, centuries before UFOs were ever called such or space visitors even an option for the imagination, there was a human experience akin to UFO abduction. Our task now is to acknowledge that kinship and, if possible, to understand it.

EZEKIEL'S "CHARIOT"

There was once a group within the Jewish people—a group of men, almost certainly—who called themselves "descenders to the chariot," the Hebrew word for "chariot" (*merkavah*) being shorthand for

---

34 Possibly intuited by the two white Mississippians abducted in October 1973 from the dock in the Pascagoula River, where they'd gone to fish and were themselves fished for, by something alien and unearthly. "They could have owned us son, they had us," the older man afterward said to the younger, their words caught on a hidden police tape recorder. And we're reminded that this was a part of the country where humans did own other humans and that was still badly scarred by that wrong. The Nation of Islam's Mother Wheel, and its context in the African American UFO tradition, parallel to the white tradition yet distinct from it, is an area that cries out for exploration. Two scholars in particular, Michael Lieb and Stephen C. Finley, have done pioneering work.

35 Psychotherapists working with the Family Constellations therapy developed by Bert Hellinger have encountered this phenomenon in the children and grandchildren of Nazis and of Holocaust survivors. Joint therapy sessions have brought healing to both.

the fantastic entity that Ezekiel described in the first chapter of his book. In their convoluted, half-intelligible writings, these people spoke of undertaking mystical journeys to the merkavah-chariot on its home territory, of going there to view it as Ezekiel had. One might naturally assume that territory to be in heaven. Strangely, though, they called their journey to the merkavah a "descent" and the return from it an "ascent." We don't (yet) know why.

These men lived centuries after Ezekiel, and no doubt they read many things into Ezekiel's text that the prophet never intended. Yet if we're to make sense of their encounters with the merkavah, we need first to ground ourselves in the Biblical vision itself. "Ezekiel saw the wheel / Way up in the middle of the air," runs the African American spiritual—and that wheel has more than once been called a UFO. Was it?

"And I looked, and behold, a stormy wind came out of the north, a great cloud, with a fire flashing up, so that a brightness was round about it" (Ezek. 1:4). I read those words as a child, wandering on my own through the double-columned pages of our family Bible, and I remember going to my mother and telling her I'd read something scary. I don't know if I made my way through the rest of the chapter, which I would no doubt have found even scarier.

As Ezekiel watches, four "living creatures" emerge from the fire-cloud, essentially human in appearance but each with four wings and four faces: human, lion, ox, eagle. Then a single wheel appears, not in the middle of the air, but on the earth beside the creatures. The one wheel turns into four, rising with the creatures from the earth, "for the spirit of the living creatures was in the wheels." They're constructed as "a wheel within a wheel," their rims "high" and "dreadful . . . full of eyes round about."

Ezekiel's attention is at last drawn to a crystalline expanse over the heads of the living creatures and to a sapphire (or perhaps lapis lazuli) throne above that expanse, where a humanlike figure of blazing fire sits, surrounded by prismatic shimmering. Recognizing this as the "glory" of his God, Yahveh, Ezekiel falls on his face.

The voice that addresses Ezekiel from the throne dispatches him as Yahveh's messenger to the Judean people, a nation on the eve of its destruction. A substantial chunk of its population, Ezekiel included, have already been carried into exile by their Babylonian conquerors. Most of those who remain in the homeland will soon follow. Ezekiel is sent to preach the sinfulness and doom of their city Jerusalem. This message anchors Ezekiel's vision in the Near East of the early sixth century BCE, and it stands as an obstacle to any notion that an encounter with "ancient astronauts" is what it's about.

The idea that Ezekiel witnessed an extraterrestrial visit has been floated repeatedly since the UFO era began, with or without a linkage to modern UFO sightings. It took on its most appealing form in a 1961 article entitled "The Four-Faced Visitors of Ezekiel," by a specialist in aircraft mechanics named Arthur W. Orton. Through a close and mostly sensible reading of the Biblical text, Orton argued that Ezekiel 1 is "the account of an actual happening; the landing of extraterrestrial beings, reported by a careful, truthful and self-possessed observer." But Orton's exegesis broke down with the shift, at the beginning of chapter 2, from prophetic vision to prophetic discourse. Why should space visitors have cared so deeply about the religious violations and political blunders of a tiny, soon-to-be-destroyed Israelite kingdom? Orton couldn't answer the question and chose to ignore it. His successors have done no better.

Surely it makes more sense—nearly all Biblical scholars will tell you—to look for the key to understanding the vision not in anachronistic space-age machinery but in the mythic iconography with which Ezekiel himself might be presumed familiar. Unfortunately, this approach doesn't get us very far either. There's nothing from antiquity that's quite like the entities Ezekiel claims to have encountered.

Human-faced animals are common in ancient Near Eastern art and sculpture. The Egyptian Sphinx is a famous example. So are the immense stone lions or bulls with wings and human heads

FIGURE 7. The vision of Ezekiel, copperplate engraving by Matthäus Merian for his *Iconum Biblicarum* (1630). From the reprint of *Iconum Biblicarum* by AVB Press (Wenatchee, WA), 1981; used with permission of Directed Media, Inc.

that stood guard at the entrances to the palaces of the Assyrian kings. But animal heads or faces on human bodies, such as Ezekiel describes, are much rarer. A single human figure with four faces, comparable to Ezekiel's "living creatures"? Very rare. In those few cases where it does occur, the faces are all human and are identical. And the ancient world offers nothing that might give sense or context to Ezekiel's wheels, with their multitudinous eyes and their "high and dreadful" rims.

The merkavah resists all attempts to conventionalize it, reduce it to known categories of experience or belief, whether ancient or modern.[36] Explaining it as the vehicle of ancient astronauts is

36 Including that of some early transmitter of the Book of Ezekiel, who fleshed out

a conventionalization, forcing it into line with a space-age sense of what's real and possible. Calling it "visions of God," as Ezekiel himself does (Ezek. 1:1), is a conventionalization of a different sort. Neither is adequate. It's something unknown, indefinable, erupting from within Ezekiel yet outside his conscious control and even his normal conscious awareness.

In that sense, yes, it was a UFO, something truly "unidentified," projected into the sky, though its proper home was the psyche. More than the Bible scholars or the ancient-astronaut theorists, Jung had a handle on it when he called Ezekiel's vision "archetypal" and declared it to be "made up of two well-ordered composite quaternities, that is, conceptions of totality"—not to mention the mandala wheel, "wheel within a wheel," unifier of opposites. As such, it may not be possible to interpret the merkavah but only to encounter it. "Symbols that have an archetypal foundation," Jung wrote, "can never be reduced to anything else."

Even as a child, I felt the stirring of its numinous fearfulness. Long afterward, as my path as a fledgling scholar carried me with increasing certainty toward Ezekiel and his merkavah—that is to say, back to my teenage UFOlogy in antique and therefore respectable guise—I learned how the rabbis of the early centuries of the Common Era had regarded his vision with a mixture of veneration and dread. The beginning of Genesis and the beginning of Ezekiel were among those Scriptures to be kept away from the young: the story of Creation might be a dangerous object of study, but the merkavah was even more so. No one might involve himself with it "unless he is wise and can understand on his own," and even the

---

Ezekiel's vision of the corrupted, desecrated Jerusalem Temple (chapters 8–11) with a recap of the merkavah vision. He identified the "living creatures" of chapter 1 with the human-faced monsters called "cherubim" who, in sculpted form, stood in the Temple's Holy of Holies sheltering the Deity with their wings (10:20). In fact, the Temple cherubim bear only a distant resemblance to the "living creatures." The equation of the two is a guess, probably mistaken, at the meaning of a vision that baffled the ancients as much as it does us.

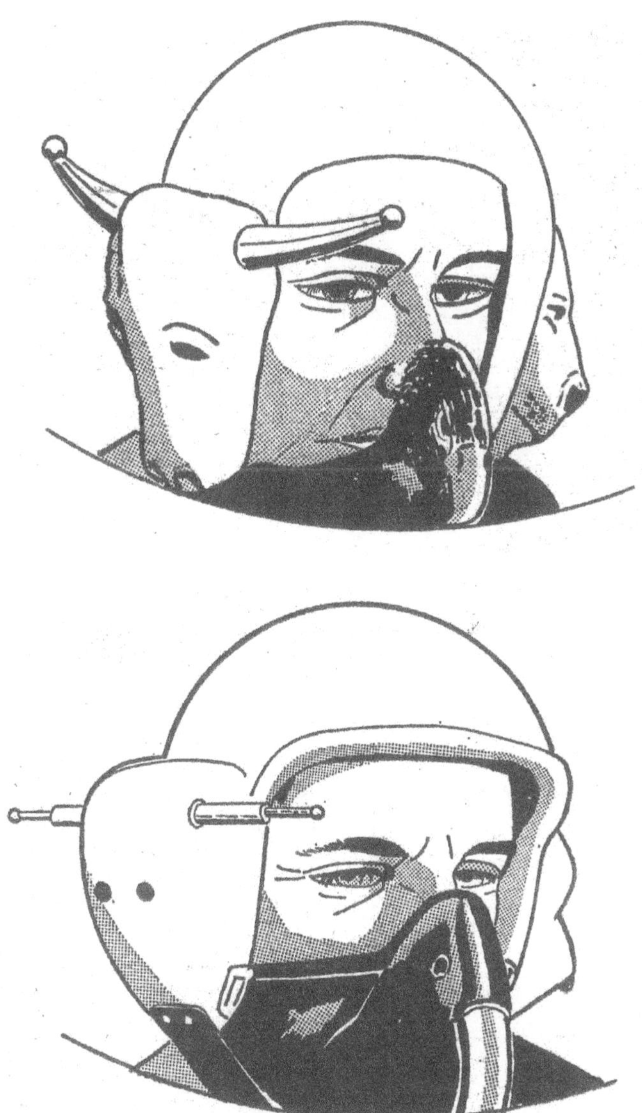

FIGURE 8. The "four faces" as Ezekiel described them (above) and as Arthur W. Orton imagined them for his "Four-Faced Visitors of Ezekiel" (below). How much better, Orton asked, could a man living six centuries before Christ have described the outfit of this extraterrestrial visitor? Both drawings by Orton, in *Analog Science Fact-Fiction* (March 1961).

wise and the understanding were at risk. Contemplate the entities described in the first chapter of Ezekiel, come to a sudden and all too accurate comprehension of them, and fire might leap out from them and burn you alive.

"DESCENDERS TO THE MERKAVAH"

Somewhere amid that ambivalent engagement of the ancient Jews with the merkavah, the men who spoke of themselves as "descending" to it had their place.

Precisely what that place was—who these descenders were, when and where they lived, what exactly they did when they "descended to the chariot," and why they thought of themselves as descending to something that ought to be in the sky—these are mysteries hardly less impenetrable than Ezekiel's vision itself. Some researchers place them in Roman or Byzantine Palestine early in the Common Era, others in Islamic Iraq several hundred years later. But all agree that these "merkavah mystics," as they've come to be known, bequeathed to medieval Judaism a peculiar Hebrew literature called *Hekhalot* (Palaces), in reference to the seven concentric "palaces" within which they imagined the merkavah to be enclosed. It's from this literature that we know them.

Were they ancient abductees? Not exactly. The relation between the experiences described in the Hekhalot literature and those of modern abductees is subtler and more complex than that, with major differences that must be given full weight. But there are also continuities, leading us into a broad range of religious phenomena that seem to encompass both.

"Rabbi Ishmael said: What are those songs to be uttered by one who seeks to gaze on the vision of the merkavah, in order that he may descend safely and ascend safely?" Thus begins *The Greater Treatise of the Palaces*, a Hekhalot text that's not so much a book as a chaotic swirl of hymns, incantations, sacred names and unearthly landscapes, with a few snatches of narrative woven in. Rabbi Ishmael and his teacher Rabbi Nehunyah ben Hakanah are the main characters. Both men were historical figures, rabbinic scholars who lived in Palestine around 100 CE. Their involvement with the merkavah and the "descent" to it was a fiction, concocted centuries after their deaths. But fiction can sometimes be a projection of a reality known to the writer, and that may be what's happening here.

Rabbi Ishmael is often the narrator. In one episode, he tells how at Rabbi Nehunyah's command he assembled the other rabbis at an entrance of the Jerusalem Temple. There he and nine fellow initiates sit at Nehunyah's feet while Nehunyah lectures on "the ways of the merkavah, descent and ascent, how the one who descends [to the merkavah] makes the descent, how the one who ascends can make the ascent."

That "descent" is a deeply frightening experience. Reading the Hekhalot, you're apt to wonder why anyone would want to make it at all. The angels you run into along the way are monstrous and horrible: "taller than mountains," their bows drawn, sharp swords in their hands. Their noses drip fire; their eyeballs, bolts of lightning. "Their horses are horses of darkness, horses of deep darkness, horses of gloom, horses of fire, horses of blood, horses of hail, horses of iron, horses of the misty cloud . . . and they eat glowing coals out of their mangers."[37]

These are not Hallmark greeting-card angels; they're as savage in their habits as they are terrifying in their appearance. Pushing other creatures into rivers of fire is standard behavior for them. They do it to each other; they do it to the human visitor who's slipped up in some way, revealing his unfitness to "see the King [God] in His beauty." But with the right magic, a human being can do the same to an angel who refuses his demands. "I will push you into the lava flow of pressing fire and set up another in your

---

37 Translated by James R. Davila. (Unless indicated otherwise, all other translations from the Hekhalot are my own.)

place," one of the descenders warns an angel, and there's no reason to think this an empty threat.

In a "heaven" so saturated with aggression and brutality, treading gingerly is a must. Voyagers need the exact names of the angels they will pass, the right seals to show them so they'll be let through. All this information Rabbi Nehunyah provides, until he mentions a detail his hearers don't understand. They beg Rabbi Ishmael to intercede, to "bring him back . . . from the vision he is viewing" so that he can clarify what he's trying to say.

Gershom Scholem, the past century's greatest scholar of Jewish mysticism, explains what's going on here. Nehunyah has been in ecstatic trance, telling his pupils what he sees in his vision of the things that Ezekiel once saw. He must be brought out of his trance so that he can respond to their questions, and Rabbi Ishmael knows exactly how to do it. A myrtle branch, infected with just the slightest taint of impurity, is placed on Nehunyah's knees. At once Nehunyah is dismissed from the world of his vision, back to normal consciousness.

Fiction, of course—glamorized, transferred into the distant past. The setting in the long-destroyed Temple is enough to guarantee that. But as I've said, fiction can be a projection of the writer's reality, and this story has the authentic feel of a shamanistic séance. The shaman journeys in spirit through fantastic and inaccessible realms. His body remains with the people who've gathered to witness his feats, while he reports to them on what his soul encounters along its way.

A parallel close at hand suggests itself: the hypnotic regression of the UFO abductee.

There are differences. The abductee is passive, put into a trance rather than actively creating it. The realm into which he or she journeys is that of memory, not of present events but of the past relived. Yet like the shaman, like the descender, the abductee is in two places at once, the therapist's couch and the extraterrestrial spaceship. This duality, this drama played out on two planes simultaneously, is a staple of films about alien abduction, from the 1975 TV movie *The UFO Incident*—a powerful and authentic portrayal of the Betty and Barney Hill episode—to the 2009 thriller *The Fourth Kind*. The stability of this feature, through nearly thirty-five years of "abduction" cinema, suggests that it reflects something fundamental about the phenomenon.

Abduction and the "descent" have something else in common. Both focus on an aerial vehicle that is *not*, as one might expect, a means for flying somewhere else. The UFO, like Ezekiel's "chariot," is itself the goal. In only about a quarter of abduction stories do we hear of some travel beyond the UFO, often though not always to other worlds, after the real business in the spaceship's examination room is done.

Several of these supplementary journeys share an odd feature that "comes as a surprise even by the standards of UFO abduction stories" (Bullard) and leads us back to the merkavah by another path. Instead of flying up into outer space, the witness goes down, whether inside the UFO or not. Bullard gives several examples, including a UFO that "plunged into the sea and came out again, then entered huge crystalline caverns which broadened into a vast underworld" and an abductee's recollection of how "beings escorted him to a beach, unlocked a rock and led him through a tunnel stretching beneath the sea." In her 1977 hypnotic regression, Betty Andreasson was frankly puzzled by her sense of having traveled outward and at the same time inward. "Did you leave this earth and go through space—to another planet?" one of the investigators asked her. "Or did this all happen on this earth?"

Betty: "I left this earth, yes, I left this earth. I believe we were in space, and somehow I believe we were in the center of the earth. Now how can you be in both?"

How indeed? And how can it be that Ezekiel's chariot, which by any rational accounting is part of the appurtenances of heaven, is reached by a process of descent? Writing nearly sixty years ago, Scholem called this "a very curious and so far unexplained change of phraseology." Sixty years of research have done nothing to explain it. But we've already seen two of Budd Hopkins's abductees insist on having gone down rather than up to the UFO. Hopkins, though perplexed at their conviction—"How'd you get there, underground?"—still couldn't shake it.

"I don't know! I don't know. We're down underground."

There's evidently something about the experience that, at least on occasion, creates a perception of descent so compelling as to overwhelm all realistic awareness that one ought to be going in the other direction. This was the case for some abductees at the end of the twentieth century—and, it would appear, for the merkavah mystics hundreds of years earlier. The lines, faint and shadowy, begin to be drawn.

THE TERROR OF THE EYES

In 1984 a conference on ancient Jewish mysticism, devoted mostly to the Hekhalot texts, was held at the Hebrew University in Jerusalem. I was invited but couldn't attend, so I sent my paper to be included in the *Proceedings*, which came out three years later. I don't think the editor was very pleased with my contribution. The next time we saw each other, he told me with a sour face that I should have sent it in a plain brown wrapper. He published it anyway.

My paper was entitled "A Sexual Image in Hekhalot Rabbati[38] and Its Implications." Its starting point was a passage describing a harrowing experience that the descender can expect to have at the gate of the "seventh palace." In that description I'd noticed something odd and uncanny, hard to put my finger on yet seemingly responsible for the visionary's terror.

Ezekiel's "living creatures," says the passage, stand by the gate of the seventh palace. So do the "Ophannim," Ezekiel's "wheels," turned by Jewish tradition into a class of angel. Whenever someone

38 The Hebrew title of *The Greater Treatise of the Palaces*.

wants to descend to the merkavah, the doors of that gate are opened to him. He goes in and stands on the threshold.

> The holy living creatures then look at him with their 512 eyes.[39] Each of the eyes of the holy living creatures is split open, the size of a large winnowers' sieve, and their eyes look as if they race like lightnings. Besides them, there are the eyes of the mighty cherubim and of the Ophannim . . . which look like torches and flaming coals. The man shudders and trembles and recoils; he faints in terror and collapses.

The angelic guards intervene, supporting and comforting the visitor. From above, a trumpet blows. "The holy living creatures cover their faces; the cherubim and the Ophannim turn their faces away." Elsewhere in the Hekhalot, the terror the heavenly beings evoke is attributed to their size, their weaponry, their propensity for violence. Here, none of these is even mentioned. It's their weird, enormous eyes that generate the visionary's dread. As soon as they're no longer staring at him, his fear is relieved.

What does it mean for an eye to be "split open"? To be comparable to a winnowers' sieve? I found the clue in another passage, where, at the climax of an erotically charged scene involving God and the living creatures, the heaven "splits open like a sieve" before the intensity of their arousal. Evidence from rabbinic literature and Greco-Roman sources confirmed that the sieve—a concave instrument whose function involved being penetrated—was used in the ancient Mediterranean world as an image for the vulva.

These "eyes" were indeed eyes, yet like those of Whitley Strieber's visitors they were something more than eyes. They were eyes like those seen by a patient of Freud's who dreamed of a woman standing by a wooden fence, facing away: "At last she

---

39 Through a multiplication process drawn from the Jewish exegetical tradition, the originally four-faced "creatures" are credited with a total of 256 faces and, consequently, 512 eyes. This of course makes them all the more frightening.

FIGURE 9. The Kilpeck Sheela—the Sheela-na-gig on the church at Kilpeck, Herefordshire, England. Photo by Nessy-Pic, via Wikimedia Commons (https://commons.wikimedia.org/wiki/File:Sheela-na-gig,_Kilpeck_Church.jpg).

turned round and gave him a terrible look so that he ran off in terror. The red flesh of the lower lids of her eyes could be seen standing out." The dreamer's associations to his dream images led back to forbidden childhood peeps between the legs of little girls, and the punishments and threats that followed.[40]

Five hundred twelve such eyes stare at the hapless descender, huge like the vulvas on the medieval *sheela-na-gig* figures—the grotesquely malformed female nudes, squatting with legs parted and hands tugging open their labia, carved onto churches with the aim (perhaps) of warding off evil through their revulsion and dread. No wonder he "shudders and trembles and recoils, faints in terror and collapses" beneath those eyes and their unblinking gaze. His archaic sexual fears have leaped out from within him,[41] unwilled and uncomprehended, to confront him at the entrance to the seventh gate. In this lies the proof that the Hekhalot are no mere paper-and-ink exercises. Beneath their turgid, garbled rhetoric hides an authentic encounter with the unconscious—just as in the UFO abductions.

---

40 Another "eye" that's more than an eye: the one that glares at the viewer out of the classic 1958 movie poster for *The Astounding She Monster* ("A CREATURE FROM BEYOND THE STARS, *EVIL . . . BEAUTIFUL . . . DEADLY*"). Film critic Tim Lucas describes the poster (easily found on the web by Googling "albert kallis she monster") as "a forceful evocation of female allure, exuding luxuriant unknowability and power." The She Monster stands voluptuous in a skintight leotard, dwarfing the male figure who crumples in fiery death-rays from two flying disks, his rifle jutting upward from a spot near his crotch. Her face is "withheld in mystery except for a single mascara-limned eye and arched brow. It seems to glow, that eye, from beneath a lioness mane of orange-yellow hair, burning forth between upheld forearms . . . " Lucas might have added that the eye is tilted as far as possible toward the vertical, located nearly on the axis running down between her breasts. Turn the picture upside down, imagine the She Monster's elbows are in fact her knees; the upward displacement of that "eye" will be apparent.

41 Like the consuming flames in another Hekhalot passage, understood in a rare burst of psychological insight to come out of the visionary himself: "The one who looks upon it, or glimpses or sees it, / his eyeballs are seized by pulsations, / and his eyeballs emit and send forth flames of fire, / and they kindle and burn him up. / The fire that comes out of the man who looks kindles him and burns him" (tr. Elliot R. Wolfson).

Now, reader, kindly look back to the beginning of chapter 4, where the cover of Strieber's *Communion* is reproduced. Hold the book so one of those eyes (preferably the left) is vertical, and the resemblance of its shape to the vulva is unmistakable.

Look deep into it. I think you'll see what I saw there, one summer day about four years after I sent my "Sexual Image" paper off to the editor, when *Communion* had come out in paperback. Namely, a smooth cleft within the blackness, running from end to end, top to bottom, one corner to the other.

This was a "split-open" eye like the ones I'd written about, from cryptic Hebrew texts more than a thousand years old. Like the Predionica mask, it was witness to the essential antiquity of those things that emerged into our awareness a little over fifty years ago, when Barney and Betty Hill sank down into their hypnotic trances.

A BROADER CANVAS

As a parallel to the abductions from outside the world of UFOlogy, "merkavah mysticism" hardly stands alone. More than one researcher has noted about the abductions what we've observed with regard to the "descent to the merkavah": they sound a lot like shamanic trance journeys.

The humiliating and sometimes painful ordeals that the abductees undergo on the examination tables—think of the needle through Betty Hill's navel—are reminiscent of religion scholar Mircea Eliade's account of shamanic initiation: "dismemberment of the body, followed by a renewal of the internal organs and viscera; ascent to the sky and dialogue with the gods or spirits; descent to the underworld and conversations with spirits and the souls of dead shamans." Shamans are attended by helping spirits, usually in the form of animals: "bears, wolves, stags, hares, all kinds of birds (especially the goose, eagle, owl, crow, etc.)." The UFO aliens often appear to abductees under the "screen" of animals, like Whitley Strieber's owl or Kary Mullis's raccoon.

Strieber, who in his later years would look back on his "visitor" encounters as "a love affair with a goddess"—who intermittently saw in the face of his beloved wife Anne "a flickering shadow of the great-eyed being I'd painted for the cover of *Communion*"—would have well understood the experience of an early twentieth-century Siberian shaman, visited in his sleep by a spirit

> in the form of a beautiful woman, who informed him that she had been the helping spirit of his dead ancestor shamans and that she would teach him to become a shaman. She also proposed to cohabit with him as his wife.[42]

"I love you," she told him. "I have no husband now, you will be my husband and I shall be a wife unto you." He resisted; the spirit was insistent. "If you will not obey me, so much the worse for you. I shall kill you." Strieber, unlike his shamanic predecessor, wasn't even offered an option. "On that night in December 1985, the most essentially and powerfully feminine presence I have ever known came to me and had me dragged out of the house and essentially beaten until I realized that she was real and I was not dreaming."

The parallels are compelling. But no sooner are you persuaded that UFO abductions are a species of shamanism, adapted to an affluent industrial society of the late twentieth century, than another set of associations comes to tempt you in a different direction.

European folklore is rich in tales of humans kidnapped or enticed into fairyland, sometimes mating with their captors. Like the aliens of the abduction tradition, the fairies habitually make away with human children, leaving their own in place as stunted "changelings" (analogous to the "hybrids" of the abduction stories). Not visitors to our planet but our neighbors here from the beginning, "the wee folk" are distinguished from us mainly by their diminutive size. In this, too, they're like the abducting aliens.

Do the sheela-na-gigs belong somewhere on this broadening canvas? No UFOlogist, as far as I know, has called attention to the "alien" quality of these powerful, repellent sculptures, found on

---

42 The description is James Davila's.

medieval churches mainly in Ireland but throughout Great Britain and continental Europe as well. That fell to feminist scholar Georgia Rhoades. "I first encountered a *sheela-na-gig* in 1994, in a shop in Avebury, England, a reproduction of the famous Kilpeck Sheela . . . : Extraterrestrial-like, bald, and holding her vulva open with both hands" (the last two features being standard for sheela-na-gigs). I don't imagine Rhoades was altogether serious about her ET comparison. It's apt nonetheless.

The purpose of these bizarre figures, what they were intended to signify, what they were in fact taken by their contemporaries to signify—not necessarily the same thing—all these remain unsolved mysteries. They've been classed as erotic sculpture, but if *erotic* means something that evokes feelings of pleasure or excitement or comfort in connection with sex, the word doesn't seem to fit. On the contrary, they seem designed to uglify sex to the extent possible.

Given the ascetic bent of the medieval Church, it's at least thinkable that this was the point. But that doesn't square with occasional hints that sheelas might be treated with reverence: coins deposited in the lap of one sheela, evidently for good luck; the stone of others worn away by caressing fingers; the testimony of late eighteenth-century writers that a sheela might be "vulgarly called the Idol." An alternative theory makes them protective charms, aimed at warding off malign influences that might threaten the holy places to which they were attached. (A wide range of ethnographic data suggests that, in many cultures, the display of the female genitalia was supposed to have this effect.) It's unlikely we will ever know for sure.

Most observers have seen the sheelas as depicting old women. But young women and at times even children are also possibilities. Rhoades writes that "some of the characteristics of the Kilpeck sheela are childlike: very large eyes, bald, no breasts"; she adds that "perhaps for some of us, the connection to children is so disturbing that we refuse to see." A fourth option, even more disturbing, is suggested by the prominence of the ribs on some sheelas:[43] that they're the dead, or on the borderline between the living and the dead.

"Extraterrestrial-like"? Only if UFOs are considered extraterrestrial, which is precisely what I doubt. The habitual baldness of the sheelas connects them with the UFO aliens, at least in the post-*Communion* era—but going back farther; think of the ETs in *Close Encounters of the Third Kind*—who are invariably hairless, even though there's no obvious reason why beings who are humanoid in other respects should be without hair. Nor is the reason for the sheelas' baldness self-evident.

This parallel, of what seems an unnecessary feature, suggests that both are denizens of the same region of the human unconscious, capable of emerging in the Middle Ages and at the end of the twentieth century. Look again at the image of the Kilpeck sheela earlier in the chapter (figure 9). Then imagine Strieber's "visitor"—goddess? lover?—with her genitalia in their proper place, not migrated upward to be her eyes. The two, admittedly, are not twin sisters, but they're at least second cousins. The major differences? The sheela has a broader nose. And the sheela is smiling, not cryptically as on the *Communion* cover, but merrily and fully.

I begin to feel a tinge of unease. Is our canvas broadening too rapidly, too heedlessly? Are we succumbing to what one Bible scholar has called "parallelomania," harping on possibly fortuitous resemblances and ignoring differences? Jerome Clark, one of American UFOlogy's foremost thinkers, would no doubt say so. In a penetrating essay on the "psychosocial hypothesis" in his *UFO Encyclopedia*, Clark protests that for its advocates, "similarities, however slight, matter more than differences, however substantial. In science one must note similarities, of course, but one must also isolate differences. Psychosocial speculators seem to regard differences as irrelevant."

---

43 Like the one embedded in the town wall of Fethard, County Tipperary, Ireland, featured along with the Kilpeck sheela in the Wikipedia article "Sheela na gig."

As if to illustrate Clark's point, in my drawing connecting lines between abductions and "descents to the merkavah" I ignored at least one major dissimilarity: The abducting aliens are normally small humanoids. The aliens of the Hekhalot literature are giants of near-cosmic proportions.

Clark's criticism is well taken. It should function, though, as a blinking yellow "proceed with caution" light, not a steady red "stop." I learned this as a graduate student in Biblical studies: "similar" and "dissimilar" are not an either/or choice, but a both/and. No two narratives could be more dissimilar than Genesis chapter 1, with its orderly unfolding of creation under the benevolent direction of a single deity, and the creation myth of ancient Babylonia, which has our world come into being through a monster-movie battle between the gods and the creatures of the wild waters. Yet the smooth surface of the Genesis story masks a myth much like that of the Babylonians, which haunted the imaginations of peoples across the ancient Near East, ancient Israel included.

Set Babylonian and Israelite creation accounts side by side, and the dissimilarities will far outweigh the similarities in both number and visibility. But the deep story lies in the similarities. So too with shamanism, "merkavah mysticism," and their twentieth-century incarnation: the UFO abduction.

What is this "deep story"? Like the six blind sages of the Indian fable, feeling their way around the elephant that in its totality is beyond their power to imagine, we can grasp elements of it. We remain mostly in the dark about what unifies them.

It's a human story, perhaps not entirely universal, yet with a demonstrated knack for transcending both history and geography. Sex is an important part of it—not, however, experienced as the transient relief of an itch below the navel, but as a living god(dess) into whose hands it's a fearful thing to fall.[44] Often it involves a

44 Paraphrasing Hebrews 10:31.

descent, reported by people who don't understand why they should be descending to locations normally regarded as celestial yet who can't deny that this is what's happening to them.

The place where they're descending is surely the unconscious, the descent into which is a metaphor but, it would seem, one that naturally occurs to the mind. What they find there will be conditioned by their cultural expectations—hence the "differences"—but with subtle continuities. The abductees are taken into a circular spaceship and examination room. The "descenders to the merkavah" pass through seven concentric "palaces."

This is a realm where the distinction between human and animal starts to blur. The Predionica mask lies on the borderline between the two; we recall the animal spirits of the shamans, the animals that morph into UFO aliens. Is this an aspect of a more profound fusion: of the "I" with the "not-I," the alien, the Other? And if so, what of the ultimate not-I: death?

So far, we've seen a few hints of death as a theme in this "deep story." Whitley Strieber's abducting visitor appears to have been identical in his unconscious mind with his fictional Janet O'Reilly, who in turn is death incarnate. There may be a similar allusion in the skeletal ribs of some sheela-na-gigs. Strieber's now deceased wife, Anne, sifting through the thousands of letters her husband received in response to *Communion*, was struck "that the dead and aliens seemed often to show up together in the lives of witnesses." One day, a few months after *Communion*'s publication, Strieber stepped into his wife's office and saw a yellow sheet posted to the wall, listing the recurrent themes she'd gleaned from the letters. At the top of the sheet Anne had written: "This has something to do with what we call death."

"A MAN IN CHRIST"

One corner of the canvas remains to be filled in. This is the single abduction-like experience from antiquity that's told in the words of the person who actually underwent it—and who, very strangely, speaks as though it happened to someone else. The experiencer was Saul, "a Jew from Tarsus in Cilicia, a citizen of no mean city" (Acts 21:39), better known to posterity as Paul the apostle.

> I must boast; there is nothing to be gained by it, but I will go on to visions and revelations of the Lord. I know a man in Christ who fourteen years ago was caught up to the third heaven—whether in the body or out of the body I do not know, God knows. And I know that this man was caught up into Paradise—whether in the body or out of the body I do not know, God knows—and he heard things that cannot be told, which man may not utter. On behalf of this man I will boast, but on my own behalf I will not boast, except of my weaknesses.[45]

Was Saul/Paul a "merkavah mystic"? Gershom Scholem thought so. Or, to use Scholem's more nuanced language: "It is obvious that Paul . . . was speaking of an idea with which his readers were familiar, a Jewish conception that he, as well as his readers in Corinth, had brought over into the new Christian community." This idea was the journey to the merkavah.

True, there was an important difference. The descent to the merkavah was an active undertaking, done on human initiative and against the ferocious opposition of the celestial beings. Paul's experience comes across as something unwilled, imposed on him. *Caught up*—the words Paul uses are passive forms of a Greek verb that means to "snatch away, carry off . . . seize hastily, snatch up . . . seize, overpower, overmaster . . . captivate, ravish . . . plunder."

Or "to abduct." With himself as abductee.

But why does he speak as though he weren't the one abducted? As though the abductee is a "man in Christ" from whom he

---

45 2 Corinthians 12:1–5 (RSV). This portion of the composite text stitched together as the "second epistle to the Corinthians" seems to have been written approximately 55 CE, which would place the experience it describes—not, apparently, to be equated with Paul's famous road-to-Damascus vision of Acts 9:1–9—around the year 41.

distinguishes himself? (Although, unless the "man in Christ" *is* himself, his appeal to "this man's" experience makes no sense.)

The answer lies in what Jeffrey Kripal calls "the ancient human experience of being not one but two"—the feeling (as a Sioux medicine man described it) of "something within us that controls us, something like a second person almost." Another experiencer recalled: "It was as if I had split into two parts. One part was watching this mantra arise within me, while the other part of me *was* the mantra." Paul, too, had a "second person" inside, that he felt as distinct from his familiar ego-self: the unnamed and possibly unnamable "man in Christ." Equipped with "this man's" authority, he could "boast," assert himself to his skeptical, at times openly jeering audience.

For Paul's relations with his one-time admirers in Corinth had turned sour and nasty. The men and women he'd taught and nurtured had come under the sway of rival preachers, promoting a different and for Paul reprehensible version of the "good news" of the Messiah Jesus. They'd turned against Paul, mocked him as a wimp, powerful with his pen but not much else. No wonder he seems to write with gibbering rage—"I am talking like a madman"—while reeling off his accomplishments in the Messiah's service. The sufferings he's endured. The perils he's faced. The "visions and revelations" when, as the greater *him* that was the man-in-Christ, he was snatched up into paradise in the third heaven.[46]

He must have seen something there ("visions"), but he doesn't tell us what it was. He puts more weight on what he heard: *arrheta rhemata*, a dazzlingly paradoxical phrase which the Revised Standard Version of the Bible translates as "things that cannot be told" but which literally means "unsayable words." (If they were

46 Ancient Jewish cosmology envisioned multiple heavens arching, dome-like, over the flat disk of the earth. The usual number was seven, possibly a distant echo of the Greek scientific theory of seven planetary spheres enclosing a spherical earth. Three-heaven models, however, occasionally crop up, and Paul was apparently referring to the highest heaven in one of these.

unsayable, how could he have heard them? There's the paradox.) Some nineteen hundred years later Betty Hill was shown a book, written in symbols "nothing like I had ever seen before," aboard the UFO onto which she'd been abducted. Her captors told her she could take it home with her, but then reneged. Those words, whatever they may have been, remained unsayable and unsaid.

But some abductees have come away with souvenirs of their experience, and so did Paul.

> And to keep me from being too elated by the abundance of revelations, a thorn was given me in the flesh, a messenger of Satan, to harass me, to keep me from being too elated. Three times I besought the Lord about this, that it should leave me; but he said to me, "My grace is sufficient for you, for my power is made perfect in weakness" (2 Cor. 12:7–9).

For decades and indeed centuries, Bible scholars have debated what this "thorn" might have been—"epilepsy, headaches, sinusitis, eye disease, depression or other malady"—and eventually given the problem up as insoluble. The UFOlogists might have helped them out.

"Implants" have been part of the abduction tradition since 1977, when Betty Andreasson remembered under hypnosis a "little ball with little prickly things on it" embedded in her left nostril. Since then, scores of abductees have lived with the sense of alien matter lodged in the intimate space enclosed by their skin. Whitley Strieber was among them. In May 1989, he experienced something inserted into the upper edge of his left ear; he felt its presence afterward as a lump, occasionally red and sore. Like Paul, he wanted it gone. A physician tried to remove it—he glimpsed it as "a white disk"—only to feel it slip away, move on its own from the top of Strieber's ear down to the earlobe.

"I reach up," Strieber wrote years afterward, "I touch my left ear, and I feel, over a quarter of a century later, the same agonizing nakedness and vulnerability I felt when I first realized it was there."

That the implants—sometimes, yes, thornlike in their appearance—invariably turn out when retrieved and analyzed to be mundane earthly substances, is beside the point. What matters is the subjective experience of alien intrusion into the body, as a sequel to the equally subjective experience of abduction. Both are *human* experiences, which now reveal themselves as having kept some measure of constancy over nearly two thousand years.

To put it a little differently: the "man in Christ" is caught up into the third heaven. The fleshly Paul is left with the thorn.

PART III

The UFO, Terrestrial

CHAPTER 6

"Three Men in Black"

IN SEPTEMBER 2004, I drove up from North Carolina to Clarksburg, West Virginia. My destination was the special room in the Clarksburg-Harrison Public Library that since 1991 has housed the Gray Barker Collection, the books and papers of one of the town's most peculiarly influential citizens. The collection's genial curator, David Houchin, welcomed me and spent hours chatting with me about the enigmatic man to whom the room was dedicated, passing on to me the oral traditions he'd gathered from its visitors. I spent a week there.

It was a research trip, but also an excursion into my own past. I've described in chapter 1 how, as an impressionable twelve-year-old, I'd been in thrall to Barker's mythmaking. More than forty years had passed since then. My home had shifted southward from Pennsylvania to North Carolina; I'd become a university professor, then a professor emeritus. Though I'd learned to distrust Barker, I never quite outgrew the fearful wonder his *They Knew Too Much About Flying Saucers* had inspired in me. Now I was coming to visit, for the first time, its place of origin.

The air conditioning wasn't working while I was there, which I counted as fortunate. Sweating (not unpleasantly) in the warm breezes that came softly in through the open windows, I could imagine myself transported back to the early 1960s as I sifted through the files of the man I'd never met, but whose writing set the course for my adolescence and possibly for my life.

We've spent the past three chapters with one of the central myths of the UFO lore, the alien abduction. The chapters that remain are devoted to three other myths, hardly less vital to understanding what the ensemble is about. Patterns we've noticed in connection with the abductions will repeat themselves, though sometimes with elements missing. The myths may develop *in parallel to* the wider UFO tradition (Men in Black), *as an antecedent* to it (the Shaver Mystery), or *at its very heart* (Roswell, New Mexico).

All three bring the UFO, with varying degrees of literalness, down from the sky and bind it to the life of this earth. The Men in Black, human or nearly human in appearance and distinctive mainly through their taste in clothing, are *the alien among us*. The Shaver Mystery, with its revelation of monstrosities unsuspected beneath our feet, speaks to *the alien within*. The legendry that's grown up around Roswell depicts the alien as shattered, unwilling and helpless, against our flinty deserts. It sounds the theme of *the alien dead*.

The Men in Black myth, which we'll look at in this chapter, has much in common with the abductions. Like the abductions, it has a long prehistory. Like them, it takes new shape and new power from the trauma of an individual to whom it can be traced. After a decades-long latency period, it spreads to become part of the culture, its presence taken for granted. And—modifying though not contradicting what I've just said—it's the creation not of a single person but a synergy of two, unifying opposites in a way that might set Jung nodding in satisfaction.

In the case of the abductions, the synergistic duo were the black man and the white woman, Barney and Betty Hill. In the case of the Men in Black, they were Barker of Clarksburg and Albert K. Bender of Bridgeport, Connecticut, whose opposing qualities were less obvious but just as real. Barker was the mythmaker of the pair, by which I don't mean "liar" or "hoaxer" (although he was both) but a truth teller of the most profound kind, one who brings forth and gives tangible narrative form to what's buried deep within us, its presence intuited but never quite grasped.

Bender, the hero of the myth, was a simpler sort of man. He was incomparably less gifted than Barker, incomparably less tormented.[47] Barker described Bender in the most glowing terms: Air Force veteran, executive (chief timekeeper, actually) at the Acme Shear Company's Bridgeport plant, a man whose "conversation reflects a wide knowledge of almost everything you can bring up," whose "piercing eyes seem to look right through you" yet whose warm good humor sets you at ease. Others had a different perspective and portrayed him differently. Bender was a weirdo, a loser, a thirty-one-year-old bachelor obsessed with the occult who lived with his stepfather and entertained himself by transforming a portion of their house into a "chamber of horrors" tricked out with artificial spiders, bats, and shrunken heads.

It was Bender who, in September 1953, encountered the historical three men, ordinary individuals who happened to wear dark clothing and black hats. It was Barker who transformed them into the mythic Three Men in Black, sending them forth on the journey that would take them, years after his death, to movie screens around the world. He promoted Bender, used Bender, made money off Bender. But he also believed in Bender, and when Bender disillusioned him, he fell into despair.

---

47 Though nearly four years older than Barker, Bender outlived him by more than thirty years, dying in 2016 at age ninety-four. In this respect also, the Barker-Bender pair resembles Barney and Betty Hill (see the end of chapter 3).

BARKER, BENDER, AND THE IFSB

Gray Roscoe Barker was born in 1925 in the tiny village of Riffle, West Virginia. Except for short intervals, he spent the rest of his life in his home state, mostly in Clarksburg. He died in 1984, evidently of complications from AIDS. Two documentary films, one of them a masterpiece, have been made about his life. No one has attempted a biography.

"I am neither a scientist nor a scholar," he introduced himself in *They Knew Too Much*. "Nor am I a bookie, as some people misinterpret my occupation when I tell them I am a *booker.* I also tell them I operate the largest theatrical film buying-booking agency in the state of West Virginia. Charitably, no one else has started a film buying-booking agency in the state of West Virginia."

He wanted to be a writer. His opportunity came in September 1952, when a seven-foot monster landed in a luminous UFO on a hilltop near Flatwoods, West Virginia, some ten miles from where he was born. (The incident has since been explained, plausibly if not altogether convincingly, as the collocation of an unusually bright meteor, a group of jittery witnesses, and a barn owl flying at them out of the darkness.) He pitched the story to *Fate*, a pulp magazine dedicated to the occult and paranormal. His investigative piece, "The Monster and the Saucer," appeared in the January 1953 issue.

The article was a hit, and Barker was emboldened by its success. The following autumn he would begin to publish (on an office ditto machine) a quarterly called *The Saucerian*, devoted to news of flying saucer sightings. In the meantime, he'd become the West Virginia state representative and afterward chief investigator for a Bridgeport-based organization called the International Flying Saucer Bureau (IFSB), whose president was Albert Bender. Barker had learned about Bender from the letter columns of a science fiction magazine and had written to him. Bender responded enthusiastically.

The IFSB was a thriving organization, the largest flying saucer group of its time, with several hundred members and steadily expanding. By the fall of 1953 it would have branches in twenty-seven states and the District of Columbia, Puerto Rico, Canada, England, France, Australia, and New Zealand. Its volunteers—neither Bender nor anyone else received a salary—gathered news clippings on flying saucers, investigated sightings to the best of their ability, and published a twelve-page quarterly called *Space Review*. This was dedicated to sightings and speculation about the saucers, and it was handsomely produced and printed.

In its writing and its ideas, it was amateurish, almost juvenile. Anyone who comes to *Space Review* from reading Barker, primed by him to believe that somewhere in its five issues lies the fantastic, terrifying secret that Bender discovered and then was forbidden to reveal, is in for a letdown. What happened to Bender in the fall of 1953 requires some other explanation.

THREE MEN PAY A CALL

On Sunday, September 27, two IFSB members named August Roberts and Dominick Lucchesi, friends of both Bender and Barker, decided to make the two-hour drive to Bridgeport from their homes in Jersey City, to visit Bender. Their car overheated, and they didn't get very far. But they phoned Bender and heard shocking news. "I know the secret of the disks!" Bender told them. Three men had visited him, Bender added, and had "in effect shut him up completely as far as saucer investigation is concerned."

Roberts and Lucchesi were stunned. So was Barker, to whom they passed along the information. The following Sunday, October 4, Roberts and Lucchesi drove to Bridgeport and tried to find out from Bender what had happened. But he'd been silenced, frightened nearly out of his wits. He wasn't talking.

"When did the three men visit you?" they asked.

His reply: "I can't answer that."

"Who were the men?"

"I can't answer that."

"Were they from the government?"

"I can't answer that."

"Do saucers come from space?"

"I can't answer that."

Eventually they hit on some questions Bender was willing to answer. The saucers are "going to be both good and bad" for the world. The world won't come to an end but "there will be changes in everybody's life." The truth will be "frightening" even to those familiar with the saucers, who expect something "unusual and fantastic"; just imagine how it will impact those unprepared for it. "They were pretty rough with me," Bender said of the three men, adding that two of them did the talking while the third stood watching, his eyes fixed on Bender.

"Did you notice what the men wore?" Roberts and Lucchesi asked.

"They wore the same type of clothes and hats," was Bender's answer. "Dark clothes and black hats."

Black hats but only "dark" clothing. It was Barker who would later shade Bender's description, ever so slightly, into "black suits." In this shift, the three men's mythologization would begin.

Barker was baffled. That was what he claimed in *They Knew Too Much About Flying Saucers*, and although on a few occasions—well, many occasions—he was known to bend the truth, on this point we can believe him. His friend James Moseley, who knew Barker better than anyone else (Barker's family included), recalled that "he seemed genuinely to believe that Al Bender somehow had stumbled onto the real nature and origin of flying saucers and been hushed up by government or alien agents."

Correspondence in the Barker Collection bears this out. In a letter to UFO author Morris K. Jessup, about a year after the IFSB closed, Barker wrote: "There is a lot involved here I would like to know, and I feel I am uncovering it bit by bit." "Right now," he wrote to Jessup ten days later, "it seems that the whole question of saucers can be resolved by looking deep into people's minds for delusions—or—there is something involved so fantastic and perhaps even terrifying that we might be better off not knowing it." This cryptic remark, which Jessup seems (from his reply) not to have understood, makes sense only as an allusion to some "fantastic" discovery that Barker truly imagined Bender to have made.

The October 1953 issue of *Space Review* announced itself the final one. The IFSB would be reorganized into a restricted-membership society no longer concerned with flying saucers; members would be refunded for any outstanding issues. The flying saucer mystery, readers were told on the first page, "is no longer a mystery. The source is already known, but any information about this is being withheld by orders from a higher source. We would like to print the full story in *Space Review*, but because of the nature of the information we are sorry that we have been advised in the negative."

To which the writer—Bender, presumably—added: "We advise those engaged in saucer work to please be very cautious."

We'll never be sure precisely what happened. We may, however, allow ourselves an educated guess.

In 1953, Senator Joseph McCarthy was at the height of his power and influence. Fears of Communist subversion were everywhere. J. Edgar Hoover's FBI was active in ferreting out Communists and their suspected sympathizers, the "masters of deceit" who hid behind a thousand disguises. The IFSB got onto the FBI's radar screen late that August, when one of Barker's "Chief Investigator" business cards made its way into the hands of an FBI agent who showed up in Barker's office in Clarksburg inquiring about the organization. The word *International* in the group's name must have set alarm bells ringing. It was to be presumed a Communist front.

The notion seems grotesque today. In the context of 1953, it made perfect, if paranoid, sense. In January that year, a panel of scientists had met under the CIA's aegis to evaluate UFOs and what threat, if any, they posed to American security. The panelists' conclusion was that they didn't exist and therefore posed no threat. Popular belief in them, however, could be dangerous, masking the entry of hostile aircraft into our air space. Amateur UFO groups therefore "should be watched. . . . The apparent irresponsibility and the possible use of such groups for subversive purposes should be kept in mind."

And so IFSB President Albert K. Bender needed to be paid a visit.

"God, but you're all over the place!" one of the three men exclaimed, looking at the map on Bender's wall that showed the distribution of the IFSB's branches.[48] Like a cancer, like Communism itself, Bender's organization was spreading across the world. It had to be stopped.[49]

They told Bender a horrific story of their own invention—we have no idea what it might have been—scaring him into dropping his research activity. In case that didn't suffice, they added a more straightforward threat. "I suppose you know you're on your honor as an American," one of them told him before leaving. "If I hear another word out of your office you're in trouble."

Over the coming months, Bender's belief in their story began to fade, and with it the idea that UFOs had any significance at all. But the fright he'd received stayed with him, and his saucer pursuits came to seem like a bad dream, a "nonsensical" business to put behind him for good. Besides, he now had other things on his mind. The year 1954 found him wooing Betty Rose, a petite,

---

48 As Bender reported it in his October 4 conversation with Roberts and Lucchesi. Michael D. Swords, whose similar but somewhat divergent explanation of the IFSB's closing inspired my own, lays proper weight on this detail. "The men were astounded at how widespread and cosmopolitan IFSB had become so quickly."

49 Even at the time, some guessed this might be the reason for the IFSB's disbanding. Bender had to personally assure the group's British representative that "neither suspected Red activity nor dishonesty was the cause of its dissolution"—an assurance given in good faith, if the visitors didn't reveal their true motives. He later was to speak of the "fantastic rumor" that the IFSB was "a Communist organization, forced to shut down by the government."

charming redhead from England whom he'd met by correspondence through the IFSB. They married that October.

For the historical three men, it was mission accomplished. For the mythical Men in Black, the mission had just begun.

THE GOSPEL ACCORDING TO BARKER

"I'm going to say something blasphemous here," curator David Houchin told Bob Wilkinson, interviewing him for the marvelous 2009 documentary *Shades of Gray*. "Gray Barker has written one of the Gospels."

They Knew Too Much About Flying Saucers is indeed Gospel-like, though not quite in the sense Houchin intended. Drawing on older traditions, actual events, and actual reports of purported events—slightly retouching them, here and there leaving out inconvenient details and emphasizing the convenient ones—but most of all through combination and juxtaposition, Barker created a dark new gospel of strange things in the sky and stranger things on earth. It's utterly fantastic, alien to our idea of reality. Yet it conveys a sense of coherence and authenticity, which grows stronger as you come to recognize how deeply rooted it is in the worlds through which Barker moved, how little of it he needed to invent.

This was Barker's masterpiece. Struggle as he might—he wrote ten more books and uncounted numbers of words in other forums—he could never produce anything like it again. He may have realized that, and it may partly explain the bleak despair that overtook his later years.

For he did despair—of himself, of the avocation-turned-business to which he'd dedicated himself. "UFO is a bucket of shit," he intoned in a poem that might have served as his obituary. "And I sit here writing / While the shit drips down my face / In great rivulets." The squalid pranks that became his characteristic, in which he and his friend Moseley took such delight, stemmed not from impish high spirits but from a misery so entrenched it could be soothed only by making fools of others.

UFO author John Keel—who carried the torch of the Men in Black through the 1970s, who coined the acronym MIBs by which they've come to be known—understood this. "Gray turned into a total hoaxer," Keel told an interviewer. "At some point, and I never could find out what really happened, he just gave up and he said, 'Well, what the hell, we might as well have fun with this.' And so you have to be very careful with the stuff he published after 1959, because you don't know whether he's making it up."

That was the later Gray Barker. It doesn't apply to *They Knew Too Much About Flying Saucers.* There, Barker was for real.

The book's themes: Silence. Danger. Warning. "We advise those engaged in saucer work to please be very cautious," were Bender's words in the final issue of *Space Review.* And *They Knew Too Much* ends, apart from its two-page epilogue, with the admonition: "And for God's sake be careful, Gray!"[50]

"I have a feeling that some day there will come a slow knocking at my own door," Barker writes in the epilogue. "They will be at your door too, unless we all get wise and find out who the three men really are."

That "slow knocking" hadn't yet happened, and Barker wondered why. "Why hadn't the three men visited me?" Wasn't he important enough? Sure, he'd received the usual "telephone calls, often with no one at the other end, that plague all saucer researchers." In his later, prankster years, he would make enough of those calls himself. But these were only "cranks and harmless crackpots." Where were the three men in black?

> I often thought it might be worth being silenced and warned to keep quiet about what I knew if I could actually have something definitely *confirmed* as to the origin and purpose of the saucers.

---

50 Written to Barker by a New Zealand UFOlogist, allegedly visited by a "bloke" from whom he learned "too much" about UFOs for his own good.

> Maybe I will some day experience that cold feeling of mingled satisfaction and fear, of triumph and defeat. I hope not.

Something genuine, all the more powerful in its ambivalence, speaks through these words. It speaks in disguise, but with unmistakable integrity. If you ask me, what was it? I will answer with a question:

What did it mean to be a closeted gay man in 1950s West Virginia?

Of Barker's sexual orientation, there's no doubt. It was common knowledge, normally left unspoken, among UFOlogy's cognoscenti. He wrote, as fiction, autobiographical accounts of his prowls through Clarksburg's sleazier locales in search of partners. A scandal, apparently involving sodomy with underage boys, landed him in court late in 1962. He was put on probation, assigned a court-appointed psychiatrist. His family, isolated and living far from Clarksburg, remained in the dark. "I didn't learn nothing of the gayness until after his death," his niece remembered years later, adding: "Back then you didn't talk about people being gay."

No. You didn't. We'll never know what went on inside Gray Barker as the realization dawned that there was something about his essence as a male that was, for his time and place, literally unspeakable. We can be sure, however, that it took place in a state of enforced, absolute silence.

The three men never "visited" him with their threats and warnings. They dwelt with him day in and day out. He knew what it was to have a secret too terrible to be revealed; he felt in his body and soul the forces that kept that secret hidden, made it impossible to imagine. Not a hint of this surfaces in *They Knew Too Much About Flying Saucers*. Yet it pervades the entire book.

"Then the world isn't going to come to an end?" Lucchesi and Roberts ask Bender, and the world's ending is a recurrent theme in *They Knew Too Much*. This was Gray Barker's experience: a careless action, a word too revealing could have brought his world to a sudden end. He knew that. He conveyed it to his readers.

I was one of those readers. My terrible secret wasn't Barker's—I've described it in chapter 1; it was the knowledge no one could speak of, the knowledge I would not admit to myself, that my mother was dying. Yet there was enough in common that I knew in my gut: Barker spoke the truth. "Deep calleth unto deep," says the Bible (Psalm 42:7), and like so much in the Bible—like so much in the gospel according to Gray Barker—this is absolutely true. Gray Barker's deep unconscious called out to me through the pages of his book. My deep unconscious answered.

So did the culture's. Which is why *Men in Black* became four Hollywood movies, and why the hit TV series of the 1990s, *The X-Files*, draws on themes that Barker introduced in the 1950s. But that's getting ahead of our story.

ANTECEDENTS

We've seen this before, with Barney Hill and the alien abductions. An individual's trauma is injected into the culture. It spreads beneath the skin; it manifests itself on large scale years or decades later. Yet, though that individual—Barney Hill, Gray Barker—is the fountainhead from which the myth springs, it has a prehistory as well.

A Man in Black appears at the very dawn of the UFO era, in the bizarre and tragic episode known as the Maury Island incident, which unfolded in Tacoma, Washington, in the summer of 1947. A certain Harold Dahl, who claimed to be a harbor patrolman but in fact made his living selling lumber he'd salvaged from the waters of Puget Sound, reported having been out on his boat on June 21 when he spotted six doughnut-shaped objects in the sky. One of them seemed to be in mechanical trouble, circled in the air by the other five. After discharging a heavy dark slag, the object flew off with its five companions.

At seven the next morning a man showed up at Dahl's home, inviting him to breakfast in a café. The man seemed to be about forty, "wore a black suit, was of medium height, and there was nothing unusual about his appearance." But what followed showed that there was something indeed extraordinary, not to say supernatural, about the man himself. As he and Dahl waited for their breakfast to arrive, the stranger related to Dahl down to the minutest detail what Dahl had seen the day before, what he and his crew had experienced. This was proof, the stranger told Dahl, "that I know a great deal more about this experience of yours than you will want to believe."

The man left Dahl with a warning: "if he loved his family and didn't want anything to happen to his general welfare, he would not discuss his experience with anyone."

We have only Dahl's word for all this, and as it turned out Dahl was lying. The sighting over Puget Sound never happened; the six doughnut-shaped objects never existed. This eventually became clear, but not before two Air Force officers who'd flown in from California at the end of July to investigate Dahl's story were dead. Their plane had crashed on their return flight, killing them both.

It's not quite clear when the Man in Black first entered the story. My own guess, although I admit there's some evidence to the contrary, is that Dahl invented him sometime after the plane crash. Originally Dahl spoke only of the malfunctioning UFO, which in retrospect might seem a foreshadowing of the doomed airplane. Once the two officers were dead, his storytelling instincts led him to the next step. A black-clad stranger, Death personified,[51] had paid a prophetic visit in advance of the real thing.

There were older precedents. The Man in Black, sometimes explicitly called by that name, is a stock figure in the confessions of

---

51 Like the ominous "old man dressed in black and enwrapped in black" of Talmudic legend, who encountered a Jewish high priest in the Holy of Holies of the Jerusalem Temple, his appearance conveying to the unfortunate man that he was doomed to die within the year. I'm not suggesting any direct influence of this ancient story on Dahl or any other participant in the drama he set in motion. Rather, I'm proposing that the Man in Black appears in diverse cultures as a representation of death, and that some of the modern riffs on the theme can be understood through this symbolism.

seventeenth-century witches. He's the Devil. Or, perhaps, he's an indeterminate archetypal figure—a "UFO" of his era—whom the witch-hunters found it reasonable to identify with the Devil.

He appeared in Scotland in 1670 as "a man in black cloaths with a hat on his head, sitting at the table." In England in 1682, he was "a gentleman in a field . . . his apparel . . . all of black." By century's end, he'd crossed the Atlantic. Tituba, the slave woman from Barbados whose graphic testimony set the Salem witch trials in motion (1692), told her rapt audience how "a tall, white-haired man in a dark serge coat" had offered her "pretty things" and "tell me he God and I must believe and serve him six years."

The UFOlogists have found special interest in a story from Norway in 1730, after Europe's witch-hunting vogue had passed. A thirteen-year-old peasant girl named Siri Jørgensdatter told her local ministers—who took her seriously, though no one else did—how her deceased grandmother had been a witch who'd flown with her on a sow's back to a feast with the Devil. "On the way they met three men dressed in black whom the grandmother referred to as 'grandfather's boys.'" The Devil himself, also in black, was "grandfather."

This seems a perfect analogue to Albert Bender's three men in black. No more so, however, than the three men "all dressed in black" who came down from the moon in 1683 to torment Abraham Cardozo. Here we find them outside the European Christian cultural sphere, though admittedly not far outside it. (As we saw in chapter 2, Cardozo, though Jewish, had been brought up a Catholic in Spain.) It's unlikely that Gray Barker had read about Siri Jørgensdatter's testimony. It's impossible that he'd read Cardozo's, which was first translated from the Hebrew (by me) long after Barker's death.

Coincidence? Never to be ruled out. But an alternative option needs also to be considered: that Bender's historical experience with three frightening visitors had summoned something from the collective unconscious into the pages of *They Knew Too Much*

About Flying Saucers: the alien, be it demon or Devil or death itself, that moves among us, haunting and dominating us, forcing us into terrified silence about those truths of which we yearn to speak. This image resonated, in widening circles. In the late twentieth century, it became first a staple of the UFO tradition, then part of the shared American cultural awareness.

BENDER REDUX

In 1962, six years after *They Knew Too Much*, Barker brought Bender back on stage for an encore. Bender's own book, *Flying Saucers and the Three Men*, published under the imprint of Barker's Saucerian Books, revealed at long last who the three men were and what they'd told him. As an extra bonus, it explained why people weren't seeing flying saucers anymore. (The great UFO waves of the 1960s, which would make nonsense of Bender's explanation, were still in the future.)

The three weren't government agents. They weren't even "men." They took human form—albeit with strange glowing eyes—so as not to scare Bender out of his wits, but in their proper shapes were hideous creatures like the Flatwoods monster. They came from outer space but maintained a base in Antarctica, carrying out a time-limited mission for the benefit of their home planet. They gave Bender a small metal disk, telling him that when he wanted to contact them, he should hold it tightly in his palm and close his eyes, while repeating the word "Kazik."

They could materialize and dematerialize at will, and in the same fashion they teleported Bender to the interior of their spacecraft. There they implanted in him an "impulse" that would cause his body to disintegrate if he ever revealed to anyone what had befallen him. He must preserve absolute secrecy until such time as his Kazik disk should disappear. When that happened, he would know that they'd left our planet for good. Then he could speak freely.

In late 1960 the disk vanished. Two years later he published his book.

Hardly anyone took it seriously.[52] Even Barker, in "Epilogue by the Publisher," expressed reservations. Maybe Bender had let himself get tangled up with "occult forces which he misinterpreted as representing interplanetary visitation"; maybe he was just hallucinating. The real three men in black, Barker suggested in an epigram that echoed through the UFO world of the time, were named Boredom, Frustration, and Disgust.

Above all, Disgust. Barker's friend Moseley has plausibly suggested that the absurdity of Bender's tale was what finally shattered Barker's faith that there was some genuine mystery in the flying saucers, drove him to the dismal conviction that the UFO was "a bucket of shit." To those of us reading it in 1962, *Flying Saucers and the Three Men* seemed pure inanity. Only in retrospect can we see there was something more.[53]

Bender's book foreshadowed the abduction tradition, then still in utero. (Betty and Barney Hill had their precipitating UFO experience the previous September, but they hadn't yet begun to undergo hypnotic regression.) It was written in the pattern of the flying saucer "contactee" literature of the 1950s. Yet it broke the mold with extraterrestrials who weren't loving space brothers but coldly efficient exploiters come to Earth to make use of its resources and content to leave humankind to its fate afterward. Meanwhile they regularly abducted humans, partly out of necessity, partly from

---

52 At least among the UFOlogists. The Bender file in the Barker Collection contains a letter from Bender (July 21, 1962) reporting that "the Vice-Pres. of Acme Shear called me on the phone today and told me how much he liked the book and is a firm believer." The same letter complains that Barker doesn't write and won't return Bender's phone calls—a marker of how their relationship had soured.

53 And, indeed, more to Bender than present-day UFOlogists are apt to give him credit for. Asked by Roberts and Lucchesi to suggest a subject for a science-fiction story, Bender replied: "Suppose there was another world out in space, and there the people were black. What do you think would happen if they came to this planet? Do you think they would help the colored or the white people? You know the prejudices that exist here, and if they came to Earth, what do you think would happen?" This was 1953; the landmark events of the civil rights movement hadn't yet happened. Yet Bender was alive to "the prejudices that exist here," and intuited the UFOs' potential to mirror the society's racial torment.

what appears to be sadistic amusement. They told Bender they'd "carried off many of your people to our own planet" to experiment on them and exhibit them, as well as "to use their bodies to disguise our own." Bender himself they treated, not exactly cruelly, but with stony indifference to the toll their visitations took on his health and peace of mind.

The examination table is here—in the form of "a strange-looking table reminiscent of a hospital operating table" upon which Bender is laid. So is the implant theme: apart from the "impulse" that will turn Bender to dust if he says anything out of line, he suspects the aliens may have left him with a physical implant that's causing his persistent headaches.

Paralyzed and helpless on the "operating table," Bender undergoes a sexual violation that's as close to those of the 1990s abductions as one could expect from the buttoned-up world of pre-sexual-revolution UFOlogy. "Three beautiful women, dressed in tight white uniforms"—a photographic negative of the three men in black—approach him, caress him, strip him "naked as the day I was born" and pour liquid all over his body.[54] His body grows warm, they massage every part of it "without exception." This is supposedly happening in November 1953, about the same time that in real life Bender's dormant libido was beginning to assert itself, as we gather from his courtship of Betty Rose the following year. An unanticipated side effect of an encounter with three men in black: the recovery of one's natural heritage as a sexual male.

MIBs

Meanwhile, others had begun to see men in black. A casebook published in 1997—the same year that the cinematic *Men in Black*

---

54 Antonio Villas-Boas (see chapter 4) was also stripped and anointed with a thick transparent liquid in preparation for sex with his spacewoman. If I didn't know better—it wasn't until 1965 that more than a handful of English-speaking UFOlogists heard of Villas-Boas—I would say that Bender knew his story and was imitating it.

made its debut in movie theaters—records some sixty "MIB" incidents, the lion's share of them from the 1960s.

Normally the MIBs appear singly or in pairs. The classic trio does occur from time to time, but it's infrequent.[55] The data is unruly and confusing, and it's hard to draw the boundaries between the actual MIB manifestations and other possibly related events that attach themselves to the witnesses' stories. These may be paranormal or just peculiar and annoying, like telephones that make weird noises on the line or go inexplicably dead. Occasionally a bit of symbolism provides a clue to the meaning of an event, as when "a man in a black hat and cloak" is seen carrying a sickle, like the traditional embodiment of death. MIB-themed pranks, parasitic on the burgeoning tradition and sometimes very cruel, have been known to happen.

A Maine physician named Herbert Hopkins, a brilliantly talented man of medicine with a long interest in occult and spiritualistic phenomena and (according to his nephew) with a significant drinking problem, told a particularly strange story. He'd been engaged in the hypnotic regressions of a UFO abductee, and he'd made tapes of those regressions. On the evening of September 11, 1976, a man in black showed up at Hopkins's home to demand he destroy those tapes.

The visitor was tall and thin, with a black suit, black tie and shoes, pants with a razor-sharp crease that didn't flatten even when he sat down. He wore a derby—an unusual article of clothing for 1976, yet shiny and new—which prompted Hopkins to think, "This guy looks just like an undertaker." The derby is reminiscent of the MIBs' reported habit of driving obsolete cars that seem brand

---

55 As in one bizarre case from 1968, where the three men appeared in the shapes of . . . Gray Barker, James Moseley, and John Keel! This is oddly parallel to what Cardozo describes from 1683: the three men in black, initially seen on the moon, took on the appearances of Sabbatai Zevi, Sabbatai's prophet Nathan of Gaza, and the sixteenth-century Kabbalist Isaac Luria.

new. Along with Hopkins's "undertaker" association, it suggests a link with the archaic, the ancestral, the dead.

The MIB had another odd feature, which Hopkins realized when the man brushed his "ruby-red" lips with the back of his glove and the color came off, leaving a slit of a mouth behind. "I said to myself, 'This guy is some kind of queer. He's wearing lipstick!' "—and at this point in his tape-recorded narrative, Hopkins laughs.

Soon afterward, Hopkins watched in amazement as the man dematerialized a penny that Hopkins held in his palm. The coin became blurry, then faded away, never (the man told him) to be seen again "on this plane." The man spoke of Barney Hill, who died because he "knew too much"—those exact words—because "he did not have a heart, just as you no longer have a coin." The same would happen to Hopkins unless he destroyed the abduction tapes and correspondence, and everything he had that related to UFOs.

Which, after the stranger left, he proceeded to do.

It's hardly possible that the event took place as described. The witness is flawed; his story filled with fantastic details which, if taken at face value, would leave reality as we know it in shambles. What he relates may have been an alcohol-fueled hallucination or a fantasy so vivid that he afterward took it for a memory. Saying this, however, is not the same as denying it any significance.

Its homosexual overtones are particularly interesting, in the light of what we've seen about Gray Barker (whose fingerprints appear here and there in Hopkins's narrative).[56] The abduction story that Hopkins was engaged in exploring hints at a gay relationship. The two abductees were very young men who lived together in a trailer; they may have been lovers, or possibly not; Hopkins may

---

56 The claim that Barney Hill "knew too much" is an obvious echo of Barker. The MIB's disappearing-coin trick is reminiscent of the vanishing of Bender's Kazik disk, while the threat that Hopkins's heart will be dematerialized suggests the "impulse" that would "disintegrate" Bender's body. On at least one occasion, Barker was photographed wearing what appears to be lipstick.

have been unsure. The uncertainty may have evoked unconscious anxieties about homosexuality. These took embodied form in the apparition of "some kind of queer" possessed of extraordinary and fatal powers, who came to him by night, home alone, his family gone to a movie and not expected back anytime soon.[57]

Seen from this perspective, Hopkins's Man in Black externalized the uneasiness he felt over the abduction case in which he'd gotten himself so deeply enmeshed, gave him his justification for purging all traces of it from his home. Destroy it all! the apparition commanded. Perhaps with a measure of relief, Hopkins obeyed.[58]

MEN IN BLACK AND *X-FILES*

"Have you heard of men in black?" a lady was asked, presumably not long after 1997. She exclaimed in response: "Of course, everyone's seen *Men in Black*!"

The woman had no interest in UFOs, hardly any knowledge of the subject. The names Gray Barker and Albert Bender, far less Herbert Hopkins, would have meant nothing to her. But thanks to its dazzling silver screen success, the mythos of an obscure, disreputable West Virginia promoter was part of her world, a recognized feature of the cultural landscape. The original *Men in Black*, opening in over three thousand theaters across the country, was the second-highest grossing film of 1997 (after *Titanic*). Fifteen years later, *Men in Black 3* surpassed it to become the highest-grossing film in the Sony franchise, drawing millions of moviegoers not

---

57 Think of the apparitions that plagued Morton Schatzman's patient "Ruth," described in chapter 2.

58 There's other evidence that sexuality was a troubled issue for the Hopkins family, which they transformed into tales of strange visitations. Hopkins's son John reported a visit to him and his wife Maureen from a bizarre couple, a man and a woman, thirteen days after his father's MIB encounter. Underlying this story is John and Maureen's regular practice of mate-swapping, which they engaged in along with alcohol and drugs until eventually Maureen shot John dead in their backyard.

only in this country but in Japan, Germany, and the UK as well. Of course, she'd heard of men in black. Hadn't everybody?

But what did "everybody" know about them from the movies named after them?

> Here come the Men in Black
> The galaxy defenders;
> Here come the Men in Black
> They won't let you remember.

That was the refrain of the soundtrack of the 1997 film, carrying on the Barker-Bender tradition more than forty years after it first appeared in *They Knew Too Much About Flying Saucers*. With a twist, however, that reminds us that the abductions came in between. In 1956, the Men in Black interdicted only the free expression of what you'd discovered or experienced. In 1997, they went after your memories themselves.

Yet these were the *good* guys of the *Men in Black* movies, which eventually multiplied into three (and now four). In this respect, the original *Men in Black* was a reaction against the hit TV series of its time, *The X-Files*.[59]

In July 1997, when *Men in Black* was released, *The X-Files* had finished its fourth season. UFOs had been central to that show from its beginnings. Its pilot episode (September 1993) was about alien abductions and the implants left behind in the victims, one of which is retrieved by FBI agents Fox Mulder and Dana Scully but suppressed, as UFO evidence normally is, by their higher-ups. Mulder's obsessive pursuit of the paranormal is explained by his little sister's having been abducted when he was twelve. The name given to his partner Scully is sometimes explained as a nod by the show's creators toward Frank Scully, author of the 1950 bestseller *Behind the Flying Saucers*. MIBs as such, however, remain marginal

---

59 Pointed out to me by film scholar Barna Donovan.

to *The X-Files* plotlines, and a moment's reflection will suggest why. The show's watchwords "Trust no one" would make little sense in a world where the sinister truth-suppressors wear uniforms identifying them as such.

The X-Files drew instead on a more indirect spinoff of the gospel according to Barker. The 1980s had seen the burgeoning of a baroque counterhistory of the postwar period, in which the UFO aliens not only had landed, but were in intimate collusion with the US government.

At the end of 1984, a document came to light that claimed to be a briefing paper written for Dwight Eisenhower in November 1952 by the head of the CIA. It informed the president-elect of the existence of Operation Majestic-12, a supersecret group of twelve leading scientists and military and intelligence officers charged with studying the crashed disk at Roswell and the alien bodies found near it.[60] The Harvard astrophysicist Donald Menzel, famous as a vocal, bigoted, and effective debunker of all things UFOlogical—the author of three books declaring UFOs to be nonsense—was one of the twelve. Whoever forged the "MJ-12" document, as it's come to be called, must have had a quirky sense of humor. But he or she conveyed a serious message, not lost on the creators of *The X-Files*: people can be the opposite of who they seem. You never know who you're dealing with.

MJ-12 was only the start. The legends grew more elaborate and fantastic. Not only had there been other crashes besides Roswell, all of them naturally covered up; not only were the remains of the disks and their pilots being kept by the military at Nevada's supersecret Area 51—but the government had even made contact with the aliens in 1964, and a few years later had made a pact with them. The aliens would share their technology; in return, the government would allow them to abduct a specified number

---

60 Roswell, which had lain in near-total obscurity for almost three decades, was rediscovered in 1978. See chapter 8.

of Americans to experiment on, Nazi-style. But the agreement broke down. A bloody confrontation in 1979 ended in a stand-off, with the aliens left entrenched in underground bases in our Southwest.

Meanwhile we ordinary folk go about our business, blind to all this, imagining (for example) that the Strategic Defense Initiative of the Reagan years was directed against the Soviet threat rather than the extraterrestrials who were its real target. The truth was out there, as *The X-Files* would have it. But only a few dogged investigators, like Mulder and Scully on the next decade's TV screens, struggled to peel away the layers of official duplicity that kept it hidden.

Gray Barker died in December 1984, the same month that MJ-12 was discovered (or more likely fabricated). The Men in Black were the villains of *They Knew Too Much About Flying Saucers*; Barker considered the possibility they might be government agents. He didn't take the next logical step, though, of villainizing the government. "Surely," he wrote, "the government, more than we saucer investigators, was in a position to know what was best for the country." Bender was put "on your honor as an American" not to reveal the secret, and Roberts, Lucchesi, and Barker himself all respected such a promise.

This was in 1956, an era when three out of four Americans trusted the government to do right "always" or "most of the time." Then came Vietnam; then came Watergate. By the mid-nineties, the times they had a-changed. The "trust" figure, as measured by polls, had plunged to the dismal level that it's at today: around 20 percent. Government was at best impotent to protect its citizens. At worst, it might be complicit with those who'd use us as experimental animals. Such was the matrix of belief out of which *The X-Files* grew.

In *Men in Black*, the system of values is turned upside down. The suppression of truth is not a crime but a civic necessity. The suppressors are given the likable human faces of Will Smith playing the young and black Agent J, and Tommy Lee Jones, the middle-aged white Agent K, who's charged with initiating his new partner into the ways of the dark-clad brotherhood.

"We ain't got time for this cover-up bullshit!" the Will Smith character cries out. His mentor sternly rebukes him: "The only way these people get on with their happy lives is they do not know about it"—"it" being the penetration of human society by thousands of covert extraterrestrials. This soothing ignorance is what Agents J and K are here to maintain.

Not that ETs are necessarily a bad lot. The vast majority, the Jones character explains, are law-abiding creatures who've come to Earth to make an honest living. But a few rogues among them menace the planet and must be kept under surveillance. Hence the MIB, "a secret organization that monitors alien activity on earth."

Another reversal: the Men in Black, walking among us as aliens, are the ones charged with keeping the real and possibly deadly aliens under control. Yet their own alienness, though softened and attenuated, is still potent enough to set them apart.

A mighty brotherhood—they have the power to overrule any organ of government known to the public—they're also a profoundly lonely one. They'll never be recognized for their work in saving and sustaining human civilization. And they never, never get the girl. Beautiful and tender ladies pass through their orbit; there's attraction, requited and reciprocal—and hopeless. Ordinary earth women are beyond their sphere, and in *Men in Black 3*, where the MIB are expanded to include Women in Black, fraternization within the organization is forbidden. Celibate as monks, unseen and unsuspected, they shelter us daily from horrors beyond our imagining.

The opening sequence of the 1997 movie conveys the MIB's supreme authority, as well as the double meaning of *alien* that's key to the film's message. A truckload of illegal Mexican immigrants has been stopped by border control authorities. The officers are in the midst of browbeating the hapless passengers when the Jones character steps in. He speaks kindly to the newcomers in Spanish, welcomes them to the United States. The immigration police are thanked and told to get lost. These Mexicans are "good" aliens; they pose no threat. There are, of course, aliens of another kind, as we discovered one fine September morning four years after the original *Men in Black* came out.

There's no doubt that communications professor Barna Donovan is right. The movie's subtext is "multiculturalism, integration, and the problematic issues around immigration," which the passage of twenty years hasn't made any less problematic. But there's another, deeper layer as well. Again and again, the theme of *effacement of memory* crops up. The Jones character and, after he gets the hang of it, the Smith character point a blinking tube called the "neuralizer" at innocent bystanders who've seen terrifying, uncanny sights that no one ought ever to see. Presto! their memories vanish. They "remember" of the event only what the Men in Black tell them they should.

The soundtrack, intoned by Will Smith, says it all:

> The title held by me, M.I.B.
> Means what you think you saw, you did not see . . .
> Hypnotizer, neuralizer
> Vivid memories turn to fantasies . . .
> Cause we see things that you need not see
> And we be places that you need not be . . .

What you think you saw, you did not see. As a teenager, I saw my mother's gradual slide toward death. I also didn't see it. Denial, they say, is not just a river in Egypt; at times it's a prerequisite for survival. The Men in Black are bullies but also saviors. ("I know we might seem imposin / But trust me if we ever show in your section / Believe me, it's for your own protection.") I think of Bender's haunting image of the "impulse" within him, capable of disintegrating his body so that "very little will be left of it." That's what Barker's sexual impulses could have done to his life—and on one occasion came very near doing—if they hadn't been ruthlessly checked. Courtesy of the Men in Black, who see things that you need not see and be places that you need not be.

In the poster for the original movie they were two: black-suited, eyes hidden behind dark glasses, arms crossed as they menacingly faced the viewer. Similarly with the mediocre and forgettable 2002 sequel. But in 2012, when the third of the series appeared, they'd become a trio: Will Smith, flanked by Jones on one side and by Josh Brolin, playing the Jones character's younger self, on the other.

Men in Black 3—Three Men in Black. The circle back to *They Knew Too Much About Flying Saucers* is complete.[61]

---

61 It's curious that the latest cinematic iteration of the theme, released in June 2019, is entitled not *Men in Black 4* but *Men in Black: International*—as if the number 3 has a special significance, marking a limit that ought not to be surpassed.

CHAPTER 7
Shaver Mystery

BEFORE BARKER, there was Raymond Palmer, and before flying saucers, there was the Shaver Mystery. Call it a prelude to the grander drama of the UFO, which erupted into the American consciousness just as the Shaver Mystery was beginning to fade. Or call it a dress rehearsal. Or, to take the most extreme position, the matrix out of which the UFO was to emerge.

The name Shaver Mystery, given by Palmer, clung to it from its beginning. It's not immediately obvious, though, what there was about it that made it a mystery to be solved rather than a story to be passively absorbed or a myth to inspire, to awe, possibly to terrify. It's called by Richard Shaver's name even though it was Palmer's at least as much as it was Shaver's. It was the synergy of the pair, to use that word once more, that made it possible.

They were an odd couple, as visibly a "unification of opposites" as were Betty and Barney Hill. Shaver, of Pennsylvania farming stock, was brawny and ruggedly handsome. Palmer was a city boy from Milwaukee, whom a spine-shattering childhood encounter with a beer truck had turned into a spindly-limbed, hunchbacked dwarf. Their religious views were starkly different.[62] Shaver, the creator—or recipient, he would say—of a rococo mythology filled with uncanny beings, was fiercely atheist. All that counted for him was material reality, though not a reality that any scientist would recognize as such. Palmer, for all his eager though not unrestrained pursuit of the fast buck, was a believer in the power of the Spirit, the guiding hand of the being he called the "Deliberate Manipulator."

As a child and again as a man of twenty, Ray Palmer had lain in hospitals on the edge of death. The doctors were emphatic: he was a goner. They gave him no chance. Both times, through Spirit, he summoned himself to life and walked out into the sunlight, crippled but vigorous. Where Shaver brought a nightmare vision of an earth that was a sun-poisoned, monster-ridden hell, Palmer brought a glowing faith in redemption through Mystery. This was the deepest meaning of the "mystery" in the Shaver Mystery, as well as its link with what would become the UFO.

MANTONG

It began with a letter.

The letter arrived in Chicago, in September 1943, at the editorial offices of the venerable science-fiction pulp magazine *Amazing Stories*. It came from someone in Barto, Pennsylvania, calling himself "S. Shaver." Obviously a crackpot, thought Howard Browne, the editor on fan mail duty. He snorted in contempt and tossed the letter into the wastebasket.

This, at any rate, is the legend that surrounds the Shaver Mystery's birth. Legendary also is how thirty-three-year-old Ray Palmer, who outranked Browne at *Amazing Stories*, went diving

---

62 A point emphasized by religious studies scholar Jeffrey Kripal.

into the wastebasket to rescue the letter and arrange for its publication in the letters column of the January 1944 issue. The letter was headlined "An Ancient Language?"

> Sirs:
>
> Am sending you this in hopes you will insert in an issue to keep it from dying with me. It would arouse a lot of discussion.
>
> Am sending you the language so that some time you can have it looked at by someone in the college or a friend who is a student of antique time. This language seems to me to be definite proof of the Atlantean legend.

There followed an interpretation of the twenty-six sounds represented by the letters of the English alphabet. Each sound had its meaning; when put together in a word, they yielded a compound meaning in which the word's hidden significance was revealed. *A* was "animal," often shortened to "an." *B* was "be," to exist. *D* was "de," a powerful and sinister symbol for the "disintegrant" force in the universe, the impulse that drives toward chaos and destruction. The opposite of "de" was "te," the positive "integrant" force, represented by the letter *T*, which is the origin of the cross symbol . . . and so on, through the alphabet.

"A great number of our English words have come down intact," Shaver wrote. He gave examples: *trocadero*, used for the theater, was a compound of "tero see a dero" (T + RO + C + A + DE + RO), "good one see a bad one." (The *tero* and *dero*, "good ones" versus "bad ones," were to play a central role in Shaver's mythology.) "This is perhaps the only copy of this language in existence," he wrote, "and it represents my work over a long period of years. It is an immensely important find, suggesting the god legends have a base in some wiser race than modern man."

"Come down intact"—from what? Later, Shaver would explain: from Mantong, the primordial language of the cosmos (man + tongue), spoken by the extraterrestrial races of "Atlans" and "Titans," who once colonized the earth and from whom we're descended. He would also make clear that the discovery of Mantong wasn't his own achievement, as he implied in his letter. He'd learned it from personal contact with other offshoots of these "Elder Races," human but not quite human, who dwell in the caves that honeycomb the earth beneath our feet. For the present, though, Shaver contented himself with setting forth his linguistic theory, which he predicted would "arouse a lot of discussion."

This was an understatement. Looking back, Palmer would compare what happened in the *Amazing Stories* mailroom to the scene in *Miracle on 34th Street* where the sacks of mail stuffed with letters addressed to Santa Claus at the North Pole are wheeled into court. He put the number of letters at fifty thousand. This was surely an exaggeration. But it's just as certain that Shaver's exercise in do-it-yourself philology—English was so close to ancestral Mantong that you could trace its words to their roots without bothering with foreign languages—called forth a response the like of which had never been seen.

Needless to say, Palmer heard cash registers ringing. He edited a pulp magazine; circulation figures were his life's blood. But there was more than that to his fascination with this strange, unheard-of correspondent from Pennsylvania.

Palmer was the ultimate autodidact. His broken body had kept him from going to school with any regularity. Yet as a teenager he'd devoured boxful after boxful of books from the Milwaukee Public Library—sixteen books a day, by his estimate—with astronomy, ancient history, and mythology among his favored subjects. As magazine editor, he drew his readers with him into a shared investigation of the mysteries of existence. Their responses, he claimed, were his real education.

As far as Palmer was concerned, truth didn't come from the elite "savants" who'd brainwashed us with their orthodox science, their conventional history, the official philology of their dictionary derivations. Its guarantors were the ordinary people in their multitudes, speaking "from some inner hiding place of the human mind." And now this Shaver, with his revelation of the secrets of human language and through it a history never taught in schools, had raised a banner behind which they all could march.

TWO TALES OF LEMURIA

The two men struck up a correspondence. On Christmas Day 1943, Shaver sent Palmer a 10,000-word manuscript entitled "A Warning to Future Man." Over the months that followed, Palmer turned this into a 31,000-word story that he ran, under Shaver's name and the title "I Remember Lemuria!," as the cover story for the March 1945 issue. (It appeared on the newsstands on December 8, 1944; wartime paper shortages had reduced the once monthly *Amazing Stories* to a quarterly.) Their partnership as author and editor would continue into the 1950s, long after the Shaver Mystery had faded.

But who exactly was the author? Where did Palmer's editorial role stop? It's often impossible to tell, and the problem is most acute with that first Lemuria story, where Palmer seems to have taken full control, imposing his agenda and passing off his own ideas and images as Shaver's. The original manuscript Shaver sent Palmer no longer exists. We have to guess at what it contained from what Palmer afterward did with it.

"Sensational 'racial memory' story" ran the blurb for "I Remember Lemuria!" on the magazine's cover. By *racial memory*, Palmer meant collective memory, the shared memory of the human race that transcends generations and centuries. The idea is expressed in words attributed to Shaver in a "foreword" promising that the reader "will forget that I am Richard Sharpe Shaver, and instead, am what science chooses to very vaguely define as the racial memory receptacle of a man (or should I say a being?) named Mutan Mion, who lived many thousands of years ago in . . . one of the great cities of ancient Lemuria!"[63]

"Attributed" to Shaver, but almost certainly not written by him. Racial memory was Palmer's thing, not Shaver's. Palmer

---

63 Just what's intended by "Lemuria" and what it means to "remember" it will occupy us presently.

was fascinated by the mysteries of memory, of his own memories that stretched back to infancy and beyond. He remembered, or thought he remembered, having been nursed by his mother as she sat by the window of their apartment, naked and beautiful, her hair red-gold in the sunlight and flowing to the floor. He remembered, impossibly, having seen Halley's comet, which had visited the year he was born but was gone from the sky while he was still a fetus in the womb. He thought that Shaver's claims of actually having been in the caves, which Shaver had already shared with him, would be too much for readers to swallow. If they were to accept Shaver's stories as historical fact, calling them "racial memories" was the only way to go.[64]

And Shaver's stories *were* fact; Palmer insisted on this. "For the first time in its history," he wrote in the prepublication hype for Shaver's debut story, "*Amazing Stories* is preparing to present a true story. . . . We aren't going to ask you to believe it. We are going to challenge you to disbelieve it . . . take it or leave it. But *we* believe it to be *true*."

"I Remember Lemuria!" is a tale of Paradise lost, Miltonian in its theme and some of its details, if not its literary quality. The Paradise equivalent is Earth, or rather the caverns that extend down to the core of the earth, into which the Atlans and Titans have descended to escape the poisonous rays of our dying sun. There they've built thriving cities, high-tech and harmonious, given to the pursuit of scientific learning and wholesome enjoyment. "Variforms" from multiple planets, web-footed Venusians and green-eyed girls from Mars, mingle and interbreed with the Atlans and Titans, who themselves came originally from space.

---

64 He was soon to backtrack, endorsing Shaver's claim of personal experience with the caves, regretting he'd "perhaps harmed the credibility of an incredible story by trying to make it less incredible." But this was only after readers' enthusiastic responses to "I Remember Lemuria!" had assured him they didn't find it incredible at all.

But something is horribly wrong. Unbeknownst to nearly everyone, a renegade Elder from among the Atlans has seized power, aided by hordes of vicious creatures called "abandondero" or (normally) just "dero."[65] These were originally human, but have been degraded by the sun's killer rays into malformed dwarfs—stupid, cannibalistic, savagely cruel. Unlike the comfortably exotic variforms, these beings are genuinely, frighteningly alien.

The power of the rebel Elder and his dero must be broken, the Atlans and Titans relocated to a distant planet where there's no sun to bring them disease and death. This is accomplished under the leadership of Princess Vanue, chief Elder of an extraterrestrial race called the Nortans—a ravishing female eighty feet tall, possessed of immense physical power and an erotic charisma that turns every male in her vicinity into her adoring, panting servant. (I suspect she's Palmer's creation and that she mirrors his "memory" of nursing with his mother, naked and lovely like Vanue and, in proportion to his infant self, nearly as gigantic.)

The Elder Races are evacuated from this tainted Earth. Some, however, are left behind, and we're their descendants. Ignorant of our origins, we walk about under the sun, which after 12,000 years is still dying and poisonous. Thanks to that sun, our lives are brief and sorry affairs, far from the near-immortality of our ancestors. Beneath us, unknown to us, the swarms of dero remain entrenched in their subterranean caverns, growing more perverted and sadistic with each generation.

Though abysmally stupid—the rank stupidity of evil is a recurring theme with Shaver—the dero are heirs to the wondrous

---

65 *Abandondero* because they come from "abandoned caves and cities." Alternatively, they're the ones "abandoned" on Earth after the Elder Races decamp for the stars. *Dero* is normally treated as a contraction of "detrimental robot" or used to refer to a "condition" of "detrimental energy robotism." But the dero aren't robots, and elsewhere in the story *ro* is used for a human being, or specifically a male human being. Combined with the sinister *de* symbol, it would seem to mean "evil person," as in the etymology of *trocadero* in Shaver's original letter. This, of course, is exactly what the dero are.

machinery left by the Elder Races. With their "stim rays," they enhance the debauchery to which they're addicted. With their "disintegrating rays," they torment people on the surface, stirring up unrest and wars, causing crashes and train wrecks and cerebral hemorrhages. They're responsible for belief in religion (says the atheist Shaver), presenting themselves to our imaginations as demons and goblins, ghosts and gods. Have you ever (asks Palmer) experienced an impulse to help a blind man across the street but then "you trip him and laugh as he falls into a mud puddle"? If so, you know what it is to think like a dero.

The second Shaver story, "Thought Records of Lemuria," appeared in the June 1945 issue. Here it does seem to be Shaver's voice, not Palmer's, that we hear. The setting is the present, and the narrator-protagonist is a steelworker in a Detroit auto plant, as Shaver was from 1932 to 1934, driven half mad by voices from his welding gun. He hears savage commands: "Put him on the rack. . . . It'll pull him apart in an hour! . . . Nice and slow, so he suffers plenty!" He hears screams of agony. The narrator's name is given as Richard S. Shaver, and the story, for all its fantastic elements, is in large measure autobiographical.

Afraid he's losing his mind, narrator Shaver flees Detroit. He winds up in a state prison, from which he's helped to escape by a beautiful waif with huge sightless eyes, almost but not quite human. She's one of the "tero,"[66] the beleaguered minority among the cavern dwellers who, though impoverished, remain civilized and decent. Led into her underground world, he beholds through the equivalent of a television screen a scene like the ones he heard through his welding gun. It's the dero in the act of torturing their captives for no purpose but sadistic delight. "You see," the blind girl tells her horrified guest, "they will not allow their victims to die, but keep them alive through every torment by the use of the beneficial rays."

---

66 Recall that *te* in the Mantong alphabet is the positive "integrant" force, the opposite of *de*.

> This is our enemy's pleasure palace; a Hell for helpless victims of their lust for blood and pain. From immemorial times, they have had such Hells in the underworld, and it has never ceased. You see, you surface Christians are not so far wrong in your pictures of Hell, except that you do not die in order to go there, but wish for death to release you once you arrive. . . . There has always been a Hell on earth, and this is one of them.

"I REMAIN IN THE CAVERNS"

Shaver wrote the story in January 1945; it was published some two months later. This was an era of hells on earth. Hitler's deroesque death camps were being revealed, one horror after the other, by the advancing Allies. Soon the most hideous display of disintegrant energy the world had seen or imagined would level Hiroshima and Nagasaki, casting a permanent shadow over the human future. You'd have to be blind not to see the Shaver Mystery as a parable of its time.[67]

Yet it's also rooted in the central fact of Shaver's experience, which he spent much of his life denying, obfuscating, distorting. The ten years that preceded his Mantong-alphabet letter to *Amazing Stories* were spent mostly in mental institutions.

First in Detroit in July 1934, at the instigation of his wife's family, who disliked him partly because he wasn't Jewish, partly because they thought him a lunatic. He'd been hearing voices through his welding gun at the auto plant where he worked, much as he described in "Thought Records of Lemuria." The voices began to follow him home. "He hears 'echoes' of voices talking about him," a court document states, recommending he be committed, and an examining doctor found "a definite consciousness of a 'dual mental personality.' When he speaks he wonders if his words are uttered by someone else."

---

67 Shaver himself noted the parallel: "Just so has Hitler, a *dero*, caused the weight of an entire nation of men to be thrown on the detrimental side of the scales. Other men are not smart enough, or well enough intentioned, to remove one Hitler. Notice the world conflagration resulting from the devotion of one nation to a detrimental energy robot."

Shaver would later tell Palmer that mental hospitals are dero hells "where they torment their victims for years without anyone listening to the poor devil's complaints—for the 'patient is having delusions.'" But at Ypsilanti State Hospital, where he stayed long term, he was given great freedom. He went home to his apartment for frequent visits with his wife, spent months with his parents on their farm in Barto, Pennsylvania. He was there at the end of 1936 when the news came from Detroit that his wife was dead, electrocuted in a freak accident with a portable electric heater.

He fled.

The record now becomes blurred and confused. For the next year and a few months, he wandered up and down the East Coast doing odd jobs, well supplied with imaginary companions. Tormenting dero traveled with him. So did helpful tero, including the blind girl described in "Thought Records of Lemuria," whom he named Nydia[68] and with whom he fell in love.

In an interview given in 1973, two years before his death, Shaver spoke of an extraordinary experience which, if there's any reality behind it, has to be dated to this period.

> I think when I really became aware of the underworld was when I was working for a fisherman down in Delaware Bay, not far from Annapolis. And, if you've ever been there, you know how the clouds—there are very beautiful cloud formations, and I noticed that the clouds were doing paintings, and somebody was painting on the clouds with some apparatus, and I could talk to them, and I did talk to them . . . mentally.
>
> And for a period of time, a whole summer and fall, I got quite well-acquainted with the people of the underworld, just by talking to them with cloud pictures and mental voices. And that's really the real beginning of the Shaver Mystery.

---

68 After a character from Edward Bulwer-Lytton's novel *The Last Days of Pompeii.*

The clouds, and the shapes seen in them, function as portals to the world below—a paradox to be kept in mind when we consider the Mystery's links to the nascent UFO tradition. It was about this time, Shaver told interviewer Eugene Steinberg, that he made his first and only visit to the caves.

> I used to have my own shack along the beach, and I made an appointment by mental telepathy. She[69] said it would be possible to visit and take a look around, because I asked them if it was, and they said yes.
>
> So one night they came for me, two of them, and we went down to the beach, got in a boat, and went about maybe five miles along the beach in a power boat and into a sort of smuggler's cave, sea cave, and went through maybe several miles of darkness, with very, very faint light to go by. They knew where they were going, but I couldn't see much. And there we were, inside the Earth, almost on the same level as sea level.
>
> I was there maybe four or five days or weeks, I didn't keep track. . . . They were attacked by deros and all the people I knew were killed, and why they didn't kill me, I don't know.
>
> When there wasn't anybody there anymore but dead people, and I didn't know which way to turn or where to go, I got in a boat and went back the way I'd come, and came out alone, went back to my shack. They wanted to know where I'd been, and I told them I'd been drunk. And that's the way it was.

As in the Book of Job—"I only am escaped alone to tell thee" —boating back across the Styx, returning from the realm of the dead. The mythic, archaic overtones of this story, which may or may not have its origin in some actual bout of drunkenness of the lonely wanderer, are too plain to be missed.

---

69 Nydia? The context gives no indication who's meant by "she."

At first sight it seems to contradict what narrator Shaver says at the end of the "Thought Records of Lemuria" story: "I remain here in the caverns." But only at the literal level, where none of this really happened anyway. Understood as psychological testimonies, both are accurate. Shaver fled the caverns but also remained there. He would remain there for the rest of his life.

"I have become one of the underworld," says Shaver the narrator, "of those who have been called trolls, gnomes and goblins in the old days." The voice from behind the curtain is Shaver the author, who knows that what he's undergone during his wanderings and incarcerations has set him apart, made him almost a different species from ordinary humanity. "I bid the surface earth farewell. I remain here in the caverns, absorbing wisdom . . . and loving . . . my little blind maiden."[70]

PALMER AND LEMURIA

Palmer believed him, or he made a show of believing. He must have realized that, translated into psychological terms, Shaver's vision of the subterranean world was far from the absurdity it seemed. In an interview twenty years later with the same Eugene Steinberg, Palmer came close to saying this explicitly.

Shaver's eight years in the caves, Palmer told Steinberg, were in reality eight years in an insane asylum.[71] This had to be admitted, yet not to Shaver's discredit. He hadn't retreated into his imagination, as the psychiatrists might say. The world he'd gone into was a real world, though entered only "mentally." It was a world he shared with the

---

70 By the time he wrote the story, Shaver was living with an earthy divorcee named Dottie, who never took his revelations seriously but, as his third wife, would stick with him until the end. But his heart belonged to Nydia.

71 A year and some months after his flight from Barto, Shaver was apprehended and eventually transferred back to Michigan, to the Ionia State Hospital for the Criminally Insane, where he stayed until his discharge in May 1943. Subtracting his period of freedom in 1937–38, this comes to about eight years. Palmer seems not to have realized there was more than one institution involved and to have imagined that Shaver spent all eight years at the Ypsilanti State Hospital.

fifty thousand readers of *Amazing Stories* who'd written to report the same experiences, to say they'd heard voices saying the same identical things, as though all tuned in to a hidden radio station. Shaver's mythical caves and his real madhouses functioned interchangeably as metaphors for something dark and hellish within us, nevertheless concealing a marvelous machinery—*mech*, to use Shaver's word for it—which, once recognized, could heal our lives.

Somehow interwoven with a place called Lemuria.

This word quickly became shorthand for the entire Mystery, starting with the titles of the first two stories in the Shaver cycle. (There would be dozens more.) Yet it's never entirely clear what's meant by it. In one of his long, learned-sounding footnotes to what's ostensibly Shaver's writing, Palmer explains it as a name given to Earth by "the first Atlan colonists," and the Lemuria = Earth equation is certainly correct. It falls far short, however, of conveying the name's full resonance.

For the occultists, Lemuria was a lost continent sunk beneath the waves of the Indian Ocean, corresponding to Atlantis in the Atlantic and to Mu in the Pacific. Unlike Atlantis and Mu, which are pure legend, Lemuria was originally a scientific hypothesis: a prehistoric land bridge that once connected India with South Africa and would explain, among other things, the distribution of the weird little monkey-like mammals called lemurs. Lemuria, "land of the lemurs," was proposed as a name for this sunken bridge, and the name stuck.

Shaver drew his names for primordial Earth and its dwellers from lost continents. In "I Remember Lemuria!", Earth is Mu or Mother Mu. One race inhabiting it is the Atlans; its place names are spinoffs of *Atlantis* or *Atlantean*. (We've seen that in his letter to *Amazing Stories*, he declared the Mantong alphabet "definite proof of the Atlantean legend.") At first sight this seems puzzling; obviously the entire earth can't be a sunken continent. Not unless the ocean waters, in Shaver's unconscious thought, are symbolic of the forgotten past and the amnesia that enshrouds it.

It seems to have been Palmer, not Shaver, who was drawn toward *Lemuria* as the particular name for this planet as it once had been.[72] In the books of ancient history and mythology that he soaked up during his invalid childhood, he's likely to have encountered a Lemuria different from the sunken continent yet complementing it in his imagination.

The ancient Romans knew the *lemures* as fearsome ghosts from the underworld, from whom one averts one's eyes in dread (and after whom the spooky little lemurs were named). An "olden rite, the nocturnal Lemuria," was instituted to honor yet banish them, for like the dero, they're bad company for the living. The householder must rise at midnight and perform a series of magic rites, never looking behind his back, for the ghosts are following. Only after saying, "Ghosts of my fathers, go forth!" nine times does he dare to turn around.

This Lemuria, dedicated to the ancestral dead whose sight cannot be endured, must have fused in Palmer's mind with the land that sank into the realms of forgetfulness. It's a landscape painted by Robert Gibson Jones for the cover of the June 1947 *Amazing Stories*, the special "Shaver Mystery" issue. ("That's how it looks!" was Shaver's comment when he saw Jones's painting.)

We're inside a vast, rough-hewn cavern from whose walls emerge nearly a dozen grotesque, gigantic figures, carved like idols from jade-green stone yet looking horribly alive, their eyes keenly watchful. Grim, towering, they look down on a man who tears through them in what seems like a jet-propelled ground vehicle, fleeing machine-gun fire directed at him by other men. The driver looks neither to the right nor to the left. The stone giants make no effort to impede him or to do anything but watch. But like the Roman householder, he must not allow himself to see them. If he did, he'd be paralyzed with dread.

---

72 This will explain why *Lemuria* dominates the titles of the first two stories, yet hardly occurs in the stories themselves.

FIGURE 10. Painting by Robert Gibson Jones for the front cover of the special "Shaver Mystery" issue of *Amazing Stories* (June 1947).

FIGURE 11. Painting by Robert Gibson Jones for the front cover of the "I Remember Lemuria!" issue of *Amazing Stories* (March 1945).

Jones also did the cover painting for the issue of *Amazing Stories* in which "I Remember Lemuria!" appeared. The inspiration was surely Palmer's. The strange scene corresponds precisely to nothing in the story, yet makes vivid commentary on its theme.

An emaciated green creature, humanoid but grotesquely ugly, crouches inside a vertical glass cylinder ringed at its top and bottom by bronze-colored metal. He's trapped there, a prisoner. At a control panel just outside the cylinder stands a beautiful woman, skimpily dressed in black leather, her right hand clutching a lever. Though she's of normal human size, her headgear identifies her as the princess Vanue. Her captive, lemur-like with his huge eyes and pointed ears, is obviously a dero.

Is she preparing to blast him into space? He presses his hands, entirely human except for the talons at their tips, against the glass. His eyes stare at the woman, imploring. Though he's horribly repulsive, there's no trace of malevolence in his expression. Desolation, rather—the inconsolable grief of the forsaken child, the abandon-dero. He craves, he yearns toward the beauty on the other side of the glass, in plain sight, out of reach. And her expression, as she stares back? Not triumph, not glee, not righteous malice. Something more like astonishment, tinged with pity. One pull on the lever and she'll be rid of this creature. But will she do it?

He's a dero, a creature of evil. In his skin color, he foreshadows the "little green men" of flying saucer cliché, almost never actually reported in connection with UFOs but inescapable in the popular discourse about them. In his physiognomy and body habitus, he's a caricature of the deformed, crippled Palmer, who in his later years entertained an image of himself as "a Martian who has been transported to Earth, and abandoned." "I really am from Mars," Palmer told people he caught staring at him, and when he set about writing his autobiography, he called it *Martian Diary*.

Palmer was known to have himself painted into *Amazing Stories* covers. He appeared on the cover of the July 1943 issue as an evil scientist confronted by a beautiful woman in a low-cut dress—his secretary Elaine—her gun pointed straight at his nose. On the "I Remember Lemuria!" cover, he's done it again. The scene is a ghastly inversion of Palmer's tender fantasy, or possibly memory, of himself as an infant at the breast of his lovely, nurturant mother (whose red-gold hair this woman has, though it isn't quite flowing to the floor). She's shut off from him by impenetrable glass, her breasts locked away behind a leather brassiere. But no, I don't think she will pull that lever. These two will stay frozen, their gazes locked on each other, for eternity.

"The alien is within us," Shaver announced, conveying psychological truth with an impossible myth of a nightmare world beneath our feet. To which Palmer adds, "The alien is me."

SHAVER ASCENDANT

The war ended. Paper again became plentiful, though not immediately; *Amazing Stories* resumed monthly publication. The Shaver Mystery soared.

Of the fourteen issues published from March 1945 through January 1947, all but one included a story by Richard Shaver, and all but one of these stories were featured on the covers. The readers demanded it. So Palmer claimed, and he seemed to have the figures to back this up. The normal print run for the March 1945 issue would have been 135,000; Palmer finagled an extra 50,000; all 185,000 copies sold. The February 1946 issue, with Shaver's "Invasion of the Micro-Men" on the cover, sold 261,611 copies.

The numbers are supplied by Palmer and probably should be trimmed back drastically. But there's no doubt the Shaver Mystery was a smash hit; if it weren't, Palmer couldn't have stuck with it as long as he did. Letters confirming Shaver's claims came pouring in and were printed in a newly inaugurated department of *Amazing Stories* significantly entitled "Report From the Forgotten Past?" (sometimes with, sometimes without the question mark).

The most eccentric and endearing of these "reports" came from two brothers in Los Angeles, ages twelve and sixteen, who'd received telepathic messages in Shaver's support from their recently deceased pet turtle. More dramatic was a letter from a certain "A. C.," supposedly an Army captain, who claimed that during the war he and a fellow officer had fought their way with submachine guns out of a cave in the mountains north of Kashmir. Palmer was "playing with dynamite" by publicizing the Shaver Mystery, A. C. warned. "For heaven's sake, drop the whole thing!"

Shaver never felt sure of himself as a writer. Yet he was prolific. We know of seventy-eight stories authored or coauthored by him, initially in *Amazing Stories* and its sister pulp *Fantastic Adventures*, then—after 1949, when Palmer left the Ziff-Davis Publishing Company and Shaver became persona non grata there—in Palmer's *Other Worlds Science Stories*. Not all his stories revolved around the central mythos of poison sun, underground caves, and ogre-like dero. Most, however, gave it at least a nod.

The drama of any given story might be fictional, might have a happy ending for its characters. The background stayed grimly immoveable: a world that was Hell with no Savior to redeem it, subject to powers of evil that might be warded off but never conquered or eliminated. This was a vision that people ought to turn away from with a shudder, yet which appealed to them by the hundreds of thousands. Believing the stories to mix fact and fiction, they speculated on where one ended and the other began. This was indeed a riddle to be solved. It may have been partly what people had in mind when they spoke of the "Shaver Mystery."

Not everybody loved this mystery. A small but vocal group of hard-core science-fiction fans hated, hated, hated it. If it weren't for its truth claims, it might have been forgivable—poorly written perhaps, but that was nothing new for science fiction. But with those claims it was an outrage, a corruption and a desecration of the genre to which they were devoted.

More than that, it was a hazard to the republic. In two articles published in a fan magazine, "Calling All Crackpots" and

"Crackpot Heaven," the writer estimated that the "crackpots" who read Shaver "number at least a million in the United States. They are, in the main, adults, and have educational levels ranging from near zero to those of Ph.D.'s engaged in technical occupations." In such numbers, marching behind a man like Palmer, they could have real political clout. They might get on school boards, influence public education. The implication: they must be fought tooth and nail.

The science-fictioneers rose to the call. They made Palmer a pariah at their conventions. They bombarded publishers Ziff and Davis with letters demanding that *Amazing Stories* be purged of Shaver and all his works. (These were ignored; the sales figures were too strong to be argued with.) They passed resolutions denouncing the Mystery as antiscientific and "a serious threat to the mental health of many people." They promised to "publicize our denunciation of this perversion of fantasy fiction, and . . . also the motives of those who advance it for money and the rationality of those who advance it from conviction."

There was truth in all this. The Shaver Mystery *was* antiscientific; it *did* involve pursuit of the dollar; it *was* believed in for motives that, though far from contemptible, weren't rational in any normal sense of the word. The violence of the reaction, however, seems fevered, more than a little hysterical. The Mystery had the power not only to captivate those for whom it was intuitively plausible but also to get under the skin of those who thought it nonsense.

As, in their turn, would the UFOs.

THE COMING OF THE SAUCERS

UFOs first appeared in the American cultural airspace on June 24, 1947, when Kenneth Arnold had his sighting of nine glittering silvery objects skipping "like saucers over water" over the Cascade Mountains. They'd been part of the Shaver Mystery for over a year. When Arnold's headline-grabbing experience triggered the first of the great sighting waves and "flying saucers" were everywhere in the newspapers, Palmer was able to say, "I told you so."

In his editor's column in the July 1946 *Amazing Stories*, introducing the Shaver story "Cult of the Witch Queen," Palmer wrote:

> If you don't think space ships visit the earth regularly, as in this story, then the files of Charles Fort,[73] and your editor's own files are something you should see. Your editor has hundreds of reports (especially from returned soldiers) of objects that were clearly seen and tracked which could have been nothing but space ships. And if you think responsible parties in world governments are ignorant of the fact of space ships visiting earth, you just don't think the way we do.

"Cult of the Witch Queen," coauthored with one Bob McKenna, appeared in the same issue. The action takes place in 1939. The narrator is a strapping, muscular steelworker known to his friends as "Big Jim." Lured by a beautiful and mostly unclothed young woman who turns out to be from the planet Venus, Big Jim enters a darkened house in the slums of an unnamed city and follows her down what seem to be endless stairs, at last passing through a large door into a cavern filled with fancy, complicated equipment. The Shaver Mystery had been running for more than a year. The reader would know, though Big Jim doesn't, who lives in those caves.

These dero, however, are not the usual repulsive dwarfs, but gorgeous women with a flair for sadomasochistic orgies. Only half unwilling, Jim is conscripted into an army sent to Venus to put down a rebellion against the vampiric witch queen of the title,

---

73 The quirky philosopher of the Bronx (1874–1932), whose four books chronicled hundreds or possibly thousands of anomalous events that science ignored because they just wouldn't fit in. The classic "Fortean" event was the fall from the sky of something that oughtn't to be there—fish or tadpoles, say, or enormous chunks of ice. But Fort also found many reports of strange objects or lights in the sky, which he suggested might be visitors from other worlds. These visitors might own us humans, Fort suggested (probably tongue in cheek), as a farmer owns the animals that graze on his acres.

FIGURE 12. Painting by Frank R. Paul for the back cover of the August 1946 *Amazing Stories*.

who rules Venus at her cruel pleasure even though she's originally from Earth. The Venusians, like us and like the dero, are offspring of the long-departed Elder Races and heirs to their mech, which they've retained the secrets of operating better than anyone on Earth. This explains why spaceships, left behind by the Elders, flow freely between the two planets.

At the end, having fled the caverns and the revolting savageries they conceal, Big Jim reflects that the whole thing might have been a dream. A descent, in other words, not into the physical earth but into himself. "It was a hell of a long dream, brother, if it didn't happen," he tells the young welder (unnamed, but obviously Richard Shaver) to whom he's relating his story.

For years, Big Jim tells Shaver, people have reported "odd things . . . like chunks of machinery falling out of the sky. Strange shadows passing the face of the moon. Things that 'look like ships' crossing the moon IN FORMATION." Science is baffled by the bizarre happenings. Only through the Shaver Mystery can they be understood.

The back cover of the August 1946 *Amazing Stories*, painted by Frank R. Paul,[74] is a full-page illustration of skyborne "ships" in crescent formation, passing in front of a huge disk that the accompanying text identifies as the star Altair but that looks just like a full moon. Eleven "ships" are visible in the crescent; two others fly detached from it. They're true flying saucers, disklike but with a raised center and a point on top, which gives them a look akin to a somewhat flattened call bell and also a female breast. Through round holes at their bottoms, they discharge hordes of gigantic wasp-like creatures onto the rocky, cratered landscape below. Terrified

---

74 Who seventeen years earlier had adorned the front cover of the November 1929 issue of *Science Wonder Stories* with an enormous disk flying through interplanetary space in near-vertical position, its elongated tentacles grasping New York's Woolworth Building. On the strength of his 1929 cover, Paul has sometimes been proclaimed creator of the "flying saucer craze," but this seems unlikely. The time lag is too great, and prior to 1947 flying disks appeared only sporadically in science fiction and its art, Paul's oeuvre included.

bipeds, clothed but monkey-like, flee the swooping insects but are overtaken and seized by the huge pincers. The scene is supposed to be a planet of Altair but it might as well be Earth, with ourselves as the winged monsters' prey; an accompanying commentary on Paul's painting likens the hapless primates to "the average man . . . on our war-mad world," while the predators are "masters of all they survey." A year before Kenneth Arnold, the Shaver Mystery has expanded into the sky.

There was no way anyone could have known what Arnold was going to encounter above the Cascades or how the nation would respond. Yet, in a manner almost prophetic, the early 1947 issues of *Amazing Stories* sounded the drum rolls announcing its advent.

"Let's make a few predictions," Palmer proposed in the April issue. "First, let's predict that within a few years, we will be visited from outer space, by a ship that will be seen all over the earth as it circles the planet, but such a ship as no one could have imagined even in our pages up to now." The ship will be piloted by Titans, the Elder Races who left earth so long ago and are now returning; it will be suitably "titanic," two hundred miles long. Obviously, this didn't quite come true. But what was to happen in June of that year was close enough that Palmer could claim a hit.

In the special Shaver Mystery issue, which bore the cover date of June 1947 but went to press on March 13, Palmer quoted Shaver as having "declared that the Titans, living far away in space, or other people like them, still visit earth in space ships, kidnap people, raid the caves for valuable equipment." One of the four Shaver stories published in that issue introduced a beautiful, benevolent sorceress of the subterranean world, who at first claims to be from "a far country" but turns out to be an extraterrestrial. "There is regular commerce between this cavern world's people and the other planets," she explains to her love-smitten male visitor. The drum roll was growing louder. Something dramatic, which neither Shaver nor Palmer had any way to know about in advance, was about to happen.

FIGURE 13. The cover of the Spring 1948 issue of *Fate* magazine. Image provided by *Fate* and used with permission.

And then it happened, and Palmer was triumphant. "A portion of the now world-famous Shaver Mystery has now been proved!" began his editorial column for the October 1947 issue. "On June 25 [*sic*] . . . mysterious supersonic vessels, either space ships or ships from the caves, were sighted in this country!"

Palmer wrote those words shortly before July 4, and the massive sighting wave already underway stunningly confirmed them. Were the "flying pie-pans, discs, what have you" from space? From "underground hideouts of an unknown race"? Possibly both? And what were they doing here? All a "mystery," he declared, providing proof of *the* mystery, namely Shaver's. "We'll see more of them," Palmer predicted, "and very soon we'll find out what they are."

Shaver was less enthusiastic. He knew that interplanetary spaceships were a far less important part of his mythos than Palmer made out; he must have sensed they were about to upstage him and his Mystery. The saucers, he suggested, might be spaceships here to deliver "cargos of wonder-mech." Conversely, they might have come to loot mech from the caves, washing machines and refrigerators from the surface, to sell on other planets. Perhaps they were invaders, liberators, here to free subsurface Earth from dero domination. But that seemed too much to hope for. His prediction was the exact opposite of Palmer's, its formulation so close to Palmer's that it sounds like he was deliberately picking a fight: "I predict that nothing more will be seen, and the truth of what the strange disc ships really are will never be disclosed to the common people."

The split between the two men had begun. The Shaver Mystery's star, at its zenith in the special June issue, was beginning its long decline. Publishers Ziff and Davis were growing uneasy with it; perhaps the science-fiction fans' crusade was beginning to have impact. Under pressure from his bosses, Palmer began to qualify his endorsements of the Mystery, to fudge on its truth claims. By the middle of July 1947, he'd sent out his first tentative feelers to a new dance partner: Kenneth Arnold.

The saucers were Palmer's future. Pulling away from the increasingly chilly atmosphere at Ziff-Davis, he founded a new magazine, *Fate*, dedicated to the supposedly true mysteries of the universe. The first issue, cover-dated Spring 1948, featured Arnold's account of his famous sighting. The wildly imaginative cover painting showed Arnold's airplane amid the clouds, overshadowed by a pair of bronze-colored, metallic flying disks.[75] In 1952, Palmer and Arnold coauthored a book, *The Coming of the Saucers*, which Gray Barker was later to call "the most fascinating saucer book I had ever read."

Palmer's science-fiction magazine *Other Worlds Science Stories*, which had become practically the sole outlet for Shaver's writing, evolved in the late 1950s into a nonfiction publication first called *Flying Saucers from Other Worlds*, then just *Flying Saucers*. The disks, meanwhile, left Shaver cold. What obsessed him instead were "rock books," pictorial records of prehuman civilizations embedded inside ordinary rocks. Sawed open, these rocks served as models for Shaver's "rokfogos," paintings suggestive of Mayan glyphs, claustrophobic and suffused with tormented and sometimes violent eroticism. (Example: "Amazons Defending Against the Attack of the Ape Bats.")[76] In 1975, Palmer published an assortment of these with Shaver's commentary in a volume that also included his autobiographical "Martian Diary." The cover was illustrated with a rokfogo and bore the title *The Secret World By Ray Palmer.* No mention of Shaver on the cover or spine. Shaver bore the wound

---

75 Each with a doughnut-like hole at its center, suggestive of the holes at the bottoms of the aerial vehicles on the back cover of the August 1946 *Amazing Stories*, as well as Harold Dahl's description of the objects he claimed to have witnessed in the sky over Puget Sound (see chapter 6).

76 Shaver had talent. Since his death, the rokfogos have been recognized and exhibited as "outsider art" in places like the California Institute of the Arts, the Santa Monica Museum of Art, and Pasadena City College.

of this betrayal until his death, which came on November 5, 1975, after a brief struggle with pancreatic cancer.

"He believed in only one God, eighteen days before [his] death," his wife Dottie recalled. "Used to say there must have been more than one God because there was too many to take care of and be loved. Felt sorry for Jesus."

Interviewed in 1973, Shaver admitted to Eugene Steinberg that he was no longer sure where the dero came from. "I wish I knew. . . . I don't think they ever grew on Earth. . . . I think they came in from space as a kind of vermin chased away from other places, and that they've gotten residence in our underworld and are a terrible threat to everyone on Earth." Shaver didn't know, but Palmer did. The dero come from inside us. Trip a blind man into a mud puddle—or mock a crippled hunchback or cheat a trusting friend out of his due recognition on the cover of a book—and the dero is you.

THE "MYSTERY"

Why, after four years of tirelessly promoting the Shaver Mystery, did Palmer edge away from it, shift his signature "mystery" from the netherworld to the sky? A glib, cynical explanation lies close at hand.

The saucers, to use the language of the book title, were the coming thing. The Shaver Mystery, wildly popular as it was with *Amazing Stories* readers and those science-fiction fans who didn't loathe it, never had much impact beyond them. A quarter of a million fans is a lot of readers. But compared to the US population of the time it was miniscule, just under 0.2 percent. The other 99.8 percent may be assumed never to have heard of Richard Shaver or the dero or the underground caves. Flying saucers, by contrast, were a national phenomenon from the beginning. What wonder, then, if Palmer crunched the numbers and decided the saucers would pay better?

This theory rests on a misreading of Palmer's character. True, he was a shrewdie with an eye for the main chance. He was also a man of deep though selective integrity. He showed this in the early 1950s, when the market for science fiction shrank and it became clear there was no good living to be made from it. The real money was in soft-core porn. That was where Palmer's good friend and admirer Bill Hamling, founder of a now-forgotten "men's magazine" called *Rogue*, put his attention and cash. So did Palmer's distant acquaintance Hugh Hefner, founder of an unfortunately well-remembered magazine of the same ilk. Don't be a chump, they told Palmer. Come into the skin trade with us and get rich.

Palmer refused and stayed middling poor. His mission was to promote the real mysteries, those of the sky above and the earth beneath, which couldn't possibly be the soulless, empty, mechanical things orthodox science made of them. For the pseudomystery of what a pretty woman looks like with her clothes off, he had no time at all.

In 1965, he opened himself to interviewer Steinberg about what the saucers meant to him, what the very idea of "mystery" meant. Steinberg asked if we will we ever solve the flying saucer mystery.

"No!" Palmer replied. And this isn't a bad thing, but a good one.

Flying saucers are physically real, Palmer said, but real also in a more spiritual, metaphysical sense. Recognize that humanity's spiritual development lags far behind its mechanical prowess, he told Steinberg. Recognize that the balance needs to be restored. Then

> if there is a power somewhere which is interested in a balance on this planet, the flying saucers would be an excellent way to—just to make us think. So to prove to us exactly what they were would make us stop thinking again. We've got the problem solved, why go ahead further? So, I think the mystery is only going to deepen.

Without mystery, our minds stagnate. "If we knew exactly what the flying saucers were," Palmer told his audience at a UFO conference a few months before his death in 1977, " . . . we would have solved the mystery, returned to boredom, and stopped thinking again." The conventional textbooks numb our minds with their assurance that they possess "facts" and "knowledge," whereas all that's real is "the mysterious horizon beyond which lie unborn facts, and unresearched and unproved knowledge."

"Mystery" isn't a riddle to be answered or a crossword puzzle to be solved. It's a metaphysical state wherein lies the salvation of the human mind and soul. This was the "mystery," as Palmer called it from the beginning, that Shaver had birthed with his Mantong alphabet. Behind it lay a terrible and glorious world of "unborn facts," whose promise and splendor Palmer intuited the moment he fished Shaver's letter out of Howard Browne's wastebasket.

This was a "mystery" of things below, foreshadowing the higher mysteries that were to be manifest in the heavens. With Kenneth Arnold, the higher mystery had made its appearance. The lower could be left behind, in honored obsolescence.

How did Palmer know this would happen? With what eerie prescience did he foresee, more than a year in advance, the coming of the saucers?[77]

The best answer seems to be that Palmer felt something latent, stirring, within the communal psyche of the nation. It was this that drew him to the Shaver Mystery in the first place. It involved an unconscious equation of below with above, which on the conscious, literal level seems strange—as incongruous, perhaps, as the notion of a descent to Ezekiel's chariot.[78] Aren't "above" and "below" diametrically opposed? Yet we speak of the "depths" of space as well as of earth and sea, and for Shaver, ingress to the one "depth" could be through the other.

---

77 The claim that Palmer was "the man who invented flying saucers" and that, through the Shaver Mystery, he inspired the 1947 sighting wave and the following fascination with UFOs was first advanced in 1983 by John Keel in a slovenly but self-assured article. Later writers have parroted Keel's designation, seldom seeming very sure what they mean by it. It can be defended, if at all, only by wild exaggeration of Palmer's influence on the public at large.

78 See chapter 5.

Big Jim discovers this in "Cult of the Witch Queen." He's marched through the underground caverns to a "black and silent expanse of water, whose farther reaches were lost in the darkness." A "vast ship . . . like a submarine" is moored at water's edge, and through a journey that's never described—because it would make no sense in terms of conscious reality, but only of the unconscious where the black and silent waters equate with the blackness and silence of outer space—Jim and the others are carried on it to the planet Venus.

As we've seen, Shaver remembered having himself experienced something similar: a journey by boat into a sea cave, then through miles of darkness, until "there we were, inside the Earth." The experience was triggered by what he saw in the sky: he "really became aware of the underworld" when he noticed something strange in the clouds.

For Shaver the materialist, all this was absolutely literal if logically incoherent. Palmer understood Shaver better than Shaver understood himself. He knew the truth of the Shaver Mystery, although it was only long afterward that he was willing to say it explicitly. All these depths—of earth, of sea, of sky—were metaphors for the psyche, the unconscious.

Again and again we've seen hints of a connection between Shaver's underworld and the mythic land of the dead. Water—and the boat that crosses the water—takes you to both. Shaver's world is Lemuria, with its overtones not only of a past sunk in forgetfulness but of terrifying ghosts that linger to torment the present.

What if that ghost world, that place of death, were to burst forth upon the living?

It happened in August 1945, while the Shaver Mystery was at its height. Palmer was writing his "Report From the Forgotten Past" for the December issue of *Amazing Stories* when he heard the news of Hiroshima. He understood at once what it meant. "War has come to a horrible pass," he wrote. "It has come to its ultimate pass. With atomic energy at its disposal, the next war means the certain end of civilization."

> No longer is the destructive power of Shaver's (imaginary or not) underground science the secret of the underground. It is on the surface now. Did it, PERHAPS, come from the underground? What strange guidance might our scientists have had?

"Imaginary or not." He knew Shaver's underground was an artifact of Shaver's brain. He also knew that it was real and that it had exploded with all its terror into our world.

Nor was this the end. Palmer knew that too. The carnage of World War II having dragged itself to an exhausted finale meant no lasting victory of light over darkness, tero over dero. A new world conflict, equipped with vastly more dreadful weapons, had already begun to form. It was only a matter of time, Palmer intuited, before men and women would look into the sky—deeper, more remote and mysterious than Shaver's caverns, yet functionally equivalent to them in the unconscious—and witness the mirroring of their fears: the incursion of something unknown, alien.

As death is unknown and alien.

June 1947. The coming of the saucers. The special Shaver Mystery issue of *Amazing Stories*. The month when the Doomsday Clock first appeared on the cover of the *Bulletin of the Atomic Scientists*, signifying the annihilation not just of the individual as in generations past but of everything human.

That was also the month, according to some reckonings, when a rancher northwest of Roswell, New Mexico, stumbled on the strange debris that in the fullness of time would give birth to the most gripping, resonant, universally known tale in all the UFO mythology—a myth whose focus and essence is death.

Palmer's redemptive "mystery" had its dark shadow. This was it.

CHAPTER 8

Roswell, New Mexico

ABOUT THE UFO CRASH AT ROSWELL, two facts are certain:

The first: about noon on Tuesday, July 8, 1947, the public information officer at Roswell Army Air Field issued the following announcement to local newspaper and radio outlets:

> The many rumors regarding the flying disc became a reality yesterday when the intelligence office of the 509th Bomb Group of the Eighth Air Force, Roswell Army Air Field, was fortunate enough to gain possession of a disc through the cooperation of one of the local ranchers and the sheriff's office of Chaves County.
>
> The flying object landed on a ranch near Roswell sometime last week. Not having phone facilities, the rancher stored the disc until such time as he was able to contact the Sheriff's office,

> who in turn notified Major Jesse A. Marcel of the 509th Bomb Group Intelligence office.
>
> Action was immediately taken and the disc was picked up at the rancher's home. It was inspected at the Roswell Army Air Field and subsequently loaned[79] by Major Marcel to higher headquarters.

The second: late that same afternoon, Brigadier General Roger M. Ramey, the commanding officer of the Eighth Air Force, invited a reporter from the Fort Worth (Texas) *Star-Telegram* to his office at Fort Worth Army Air Field. This was the "higher headquarters" mentioned in the Roswell press release. There the reporter met Ramey and his chief of staff, Colonel Thomas DuBose, and Major Marcel from the Roswell base. He was shown, strewn over the floor of the office, the remains of what obviously had been a weather balloon, the foil-paper panels of the balloon's radar target prominent among them. He took pictures of Ramey and DuBose holding pieces of the wreckage and looking thoroughly pleased with themselves. This was what all the fuss had been about, Ramey told the world: an ordinary weather balloon.

Marcel, who was later to insist that this junk wasn't what he'd retrieved from the ranch and flown out to Fort Worth in packing cases but something substituted for it, was also photographed with the wreckage. His expression in the photos is, at least to me, unreadable. Is this the face of a man pressured into going along with what he knows to be a fraud and a cover-up? After more than seventy years, the wide-open, almost startled eyes and the half-smile preserve their secrets.

These are the two solid bits of data. Everything else we think we know about Roswell is assertion, recollection, speculation. Piecing it all together into a coherent and persuasive narrative is the single most complex and baffling riddle in UFOlogy. It's also

---

79 Probably an auditory error for *flown*. The announcement was dictated over the telephone rather than distributed in written form.

FIGURE 14. Major Jesse Marcel with the supposed Roswell debris, July 8, 1947. Image provided courtesy of the *Fort Worth Star-Telegram* Collection, Special Collections, The University of Texas at Arlington Libraries, Arlington, Texas, and used with permission.

the best known; for who is there in this country, and in many other parts of the world as well, for whom the name *Roswell* doesn't ring a bell? But the note sounded when that bell is rung differs from person to person.

Once the excitement of the air base's announcement died down, squelched by the weather-balloon explanation that hardly anyone thought to question, the incident was forgotten. (Roswell's most famous native daughter, the actress Demi Moore, has said that while growing up she never heard of it.) Only in February 1978 did it begin its climb out of obscurity. That was when a UFOlogist named Stanton Friedman, in Baton Rouge to do an interview, was told by the director of a TV station that he really ought to get in touch with Jesse Marcel, who had "handled pieces of one of those things." Contacted by telephone, Marcel told Friedman that the debris he'd helped to collect "sure wasn't part of a weather balloon; I knew that." What it was, however, Marcel had no idea.

More than forty years have passed since that conversation. Jesse Marcel is long dead. Jesse Marcel Jr., who'd been eleven when he was awakened one July night in 1947 to help his father sort out the debris spread across the Marcels' kitchen floor—the last survivor of those who actually saw and touched the stuff—has also died. Roswell has transformed itself from a banal mystery of fallen debris into a profound and gripping myth of mortal divinity, known the world over as the most hauntingly familiar fairy tales are known. The roots of that transformation lie in the three decades of darkness that preceded, from 1947 to 1978. They're tangled and baffling, for the most part hardly traceable. Let's enter that shadow realm and see what we can find there and what it can teach us—about the UFO, our culture, our world. About ourselves.

1947: THE DEBRIS

The J.B. Foster ranch wasn't exactly "near Roswell," as the air base announcement had it, but lay some eighty-five miles to the north-west. And what ranch manager W.W. "Mack" Brazel discovered there was somewhat shy of a landed disk. (Notice the announcement didn't say "crashed.") Interviewed late on the afternoon of July 8 for a Roswell daily newspaper and the Associated Press, Brazel described how he and his eight-year-old son had come upon "a large area of bright wreckage made up on [*sic*] rubber strips, tinfoil, a rather tough paper and sticks."

They'd made this discovery on June 14. Brazel hadn't thought much of it at the time, but on the Fourth of July he and his family "gathered up quite a bit of the debris." So he told the reporters, and there seems no way to discount his date of June 14,[80] although I do wonder what would have induced him to leave a mass of indigestible stuff lying around for three weeks where the sheep who roamed the ranch were bound to eat it and make themselves sick. For reasons that will emerge presently, those who regard Brazel's debris as having been discharged from a damaged and doomed UFO prefer to suppose he found it on or close to July 4 (as the announcement's "sometime last week" would imply).[81] The Roswell skeptics insist for their own reasons on June 14, and on balance it seems that they have the better argument.

"There were no words to be found anywhere on the instrument, though there were letters on some of its parts," the Roswell newspaper noted. "Considerable scotch tape and some tape with flowers printed upon it had been used in the construction." This doesn't sound remotely like an interplanetary spaceship. But Brazel insisted it wasn't a weather balloon either. "He had previously found two weather observation balloons on the ranch, but what he found this time did not in any way resemble either of these."

---

80 Some have suggested that Brazel was in military custody at the time he gave his interview and that he was parroting what had been dictated to him. But then why did he say, at the end of the interview, that what he'd found certainly wasn't a weather balloon? A military censor, if there was one, would hardly have allowed this.

81 Confirmed by the recollection of Brazel's daughter Bessie, who was to testify long afterward that he'd found it "right around the Fourth." But the years might have blurred Bessie's memory, and we've already seen the base announcement to have been less than strictly accurate in its details.

His daughter Bessie, age fourteen, was one of the family members who helped her father collect the debris. In an affidavit forty-six years later, she recalled how, after several hours' work, "we filled about three sacks, and we took them back to the ranch house. We speculated a bit about what the material could be. I remember Dad saying, 'Oh, it's just a bunch of garbage.'" She remembered the tape and its "flower-like designs . . . faint, a variety of pastel colors, and reminded me of Japanese paintings in which the flowers are not at all connected." The material was odd, "foil-like on one side and rubber-like on the other," and "could not be torn like ordinary aluminum foil could be torn." This would become a recurrent feature of witnesses' recollections of the debris: its indestructibility. It could not be torn or burned and if folded would pop back into its original shape.

On Monday, July 7, Brazel drove into Roswell ("to sell some wool," according to the newspaper story) and reported his find to Sheriff George Wilcox. The sheriff in turn notified the air base, which at once sent Major Jesse Marcel and another officer out to the Foster ranch to retrieve what was left of the material. Marcel arrived at his home in the town of Roswell in the middle of the night, his car filled with the debris. "He brought some of the material into the house, and we spread it out on the kitchen floor," his son remembered. "He felt it was very unusual and may have mentioned the words 'flying saucer' in connection with the material. He was certain it was not from a weather balloon."

The next day came the "landed disk" announcement, which may have been dictated by the base commander, Colonel William Blanchard. (Or possibly written by the public information officer[82] with Blanchard's approval, or possibly even without it; the point is debated.) Then Marcel's flight to Fort Worth with the debris, and a few hours later the great letdown. "RAAF Captures Flying

---

82 Lieutenant Walter Haut, who in 1991 was to become one of the three cofounders of Roswell's International UFO Museum and Research Center.

Saucer on Ranch in Roswell Region" was the headline in the Roswell *Daily Record* on the afternoon of July 8, and twenty-four hours later: "Gen. Ramey Empties Roswell Saucer." For the next thirty years, "weather balloon" would remain the final verdict on Roswell.

WHAT WAS THAT DEBRIS?

Both Brazels, father and daughter, remembered seeing flowered tape amid the debris. A physicist named Charles Moore, who in the summer of 1947 had been a hundred miles away at Alamogordo, also had a memory of flowered tape. Moore was twenty-six years old at the time, working with a team of scientists on a top-secret espionage project with the code name Mogul.

Repeatedly that summer, the Project Mogul team had sent balloon trains aloft with recording equipment and radar reflectors attached. (Their aim was to find a way to get the balloons to rise to the base of the stratosphere and stay there, where it was expected the equipment would pick up sound waves from Soviet nuclear tests.)[83] Many years afterward, Moore remembered that the material they'd used in putting together the balloon trains had included tape with "a distinctive pinkish purple pattern of an abstract flowerlike design printed on its backing."

This could hardly be coincidence. The conclusion seemed inescapable. What had gone up at Alamogordo had come down on the Foster ranch.

So the public was told in 1994, in the *Report of Air Force Research Regarding the "Roswell Incident."* Roswell was growing famous.[84]

---

83 It didn't work out. Project Mogul proved ineffective, its results unreliable. Better ways were eventually found to detect Soviet nuclear activity, and Mogul was sent to the scrap heap.

84 The following summer, the State of New Mexico would formally "proclaim June 30 through July 2, 1995 in New Mexico as 'Roswell UFO Encounter 1995' and urge all our citizens to note this occasion with the appropriate recognition." The fiftieth anniversary of the event was coming up fast; advance publicity would help draw the tourists. On July 4, 1997, columnist Molly Ivins noted that "the Air

Citizens wanted to know the truth behind the weather balloon story, now assumed to be a cover-up; at the prodding of a New Mexico congressman, the Air Force had undertaken a reinvestigation. The result: a "Balloon 2.0." The Foster ranch debris had been balloons, all right, but not ordinary weather balloons. Rather, they were the special hush-hush balloons of the now declassified Project Mogul.

The theory was and remains attractive. Aside from the striking linkage provided by the flowered tape, it explains why Brazel and Marcel were so certain that what they had on their hands wasn't a standard weather balloon: it wasn't. It explains why even experienced officers were at first baffled by the remains, why they thought them important enough to merit a special flight out to Fort Worth—and why the military suddenly turned cagey about the stuff a few hours after trumpeting its discovery on the news wires.

This explanation does, however, have its problems. There were a limited number of Mogul balloon launches in the summer of 1947. Nearly all were tracked to places other than the Foster ranch. The only plausible candidate for the ranch debris was "flight no. 4," supposedly launched from Alamogordo on June 4, about the right time for Brazel to have discovered its remains ten days later. Yet a contemporary diary entry by a member of the Mogul team says unambiguously that flight no. 4 never flew and had been canceled on account of clouds.[85]

The advantages of the new balloon theory over the old one, moreover, are less impressive than they seemed at first. UFOlogists have pointed out that while the ultimate purpose of Project Mogul was a tightly guarded secret, in its day-to-day workings it was routine scientific experimentation, using perfectly ordinary materials. We're back with the same problems: why did the

---

Force has achieved such an advanced state of dingbattery on matters sexual that it had to retreat to the safer ground of denying that space aliens have been landing near Roswell, N.M. Of course, no one believed them."

85 In the interest of aviation safety, federal regulations prohibited the launching of balloons on a cloudy day.

military men get worked up over such humdrum stuff? What can have given Colonel Blanchard the idea that they had one of the "flying discs," made headline news by Kenneth Arnold's sighting two weeks earlier, in their hands?

It's at least thinkable that the officers knew almost from the start that they were dealing with balloons of earthly manufacture. Only whose balloons? Ours? Or those sent into the sky by an enemy? How did we know that a nest of Soviet spies hadn't established itself south of the border, using their balloons to spy on US military facilities for unclear but surely nefarious purposes? Such suspicions might have been extreme and groundless, but in the early days of the Cold War they couldn't be dismissed as paranoid. Until they could be definitively put to rest—as they soon were—the debris on the Foster ranch had to be treated as serious and possibly dangerous business.

Conjecture, of course. But it's supported by the recollection of Colonel Blanchard's wife that her husband thought the debris "might be Russian because of the strange symbols on it. Later on, he realized it wasn't Russian either." These "strange symbols," sometimes called hieroglyphics, turn up again and again in witnesses' descriptions of the debris. What they might have been, as well as how they relate to the apparently decorative flower patterns on the tape, has never been cleared up. The Mogul theory provides no answer. And to invoke extraterrestrials isn't a solution, but only a displacement of the problem into outer space.

Nor do we have an answer to the more puzzling question of what prompted Blanchard to announce that his officers had recovered a landed disk, when the materials on the Foster ranch were obviously nothing of the kind. It doesn't help to suggest, as some UFOlogists have, that General Ramey pulled a switch in his office, displaying a torn-up weather balloon as the supposed debris while the real stuff was dispatched to yet higher headquarters under cover of silence.[86] Terrestrial or extraterrestrial, what Brazel found could

---

86 Which I don't believe. The photos taken in Ramey's office, though not quite identical with the descriptions given by Brazel and his daughter—the tape de-

by no stretch of the imagination be called a disk. The crashed-UFO advocates have found themselves obliged to distinguish the "debris site," where the wounded spacecraft sloughed off some of its materials, from the "crash site" or "impact site" proper, where the disk itself came to a shattering end. Wherever that impact site might have been (more on this presently), it wasn't the Foster ranch.

We're reduced to speculation. Mine is this: that the core myth, of a celestial entity descended to earth, had already begun to work on Blanchard and his subordinates, side by side with their realistic concerns about Soviet espionage. For a short time, perhaps only a few hours but long enough to issue a press release, it overrode the plain evidence of their eyes as to what lay before them. Like Jonah's gourd in the Bible, it sprang up in the day and perished that night, "emptied" (as the newspaper headline put it) by General Ramey in Fort Worth. It was then forgotten or, more accurately, unremembered.

Yet it hung on. Its reemergence three decades later is proof of that. The preternatural durability of the debris, persistently recalled by the witnesses, may be read as a metaphor for the myth itself. Resilient, tenacious, it grew and blossomed in the limbo between memory and oblivion.

Yet in its original form it was incomplete. A flying disk, whether landed or crashed, requires pilots; what had become of them? In the earliest reports, the ones we've examined so far, there's no whisper of extraterrestrials living or dead. Somewhere in the darkness and silence, that lacuna came to be filled. On October 24, 1978, the theme of alien corpses surfaced for the first time.

1978: THE BODIES

Call it serendipity: as with Jesse Marcel earlier that year, it was UFOlogist Stanton Friedman who first heard about the new development. After giving a lecture on UFOs at a Minnesota university, he was approached by a couple who introduced themselves as Vern

---

scribed by the Brazels doesn't appear in them—overlap enough to suggest the same materials were involved.

and Jean Maltais. They told a strange story, of a now deceased friend named "Barney" Barnett, who'd told them of seeing a crashed UFO, with alien bodies, in New Mexico—well, they couldn't remember just when, but it was sometime in the late 1940s.

Friedman passed this information along to his acquaintance William Moore, who set up an interview with the Maltaises. What they told Moore is reported in his book *The Roswell Incident.*[87] This book, published in 1980, was the first of what was to become a burgeoning subgenre of the UFO literature, focused on Roswell and the shadowy events of the summer of 1947.

It was in February 1950, the Maltaises recalled, that they visited their old friend Barney at his home in Socorro, New Mexico. There they heard from him the story of his UFO encounter. This is repeated by Moore in first person, in Barnett's own words—as though it were possible for the Maltaises to have remembered verbatim a conversation nearly thirty years earlier. Some fictionalizing has plainly taken place, whether by Vern Maltais (who relayed Barnett's story to Moore) or by Moore himself.

"I was out on assignment, working near Magdalena, New Mexico, one morning." That was what Barnett, who worked for the federal government as a civil engineer, is supposed to have told the younger couple. He noticed light reflecting off "some sort of large metallic object," about a mile away across the desert. He went to have a look.

He wasn't alone, it turned out. The crashed disk, 25–30 feet across, was already surrounded by a group of people who told Barnett they were archaeologists from an eastern university, which the Maltaises vaguely recalled him as having identified as the University of Pennsylvania. They'd stumbled across the disk by accident, just as he had. "I noticed that they were standing around looking

---

87 Nominally coauthored with the famed linguist and paranormal writer Charles Berlitz, like Moore's earlier book *The Philadelphia Experiment: Project Invisibility* (1979).

at some dead bodies that had fallen to the ground." There were other corpses inside the disk.

The bodies, said Barnett (as remembered by Vern Maltais), "were like humans but they were not humans. The heads were round, the eyes were small, and they had no hair. The eyes were oddly spaced. They were quite small by our standards and their heads were larger in proportion to their bodies than ours." At which point Jean Maltais put in that Barnett had "repeated several times that their eyes were small and oddly spaced."

Small eyes—that sounds all wrong. We've been trained by the cover painting of Whitley Strieber's *Communion* to expect UFO aliens to have enormous oval eyes.[88] But *Communion* wouldn't hit the bookstore shelves until 1987. When the Maltaises spoke with Moore, the American image of the extraterrestrial was informed by the film *Close Encounters of the Third Kind*, released only a year or two earlier. The cinematic aliens' eyes are slightly larger in proportion to their faces than an adult human's would be, but the difference isn't very striking. And, as can easily be seen from a Google image search, "oddly spaced" would be an apt way to describe them.

Shall we write off the Maltaises' recollections as *Close Encounters* warmed over? Hardly. The aliens in the film are childlike, gentle, and benevolent, but also totally in control of the situation. They're here to instruct humanity, guide us into an unimaginable new era of universal harmony. ("It's the first day of school, fellas," a scientist tells his awestruck colleagues as they struggle to understand the UFO's musical communications, and we grasp the tender irony: the children are teachers to the grownups.) The aliens in the Barnett-Maltais tale are similarly childlike—disproportionately large heads—but shattered and dead.

Something else is expressing itself here. It's filtered, in the Maltaises' retelling, through the cinematic culture of the late 1970s.

---

88 See chapter 4.

Yet the story has an earlier stratum as well, difficult though perhaps not impossible to separate from what the Maltaises may have contributed to it. Barney Barnett died in 1969, and the Maltaises weren't the only ones who remembered him telling of having been up close to a UFO.

Most significantly, there was Harold Baca. He came forward in response to a letter Friedman published in a Socorro newspaper, and in June 1991 UFOlogist Kevin Randle spoke with him by telephone. In the 1960s, Baca told Randle, he'd lived across the street from the Barnetts. Barney was dying of cancer, and as a good neighbor, Baca had pitched in to help the sick man's wife take care of him. There he heard the UFO story from Barney's lips. His disease, Baca remembered Barney as having insisted, had arisen from the contaminated air he'd breathed from the crashed UFO and the alien bodies.

Twenty years had passed between Barnett's experience and his illness. It's hard to believe there was any real causal connection. But the detail reflects an awareness that he'd seen something he shouldn't, that dooms those who encounter it. This is a recurrent theme in the crashed-UFO stories that cluster around Roswell: it's forbidden to see these things, forbidden to know about them, forbidden to speak of them.

The taboo's customary enforcer is the US military. "While we were looking at them," Barnett supposedly told Vern Maltais, speaking of the alien corpses, "a military truck drove up with a driver and took control."

> He told everybody that the Army was taking over and to get out of the way. Other military personnel came up and cordoned off the area. We were told to leave the area and not to talk to anyone whatever about what we had seen . . . that it was our patriotic duty to remain silent.

"This included the University of Pennsylvania people," Jean Maltais added. As might be expected, UFOlogists have poured endless time, energy, and resourcefulness into trying to track down the team of archaeologists who preceded Barnett to the crash site. They've come up with a zero. No archaeologists or archaeology students from the University of Pennsylvania or anywhere else can be found who claim any knowledge of a crashed UFO in New Mexico in 1947. They're as much a part of the myth as the aliens, their function in it symbolic. By their presence, they link the UFO to the archaic and voiceless past, the generations of silent dead whom it's the archaeologist's mission to resurrect.

Barnett's encounter took place on what he called the Flats, the prehistoric lakebed to the west of Magdalena, New Mexico, that's known as the Plains of San Agustin. The Foster ranch lies some one hundred miles to the east as the crow (or the UFO) flies. What's the connection between Barnett's story and Mack Brazel's debris?

The superficial answer—less superficial ones will presently emerge—lies in the distinction to which I've already referred, between the "debris site" (the ranch) and the "impact site." If the debris was extraterrestrial, it had to have been discharged from a UFO that, although severely damaged, was still in flight. The disk's pilots must have managed to keep it aloft for another hundred miles or so before it finally hit the ground, in the spot where Barnett came upon it.

Barnett's story thus provided one option for identifying the impact site. But as Roswell's fame spread in the early 1990s, memories began to surface of an impact site closer to the ranch. A man named Jim Ragsdale came forward with a story of how, one night during the Fourth of July weekend of 1947, he and his married girlfriend—immortalized in the Roswell literature as Trudy Truelove—had been lounging "buck naked" in his pickup truck, drinking beer, at a spot about forty miles northwest of Roswell. They spotted a mysterious "bright flash" in the midst of a fierce lightning storm. At sunrise they drove in the direction of the flash, and "came upon a ravine near a bluff that was covered with pieces of unusual wreckage, remains of a damaged craft and a number of smaller bodied beings outside the craft." They didn't have long to explore the amazing sight. A military convoy showed up shortly afterward and took charge of the area, and the lovers skedaddled as quickly as they could.

Obviously, Ragsdale's story and Barnett's can't both be true, unless we posit two UFOs having mechanical trouble over different regions of New Mexico in the late 1940s. (And which of them will have generated the materials on the Foster ranch?) But just as obviously, they're cognate, reflecting a tradition which, as Barnett's tale shows, reaches back into the dark decades between 1947 and 1978 when the myth was taking shape. That the tradition should have been internalized as personal memory is an important psychological phenomenon, which mustn't be used to cast doubts on the sincerity of its narrators. All versions are important. None can be dismissed.

1989–91: GLENN DENNIS

Roswell Army Air Field, soon to be renamed Walker Air Force Base, was located immediately south of the town. Supplying services to the base was Roswell's chief industry. When the base closed in 1967—Lyndon Johnson's revenge, I was told when I visited in 2006, for Roswell's having gone Republican—the town was all but ruined. Stores stood empty along its main streets. Only years later, with Roswell's entry into the limelight as the scene of a UFO crash, did prosperity return.

One of the businesses that thrived on its relationship with the base was the Ballard Funeral Home, contracted to provide mortuary services for the military. Glenn Dennis, who was to emerge as the single most pivotal figure in the creation of the Roswell myth, worked there in the summer of 1947 as a mortician. He was twenty-two years old, and early one July afternoon (he remembered more than forty years afterward) he received a peculiar telephone call from the base. What was the smallest size hermetically sealed coffin the funeral home could provide? the caller wanted to know. Not that there was any immediate need for such a thing. "We need to know this in case something comes up in the future."

Still, how quickly could they get it? Dennis assured him they could have it the next day.

An hour later the man called back. How would you prepare bodies that had been lying out in the desert for some time? The caller was particularly interested in what effect the preparations might have on the bodies' chemical makeup. Dennis offered to come out to the base to help with that. Oh, no, no, he was told once more . . . just in case something should arise.

Dennis then recalled:

> Approximately an hour or an hour and 15 minutes later, I got a call to transport a serviceman who had a laceration on his head and perhaps a fractured nose. I gave him first aid and drove him out to the base. I got there around 5:00 PM. . . .
>
> I drove the ambulance around to the back of the base infirmary and parked it next to another ambulance. The door was open and inside I saw some wreckage. There were several pieces which looked like the bottom of a canoe, about three feet in length. It resembled stainless steel with a purple hue, as if it had been exposed to high temperature. There was some strange-looking writing on the material resembling Egyptian hieroglyphics. Also, there were two MPs present.
>
> I checked the airman in and went to the staff lounge to have a Coke. I intended to look for a nurse, a 2nd Lieutenant . . . 23 years of age at the time (I was 22). I saw her coming out of one of the examining rooms with a cloth over her mouth. She said, "My gosh, get out of here or you're going to be in a lot of trouble."

Two MPs (the same ones as beside the ambulance?) began to escort Dennis out of the hospital, telling him they had orders to follow him back to the funeral home. But they were stopped.

> We got about 10 or 15 feet when I heard a voice say, "We're not through with that SOB. Bring him back." There was another Captain, a redhead with the meanest-looking eyes I had ever seen, who said, "You did not see anything, there was no crash here, and if you say anything you could get into a lot of trouble." I said, "Hey look mister, I'm a civilian and you can't do a damn thing to me." He said, "Yes we can; somebody will be picking your bones out of the sand." There was a black Sergeant with a pad in his hand who said, "He would make good dog food for our dogs." The Captain said, "Get the SOB out." The MPs followed me back to the funeral home.

The nurse who was Dennis's friend phoned the next day, saying she needed to talk. They met at the officers' club. She made him swear he'd never use her name. Then she told of having been present at the autopsy of three bodies unlike anything ever seen on earth.

They were three and a half to four feet tall, the nurse said, with hairless and disproportionately large heads and deep-set eyes. Two of them were "very mangled and dismembered, as if destroyed by predators; one was fairly intact." (Notice the parallel with what was supposed to happen to Dennis himself: he'd be fed to the dogs.)

> She said she had never smelled anything so horrible in her life, and the sight was the most gruesome she had ever seen. . . . She said she and the doctors became ill. They had to turn off the air conditioning and were afraid the smell would go through the hospital. They had to move the operation to an airplane hangar.

That was the last time Dennis saw his friend. Over the next several days she was transferred out; she was later reported killed in a plane crash. (As the aliens had been.) Sheriff Wilcox, who was a close friend of Dennis's father, came to his home to warn him: "I don't know what kind of trouble Glenn's in, but you tell your son that he doesn't know anything and hasn't seen anything at the base. . . . They want you and your wife's name, and they want your and your children's addresses."

Sheriff Wilcox might or might not have verified the truth of this account. But by August 7, 1991, when Glenn Dennis signed the affidavit that I've been quoting, Sheriff Wilcox was long dead.

In all the world's mythology, is there a tale more gripping than this? That its pivotal action takes place offstage as it were, like the blinding of Oedipus in the Sophocles play, only adds to its power and horror.

Just when it began to circulate is unclear. Some UFOlogists claim to have heard from unspecified "witnesses" that "Dennis had told them about his run-in at the base long before Roswell became a household word." But this is too vague to be useful. It contradicts Dennis's own account, according to which he never shared his story with anyone but his father prior to 1990. "I didn't want to get mixed up in this mess," he said—although he soon reconciled himself sufficiently to the "mess" to become (in 1991, along with the former public information officer Walter Haut and a third man) one of the cofounders of Roswell's International UFO Museum and Research Center. He presumably meant the 1990 date as an approximation. The year before, his story was already known widely enough to attract the attention of Stanton Friedman, who interviewed Dennis in August 1989.

What Dennis told Friedman was similar to the account he set down in his affidavit two years later, though differing on some of its details. In this earlier version, the officer who threatened him in the hospital was a "big red-headed colonel," and there was no mention of any black sergeant. This last detail never made sense in the context of 1947's segregated military. No African American, in or out of uniform, could have threatened to use a white man for dog food and gotten away with it. Like anything else in a myth, it's to be interpreted in terms of the meaning (shortly to be considered) that its presence conveys.

Friedman asked Dennis for the name of his friend the nurse, and Dennis answered readily enough: Naomi Self. He spelled out her last name for Friedman: S-E-L-F. As with the archaeologists on the Plains of San Agustin, the UFOlogists have poured their energies into documenting Naomi Self's existence and—in case she wasn't killed in a plane crash after all—tracking her down. As with the archaeologists, they've drawn a blank. We have records for the five nurses who served at Roswell Army Air Field in 1947; no "Naomi Self" was among them.[89] No confirmation has come to light that there ever was a military nurse of that name. In a sense, this is not surprising: Dennis admitted in 1995 that he'd made the name up.

Supposedly he did this to protect the woman and her family from reprisals. More likely she never existed, and in giving her a name so unusual, Dennis conveys to us who she is. Namely, his "self," split off from and unacknowledged by his conscious awareness, a woman who tends to the living as he tended to the dead. (Until the UFO crash, when she took his role upon herself.) In the Roswell literature she's sometimes referred to as "the missing nurse." She might more truly be called "the missing Self."

1990–91: GERALD ANDERSON

Of all the witnesses to Roswell, Gerald Anderson is the UFOlogists' least favorite. They've written him off as a liar and a hoaxer, and they have sound reason for doing so. He was caught in the act of doctoring a phone bill to "prove" a telephone interview to be only half its actual length, of forging diary entries to confirm his claims. "False about one matter, false about them all" runs the old saw, and Gerald Anderson was false about a lot of things. Yet along with his lies and fantasies, he also spoke much truth.

He first told his story in the wake of a January 1990 rebroadcast of a TV special about Roswell, which appealed to any who could shed light on the mysterious events to come forward. He was five years old in the summer of 1947, Anderson said, and he was

---

89 Though one of these nurses, Lieutenant Eileen Fanton, may possibly have served as Dennis's inspiration.

traveling in western New Mexico with his father, uncle, brother, and cousin when they came upon a crashed UFO in the Plains of San Agustin. They approached the object and explored it. They weren't alone: there was also a team of archaeologists from an eastern university, possibly the University of Pennsylvania, a "Dr. Buskirk" and several of his students. Soon another man arrived, whom Anderson remembered as looking like President Harry Truman and whom UFOlogists have sometimes identified as Barney Barnett.

This seemed like striking firsthand confirmation of the story told in Barnett's name. But cracks began to appear. Anderson's Dr. Buskirk, it turned out, really did exist. He was still alive. Anderson had described his physical appearance with great accuracy. But he wasn't from an eastern university, and at the beginning of July 1947 he wasn't on the Plains of San Agustin but on a reservation in Arizona, busy taking photographs for a book on the Apache Indians. He'd never seen any UFOs, crashed or otherwise. Anderson had known him not from the New Mexico desert in 1947 but from Albuquerque High School ten years later, where Buskirk had taught a course on anthropology in which Anderson was enrolled.

This undermines any possibility that what Anderson "remembered" really happened. But it also undermines the notion he was consciously faking it. A hoaxer, if he felt the need to provide a name and description, would have simply invented them. He wouldn't have exhumed them from the wrong compartment of his memory. Dr. Buskirk appears in his ex-pupil's recollection of a UFO crash the way men and women from our actual past appear in our dreams, in new and fantastic settings.

As in Barnett's story, after which this is obviously modeled, the scene of the crashed disk comes to an abrupt, brutal end with the arrival of the military.

"There was a captain . . . he had red hair," Anderson told Kevin Randle in February 1990. "He was an asshole. He threatened everyone with the most incredible things you could possibly believe." Initially unaccompanied by any sidekick, by September 1990 the red-haired captain has been given a black soldier as his driver, and by March 1991 a black sergeant is "definitely second in command . . . very rude, very forceful, they pointed weapons at people, they threatened to shoot people. We were summarily rounded up like cattle."

The team of red-headed officer and black sergeant, who harassed Glenn Dennis in the Roswell base hospital, turns up in the Plains of San Agustin two hundred miles away. Impossible this should be coincidence. Absurd, however, to suppose these two were historical figures, prowling New Mexico in search of UFO crash witnesses to terrorize. Dennis's story was featured in the *Unsolved Mysteries* TV show that prompted Anderson to come forward; surely Anderson was inspired to repeat Dennis's detail in a new but equally appropriate context. But he wouldn't have done this unless it had meaning for him, as it did for Dennis.

What might this meaning have been? Redheads are conventionally supposed to have fiery tempers, as one interpreter has pointed out. But this isn't the half of it. In medieval art, Judas Iscariot was regularly depicted as a redhead, marked through this trait as a man set apart and sinister. Jews have been stereotyped as having red hair. "Red head / Jewish bread / Five cents / A Jewish head," ran an African American children's taunt song early in the twentieth century.[90] Did the captain's red hair mark him as Jewish? If so, Dennis's and Anderson's pairing him with a black sergeant might express a shared anxiety—not necessarily involving any conscious racism or anti-Semitism—about minorities in American society being invested with uniforms, put in positions of power. This

---

90 No doubt modified with an anti-Semitic twist from the chant "Red head / Ginger bread / A nickel for / A ginger head." I wish I could remember where I read or heard about a Jewish tradition that Haman, the raging anti-Semite of the Book of Esther, had red hair.

anxiety, which best makes sense as originating from the 1960s onward, would then have been projected back into their memories of once-upon-a-time New Mexico.

But there's something more here as well: archaic, mythic, archetypal. I suspect the redheaded captain to be, at the level of the unconscious, an avatar of the ancient Egyptian demon-god Set or Seth, an uncanny entity bound up with the desert. This was the "red land" for the Egyptians, and Set himself is red, whether red-haired or ruddy-skinned or both. A murdering bully, he's responsible for the death and dismemberment of one god and the mutilation of another; the alien is his domain, and fearsome happenings in the sky like thunderstorms and eclipses. The millennia have changed his wardrobe but left his character unsoftened. In his twentieth-century guise, he haunts the desert flatland of San Agustin, promises the hapless Dennis that they'll be "picking your bones out of the sand." Anderson recalled how, backed up by a henchman who's black as a medieval devil is black, he "made all the threats. He threatened to have people shot. . . . He told my uncle and my father that if they didn't want to spend the rest of their life in prison they would never say anything about what they saw there, if they ever wanted to see us kids again, they'd take the kids away. They'd never see the kids, you know."

Will the adults be taken away, or the children? Either way, the children are abandoned, as are those childlike aliens, left to die on a barren, unfriendly planet.

> All of a sudden it [the one surviving alien] just turned and looked right straight at me between my uncle Ted and myself. And this is when—it was just like an explosion of things in my head, things . . . I started, you know, feeling just terrible depression and loneliness and fear and just, you know, awful, awful feelings that just suddenly burst in to my mind there. I don't know if that meant that it was communicating with me and I was the only one there that it could communicate with because I was a kid. I don't know.

> I turned and ran and I ran across the arroyo and up on the area that it had bounced off of during the crash. I was just standing there looking down at this scene, you know, at my family, and off in the distance I could see cattle grazing. I could see a windmill and could see dust trails out on the plains out there.
>
> And, oh, I was there for a while and then I came back down.

"I felt that thing's fear, felt its depression," Anderson told a reporter from a Missouri newspaper. "I relived the crash. I know the terror it went through." As in a dream, where all the characters are projections of ourselves, the alien is that five-year-old boy; the five-year-old boy is the alien. The emotional authenticity of these searing words speaks for itself.

WHAT WERE THOSE BODIES?

The man who did the most to rehabilitate Anderson's testimony was, paradoxically, a Roswell debunker. He was Air Force Captain James McAndrew, the author of *The Roswell Report: Case Closed* (1997), a follow-up to the Air Force report of 1994. That earlier report, in which the Mogul theory was first floated, had been criticized for having nothing to say about the reports of alien bodies. McAndrew stepped forward to fill the gap.

What McAndrew noticed was that the alleged eyewitness accounts of crashed UFOs, fantastic as they were, nevertheless managed to incorporate accurate descriptions of Air Force retrieval techniques. Civilians wouldn't have known this except from observation. It followed that their stories couldn't be dismissed as pure inventions. They had to be treated as accounts, distorted and exaggerated to be sure, of events that really had happened.

What were those events? McAndrew pointed to a series of experiments conducted by the Air Force in New Mexico in the 1950s; they sent balloons into the upper atmosphere with man-like dummies and then let them drop, first in free fall and then with opened parachutes. The purpose was to collect information on how pilots or astronauts might be able to parachute to earth if forced to bail at high altitudes. The dummies traveled with an array of scientific equipment, all of which had to be retrieved promptly on the ground if the information gathered by their flight wasn't to be lost. The persistent reports, of military vehicles showing up almost immediately at UFO crash scenes, made sense in this context.

Of course it wasn't true, McAndrew insisted, that the military men bullied or harassed the witnesses. On the contrary: they were on excellent terms with the civilian population, whose help they needed to carry out the retrievals. (Had soldiers been observed taking down people's names and addresses? This was so they'd know where to send reward checks.) Nevertheless, the real events seen by Ragsdale, Anderson, and others poke their way again and again through the layers of fantasy in which they're all but smothered.

"They was using dummies in those damned things," Ragsdale said of the bodies he'd seen, and Anderson recalled that at first "I thought they were plastic dolls." Both men soon came to realize that their initial impression was mistaken, that these were the corpses of alien beings. But why should it have occurred to them to speak of "dummies" or "plastic dolls" in the first place, unless conveying a suppressed awareness that that was what the things they saw in fact were?

In the heat of the New Mexico desert, Anderson felt an eerie chill emanating from the crashed spacecraft. "You know, the odd part about this was that the closer you got to it, the cooler it was . . . ice cold. It felt like it just came out of a freezer." This wasn't the sort of detail a hoaxer would invent. But a payload, just plunged to earth from subzero temperatures in the upper atmosphere, would feel exactly as Anderson described it.

There was a problem with McAndrew's theory, which the UFOlogists weren't slow to point out. The experiments he described were first performed in 1950; how could they account for events that had taken place three years earlier? McAndrew had to posit not only distortion of the witnesses' memories but also displacement of those memories in time and also in location. This seemed too implausible to be taken seriously.

Yet such things happen. I became convinced of it in 2014, when I posted to my blog a reminiscence of my adventure fifty years earlier as a sixteen-year-old UFOlogist investigating a "UFO landing" in Glassboro, New Jersey, that turned out to be a hoax by a local college student.[91] A response I received to my post first jolted me, then baffled me, then persuaded me that McAndrew's assumptions about how memory works were solid and reasonable.

The UFO was supposed to have landed in a clearing in the New Jersey woods on Friday, September 4, 1964. The next morning, September 5, was the fourteenth birthday of a lady who first posted her comment to my blog, then followed up with an email. She awoke that morning, she remembered, to find the Air Force in Glassboro in full force.

They knocked on her door; they spoke with her father. The street was closed, with no traffic allowed in or out. It was a long time before her family could even pull their cars out of the driveway. All of which illustrated how very seriously the Air Force took that UFO.

"I remember that day like it was yesterday," the woman wrote with obvious sincerity, and you usually have a good memory for significant days like your birthday. Yet I knew the Air Force clampdown couldn't possibly have happened. I was in Glassboro the following Saturday, September 12, investigating the "landing," getting soaked in the pouring rain at the "landing site," then invited home to dry out and eat dinner with a warmhearted, gracious local family. I spoke with them and with many others

---

91 See chapter 1.

in Glassboro that day and in the coming weeks. Not one soul mentioned any Air Force clampdown on the town.

I emailed the woman, telling her this. I assured her that I trusted her honesty. I confessed myself puzzled. She responded that not only she but others as well remembered the Air Force being in Glassboro early that morning, shutting down the street. She now recalled they'd come to her house twice, in uniform.

It took a few months before I realized what had happened.

In June 1967, with almost no advance warning, Lyndon Johnson and Soviet Premier Alexei Kosygin held a summit conference in Glassboro. This was a truly historic event, a major easing of Cold War tensions, which has gone down in the history books as the "Glassboro summit." Of course, the town was under the tightest possible security. Snipers with rifles were posted on the roofs of the buildings of Glassboro State College, where the two leaders met. The woman who'd written to me, I discovered upon checking a map, had lived on a street one end of which was hardly more than five hundred feet from the edge of the campus. No wonder the street was closed and her family's cars kept from leaving the driveway.

She remembered the events accurately. Only, she'd displaced them from the real Glassboro summit to a context three years earlier, which in her unconscious seemed more significant and deserving of the military's attention: the landing of an extraterrestrial spaceship in a woods just outside the town. In reality there was no spaceship and no landing, but that didn't matter: this nonevent was the event that counted. And so it was in Roswell, New Mexico.

This is how it was, as I envision it:

The memories of those who came forward as witnesses, although triggered by real events, interpreted those events in the light of the myth and thereby used them as material for the further invention and elaboration of the myth. (Remember: I don't use *myth* to mean falsehood, but the emergence and unfolding of something from the shared unconscious, which may be the most profound and terrible of truths.)

The displacement of the events back to 1947 was part of the process. So was Anderson's projection of his childhood loneliness and terror onto the UFO alien. So was Glenn Dennis's externalization of his "missing Self," what Jung would have called his unconscious feminine anima, and bestowing on her a face and personality. For the dreadful autopsy in which this projected "Self" was an unwilling participant was grounded in something that really did happen, of which Dennis must have been a part.

McAndrew tells the story. On June 26, 1956, the skies just south of Roswell were the scene of a ghastly accident. An airplane with eleven crewmen caught fire, spun out of control, and crashed. Everyone on board was killed, their bodies horribly burned. The autopsy protocol spoke of a "face completely missing," "multiple fractures of all bones of the skull," "partially cooked strands of bowel . . . over the abdomen and in the chest."

The bodies were taken to the Walker Air Force Base hospital for identification, then moved to a refrigerated room on account of their overpowering stench—much as "Naomi Self" described to Glenn Dennis. Three of the corpses, the same number as the dead aliens in Dennis's story, were autopsied the next day at the Ballard Funeral Home. Dennis didn't conduct the autopsies but, as a mortician there, he's likely to have assisted in them. Playing the role, in other words, that he assigned to his "missing Self."

He was thirty-one years old. He was familiar with death but not with death so sudden, massive, and horrific, leaving bodies so disfigured as to suggest unspeakable suffering compressed into the last millisecond of conscious existence. His mind recoiled from preserving the awful images, constructing instead a "screen memory"[92] that put him one move away from the encounter

---

92 On the concept of the screen memory and its uses by UFOlogists and their critics, see chapter 4. Screen memory has been proposed as an explanation for the

with those bodies, that transformed the corpses from healthy young airmen with whom he could identify (and whom he may have known personally) into extraterrestrials, their death agonies as alien to him as their lives on some distant planet. He rationalized that screen memory and at the same time mythologized it by displacing it into the past, attaching it (much as my Glassboro friend did) to the events that began with Mack Brazel's strange debris.

This was the decisive step in the birth of the Roswell myth as we know it out of the Foster ranch mystery. Fittingly, it was a specialist in the arts of death who brought the newborn into the world.[93]

THE MYTH AND ITS MEANING

What is the myth about? *Death*—dramatized in a tale whose tenacity bears witness to its power, yet not quite like anything in the classical mythologies. The Greeks, I once wrote, imagined the gods to be immortal. The UFOlogists know better.

UFO aliens are the modern-day equivalents of gods; this has become almost a cliché among those who doubt their reality. Fair enough: the UFOnauts ride through the sky in their chariots, inaccessible to earthbound mortals except insofar as they choose

---

Aldeburgh flying platform incident in England during World War I. A woman remembered having seen, in the air just above the level of her house, eight to twelve men standing on "a round platform with a handrail around it. This they were gripping tightly." Perhaps, UFOlogist John Harney has suggested, this was a screen memory of a dreadful event that occurred on July 16, 1917, when a German Zeppelin was shot down near the woman's home, turning into a fireball that could be seen for fifty miles, burning its crew alive. As with Glenn Dennis, the screen was a pseudomemory of the unknown and mysterious. It hid a real memory of something terrestrial, readily comprehensible, yet too ghastly for the mind to preserve without cracking.

93 Another mortician, the Japanese American Norio Hayakawa, played a leading role in Area 51's rise to fame as an adjunct to the Roswell myth, through his promotion (in 1990) of Robert Lazar's stories of flying disks and large-headed aliens at the Nevada site. Hayakawa's ethnicity as well as his profession may be significant, along with its having been on Japanese media that Lazar's claims first got international attention. We'll presently see why.

to reveal themselves. But in the classic myths the gods don't fall out of the sky, they and their vehicles shattered together. Their corpses aren't torn; their guts aren't devoured by desert predators. Nor are they frail, childlike, and sexless, with huge heads and spindly limbs. So exactly and pathetically like children, in fact, that in 2015 Kodachrome slides of the mummy of a two-year-old boy were widely believed, on no grounds whatsoever, to show one of the Roswell aliens.

Charles Ziegler, an anthropologist who in 1997 undertook to elucidate the Roswell story as "the genesis of a modern myth," found it useful to compare the UFO beings to angels. "UFO and angel stories share striking similarities," he wrote. "Both involve elusive entities that carry out their terrestrial activities unobtrusively without leaving behind physical evidence of their existence or their unearthly status, and at the deepest level both convey the same fundamental message—we are not alone." Roswell, unmatched in the UFO lore for name recognition even among those who don't know or care about UFOs, undermines this easy parallel. What would Ziegler have said if the most resonant, familiar, widely circulated angel story were to tell of a man who finds his guardian angel dead in the gutter, half eaten by dogs?

Searching world folklore for a category into which Roswell could be placed, Ziegler found a genre of tale in which "an essential item such as food or water is impounded or hoarded by a malevolent monster," to be liberated from the monster's clutches by a "culture hero." This, Ziegler thought, was the essence of the Roswell drama, with the US government cast as the monster, the UFOlogist as the culture hero, and the "evidence-based knowledge that we are not alone in the universe" as the "essential item." The tale's most compelling image, the crashed and crippled disk with its dead occupants, is thus left without meaning. It's there only to convey the abstract lesson: we're not alone.

Abstract—and without the smallest utility. We learn nothing about our fellow sharers of the universe beyond that they exist. Are they here to rescue us? Invade us? Teach us something we need to know? If so, death has silenced their lips, leaving their corpses one more riddle. As a piece of "essential" wisdom, this is pretty poor stuff.

Unless the central lesson is just that: they *are* mortal.

In the classic mythologies, gods do sometimes die. They die to be resurrected, like the Near Eastern vegetation deities who perish in the scorching summer, or the martyred reforming rabbi who's become Lord to a third of the world's population. Or they die like the Norse gods, in a final Ragnarok, a doomed battle with the forces of death and darkness. Is that the meaning of Roswell—that in the wake of Alamogordo and Hiroshima and Nagasaki, humankind's Ragnarok is here and now?

Other parallels suggest themselves, once we expand the category of what it means to be a god. There's the Greek Icarus, a human child who's all too human and childish, yet whose waxen wings make him seem a sky-riding god to the open-mouthed laborers on the earth below. "Drawn by desire for the heavens," glorying like space-age humanity in the technological prowess of his flight, Icarus flies too near the sun and finds his wings melting away. Like the Roswell UFOnauts, he crashes to his death.

Then there's the Canaanite deity, identity still controversial, who hides behind the glowing, sinister majesty of the "Shining One, son of Dawn"[94] of Isaiah 14:12. "How art thou fallen from heaven, O Lucifer, son of the morning!" the King James Bible proclaims, drawing on the Latin rendering of his name as *Lucifer*, "Light-bringer."

> For thou hast said in thine heart, I will ascend into heaven, I will exalt my throne above the stars of God. . . . I will ascend above

---

94 Hebrew *Helel ben Shachar. Helel*, like the Greek *heosphoros* and the Latin *lucifer* used to translate it, seems to have been a designation of the planet Venus as Morning Star.

> the heights of the clouds; I will be like the most High. Yet thou shalt be brought down to hell, to the sides of the pit.

In his brilliant hubris this "Lucifer" is, like us, a child of enlightenment. He'll soar to stratospheric, indeed interstellar heights, there to become "like the most High." The prophet has a chill message for him, as for the UFO pilots at Roswell: "Thou shalt be brought down to hell, to the sides of the pit."

The space age, Roswell reminds us, is also the nuclear age. We stand on the edge of a crash from which there can be no recovery.

It's a grim message, counterbalanced but not cancelled out by the vibrant gaiety of the Roswell UFO Festival that's emerged from it, celebrated the first week of each July to commemorate the mythic event. There, in the sun-drenched streets of a now prosperous Roswell, the aliens are resurrected along with their town. In posters and dress-up costumes and Mylar balloons, they're green as spring's new vegetation.[95] The festival is lighthearted but also grave, featuring an alien costume contest and an alien pet contest but also serious lectures by leading UFOlogists; life, it insists, goes on even in the presence of death. As in the hilarity of the Mexican Day of the Dead festivities, the darkness that undergirds the fun is made palatable. It is not expelled.

In the introduction to this book, I quoted two psychiatrists' intuition that at the heart of the UFO was an "unconscious concern with death and immortality." They made this suggestion in 1969, when Roswell was all but unknown. Since then it's emerged as "the seminal event in UFO history," commemorated not only locally but internationally on World UFO Day (July 2),[96] encapsulating

---

95 The dead aliens at Roswell, like UFO aliens everywhere, are never described as being green (see chapter 4). The color is symbolic, not historical.

96 Proposed in the early reconstructions of the Roswell events as the date of the crash; it's this that the organizers of World UFO Day (first observed in 2001) have followed. June 24, the anniversary of the Kenneth Arnold sighting, is also sometimes celebrated as World UFO Day, which until Roswell's rise to prominence

and symbolizing the entire UFO phenomenon. As if to say to the psychiatrists: you were right all along.

Death—the ultimate alien and at the same time the most intimate alien that can be imagined. *Death*—bone of my bone and flesh of my flesh, born with me at the moment of my birth and growing with me from babyhood onward. (This is the hidden meaning of the Roswell corpses being those of small children.) Yet also *death* through which I become wholly other than myself; indeed, as most of us secretly believe even if we profess the contrary, I become nothing at all.

"If I am, death is not. If death is, I am not" runs a modern reworking of an old Epicurean slogan. This is supposed to be comforting, an antidote to fear of death. ("Why should I fear that which can only exist when I do not?") The comfort is icy and hollow. In the face of death, logic is helpless. Only myth will serve. Thus Roswell.

Who are the extraterrestrials in the Roswell myth? They're embodiments of death in its aspect of alienness, as the redheaded captain and the black sergeant embody it in its aspect of raw terror. They're also ourselves, frail helpless children confronted by a calamity we can neither grasp nor ward off. This is why those who "remember" them tend to identify with them. Glenn Dennis will be eaten by animals, as were the ETs. His "missing Self" dies in a crash, as they did. Gerald Anderson feels the "awful, awful feelings" of the dying alien explode inside his head; for "I was a kid" and therefore kin to this unearthly being.

Lurking in the shadows, we can sense a new sort of death, a recent arrival to this world when Roswell made its first brief splash. I've already remarked on the coincidence that's hardly a

---

was the most logical choice. Is it coincidence that the nine-day period from June 24 through July 2 corresponds almost exactly to Christmas–New Year's Day at the opposite pole of the calendar?

coincidence:[97] June 1947, which saw the birth of the UFO era, was also the month when the Doomsday Clock first appeared on the cover of the *Bulletin of the Atomic Scientists*. Death had always been with us; so had visions of the end of the world. But this "end" normally meant the deliberate intervention of a benevolent God, a "new heaven and a new earth" to follow. Now Doomsday was no "Judgment Day" (the original meaning of the word *doom*), but pure annihilation, pure desolation. It would leave behind only empty sky and barren earth, God and the human spirit dead in tandem.

Translated from the mythic symbolism, this is the meaning of Roswell: Child-humanity, dreaming of heavenly dominion, crashes to permanent extinction.

Who brought this new death into the world? The 509th Bomb Group, headquartered at Roswell Army Air Field, in 1947 the only unit of any military to be entrusted with nuclear warfare. It was the pilots of the 509th who dropped the bombs on Hiroshima and Nagasaki. It was the intelligence office of the 509th that, some two years later, proclaimed itself "fortunate enough to gain possession" of the disk that never existed. How fitting that the ghastly specter they had raised—fallen divinity, fallen humanity—should make its appearance on their doorstep.

To remain latent for a generation, then burst forth to inextinguishable life.

---

97 See the end of chapter 7.

EPILOGUE

John Lennon in Magonia

ONE MORE SCENE from Magonia, complementing those introduced in chapter 2:

The date is August 23, 1974. At the center of the scene is one of the most famous individuals in the world, the former Beatle John Lennon, along with his assistant and then-lover May Pang. The episode has all but vanished from the annals of UFOlogy, despite having been what the UFOlogists would call a "close encounter of the first kind," multiply witnessed.[98] We may well wonder why.

It wasn't that Lennon was secretive about his and Pang's experience. "On the 23rd Aug. 1974 at 9 o'clock I saw a U.F.O. J.L.," says a liner note for his *Walls and Bridges* album, issued a little over

---

98 Jerome Clark's monumental *UFO Encyclopedia*, that vast resource for knowledge of all things UFOlogical—now out in its third edition (2018)—has not a single word about it.

a month after the sighting. A sketch Lennon did at about the same time, which he may have been considering for the cover illustration for *Walls and Bridges*, depicts the UFO soaring over a throng of people, all seemingly oblivious to what's over their heads. In "Nobody Told Me," one of the last songs he recorded before he was shot dead in December 1980, he included the line "There's a UFO over New York and I ain't too surprised."

Lennon, separated at the time from his wife Yoko Ono, was living with Pang in a penthouse apartment on East 52nd Street in Manhattan. It had been a hot day, but by 8:00 it had cooled off enough for them to turn off the air conditioning and open the windows. Pang had showered, and as she was drying off (as she told an interviewer fourteen years afterward), "she heard John yell to her from the outside roof, 'May, come here right now!' Startled, she ran to John and found him standing on the roof nude and pointing wildly southeastward."

"I drop the clothes and now I'm nude (laughs) and running out there," she told another interviewer. Lennon remembered the same thing. "I was standing, naked," he recalled, "by this window leading on to that roof when an oval-shaped object started flying left to right. It had a red light on top. . . . I shouted after it, 'Wait for me, wait for me!' "

It didn't wait, although it easily could have. It was a "classic" disk, luminous and silent, floating through the air less than a hundred feet away from the astonished couple. Lennon was sure he could have hit it with a brick if he'd had one. Then, ignoring Lennon's entreaties, it was gone. It stayed long enough, though, for Pang to be able to fetch a camera so they could take pictures of it. The photos turned out blank. Naturally. There was nothing there to be photographed. The UFO came from inside.

But the scene isn't just the flying disk. It's also the people who saw it. They were naked—both Lennon and Pang harp on this point in their retellings of the incident so frequently that it's impossible to believe the point was of no significance.

Where else do we hear of a nude couple confronted by a numinous presence?

"And the eyes of them both were opened, and they knew they were naked. . . . And they heard the voice of the Lord God walking in the garden in the cool of the day," says the third chapter of the Book of Genesis. And we note that this is exactly the time of day when Lennon and Pang had their experience. Adam and Eve hide themselves from that Voice—the opposite of Lennon and Pang, who step out onto the roof to greet their visitor—"and the Lord God called unto Adam, and said unto him, Where art thou? And he said, I heard thy voice in the garden, and I was afraid, because I was naked; and I hid myself."

Nudity wasn't shameful in 1974, as it had been when the Genesis storyteller wrote. The mores of the counterculture called for it to be flaunted and not hidden. But the archetypal scene remains the same: man and woman stand naked before the unknown, unidentified yet radiating power and awe. Not that Lennon and Pang deliberately set themselves to reenact the Bible story; that seems to me inconceivable. It emerged spontaneously from within them, of them yet outside their conscious control.

Three years earlier, in his best-known song of the post-Beatle era, Lennon challenged his audience to "imagine" an ideal world free of nationalities, emptied also of religion. In that world there'd be no heaven above us or hell beneath, "above us only sky." That sky is completely disenchanted (to use Max Weber's language), stripped of any transcendent significance. But the repressed has a tendency to return. One warm August night the enchanted sky reasserted itself before the eyes of the man who'd "imagined" it could be banished.

It reasserted itself as a shared vision. It expressed itself through a template hardwired into the unconscious, set down in recognizable form many hundreds of years ago in the Book of Genesis. It took the shape, for those who experienced it, of an Unidentified Flying Object.

Early in this book, I told how my eighth-grade friend Bryan and I set out to write an extra-credit paper for a science class and instead discovered flying saucers. I don't think we ever wrote that paper. That winter I did write a few chapters of a book, nominally co-authored with Bryan, which we planned to call *The Flying Saucer Mystery*. We would state the facts; we would examine the hypotheses. Then, a pair of junior Sherlocks, we'd find the solution.

My teenage quest for that solution, through my mother's sorrowful final years, has already been described. Of course I failed both to keep my mother alive and to solve the mystery of the saucers. Ray Palmer could have told me that I'd fail, that indeed it was better for me to fail, for if I solved the mystery, it would be gone and I'd be left with nothing. I would have ignored him, the wisdom of his words as far beyond me as some distant galaxy.

What's the "solution" to the mystery of what John and May encountered that August night? Would it be "solved" if I identified some unusual object in the sky, a Goodyear blimp or the like, that triggered their experience? Martin Kottmeyer, to whom I'm indebted for guiding me to the resources I've used in telling their story, has pointed out to me that they're likely to have had some objective stimulus. What that stimulus was is for me a matter of near-total irrelevance.

Nor is it "solved" by the jeering dismissal "What drug were they on?" Lennon has denied he was on any drug that night, and it wouldn't matter if he were. The UFO came from within, and whether it was evoked with chemical means or without them is an issue of secondary importance. The central question is the one I've pursued throughout this study: *what did it mean?*

Call it the religious experience of an irreligious man, unbidden and unfettered by any conscious volition. A shared experience, like Adam and Eve's as expressive of the lovers' relationship with one another as with the sacral Other that appeared to them from the sky. This doesn't "solve" the mystery either. It has the virtue, however, of restating it, placing it in a fresh context in which it can be explored.

Does that "Other" even exist? Not in the physical world, certainly as far as the UFOs are concerned. (I leave aside the question of what objective existence can be attributed to the God of Genesis.) But it can't be limited to John's perhaps overstimulated brain, or May's, or the two of theirs together. The parallel in Genesis shows that it was part of them yet also beyond them, a transcendent reality shared with others in distant times and places. Probably with their entire species.

In its essence, the UFO is a religious phenomenon. This assertion must not be confused with the shallow sneer of some debunkers that UFOs are "a religious cult." What it says is that a UFO sighting, insofar as it goes beyond simple misinterpretation of mundane stimuli, is a religious event, an experience of the numinous that arises—spontaneously, it would seem—from our internal worlds. The totality of UFO lore is a religious myth through which those who've not been blessed (or cursed) with the experience can vicariously participate in it. The myth is endorsed by group tradition. Yet fundamentally it's believed in because of a stubborn awareness, every rational objection to the contrary, that it's real and true.

This is the "hidden story of the UFO." It's a story not of spaceships and interplanetary visitors but of human beings like John Lennon and Barney Hill and Gray Barker and Richard Shaver and you and me, and our interactions with our shared unconscious, which if not "God" in the traditional sense is psychologically indistinguishable from It.

There are some regularities in the story. Not quite the patterns I searched for as a teenage UFOlogist, which I expected to reveal the unseen forces behind them like iron filings sprinkled on a paper over a magnet, but discernable nonetheless.

One is *the emergence of a mythic theme from the trauma of an individual*, who in violation of the silent, anonymous process of mythic creation, can be pinpointed in time and space. The trauma is normally bound up with *alienness*: of a black man in a racist society, a gay man in a homophobic society, a crippled hunchback in a society that values good looks and physical vigor. Or a devastating encounter with the ultimate alien, death, particularly a death that's sudden and meaningless and horrific.

Often this individual is part of *a synergistic pair*, in which it's not easy to tell who has contributed what to the developing myth. This is true of Barney and Betty Hill, Gray Barker and Albert Bender, Ray Palmer and Richard Shaver. The last case is particularly rich in subtlety and paradox. Whose trauma did the Shaver Mystery communicate? Palmer's, with the broken and grotesque body that made him seem a man from Mars, inside which his towering spirit looked death in the eye and twice triumphed? Or Shaver's, labeled a madman and confined within a hospital for the "criminally insane," although all who knew him testified to the brawny man's habitual gentleness?[99]

The myth originates within historical time, and recent historical time at that. *Yet the myth regularly proves to be age-old,* manifesting in earlier generations under different guises. The "descenders to the chariot" early in the Common Era fainted under the gaze of eyes like those that stare from the cover of Whitley Strieber's *Communion*. Albert Bender was persecuted by three men in black, like Abraham Cardozo nearly three hundred years earlier. This is one of UFOlogy's paradoxes, very likely bound up with the process by which the trauma of the one spreads to the many. As a primordial myth, universal, it was a property of the many to begin with. Now, in its new iteration, they embrace it as something

99 Both experienced hospitals as their places of trial, from which Shaver emerged shattered and Palmer victorious—the reverse of what you'd imagine from looking at their outsides. But in dealing with the UFO, it's the hidden and not the visible that counts—or rather, the hidden and its interaction with the visible.

long-known but forgotten. Or not altogether forgotten, but not quite remembered either.

And spread it does. As a rule, not immediately; that's another of the regularities we've encountered, not quite invariant.[100] First comes a *latency period*. Twenty to twenty-five years passed between Barney Hill's "abduction" memories and the flowering of abductions into a recognizable feature of American culture. It took thirty years for Roswell to return to the spotlight, forty years for the myth immortalized in *They Knew Too Much About Flying Saucers* to morph into the *Men in Black* movies.

In this process of forgetting-then-remembering, multiple factors are surely at play. It would be unwise to reduce them to a single cause, whether of individual or mass psychology. Yet at the end the myth has become a shared cultural property, recognizable to nearly everyone, evoking an emotional response of some sort even if it's only a contemptuous sneer. (This also is a form of vicarious participation.)

The UFOs remain unidentified, not in terms of the mundane stimuli that trigger their appearance but in terms of what they mean within us, from which regions of our "inner space" they come and what conditions govern their emergence. There's much that we can feel fairly sure we understand, more that we can fumblingly guess at. Yet there's even more that will continue to baffle us, that we have no choice—once we've refused the stale alternatives of believing or debunking—but to contemplate in wonder.

This is the mystery that two thirteen-year-old boys set out to "solve," that remains unsolved to this day although I think I have a grasp of its contours that I couldn't have had when I began my quest. The more I ponder it, the more it seems to me an aspect of the ancient and insoluble mystery of who we are.

---

100 The Shaver Mystery seems an exception.

We: a two-legged, two-gendered animal evolved from microbial existence through unthinking, unfeeling biological processes, capable nonetheless of thought and feeling. *We*: rational and sentient yet mortal, living and knowing we must die. Religion, in the famous definition of Unitarian minister Forrest Church, is "our human response to the dual realities of being alive and having to die." This is the religious issue at the heart of the UFO.

Long ago, the Psalmist asked, "What is man, that Thou art mindful of him? the son of man, that Thou visitest him? For Thou hast made him a little lower than the angels, and hast crowned him with glory and honour"[101]—and if there's no "Thou" to have accomplished this, as current scientific opinion has it, but only inconceivable eons of the blindness, cruelty, and terror that we call "nature," the end result is the same. In our wisdom, in our power, we're all but angelic. Yet dust we are and to dust shall we return.

Near-angel and dust, with dust always winning. So Adam is told (Genesis 3:19) in his climactic encounter with the divine Alien that reappeared, in mandala rather than human form, over John Lennon and May Pang's Manhattan apartment.

At age thirteen I didn't yet face my own death, as I may this year, or possibly next year or the year after that. I did face my mother's, and like Perseus's mirror in the ancient and impeccably true myth, the UFOs gave me a way to look into that Gorgon face and live. In a very real sense, they saved my life. How could I forget them? How could I leave them alone?

Bryan and I never wrote *The Flying Saucer Mystery*. Nearly sixty years later I've at last written it, with some alteration of its title. You are holding it in your hands.

"There is often a passage in even the most thoroughly interpreted dream," Freud once wrote, which must be left obscure, its "tangle

---

101 Psalm 8:4–5.

of dream-thoughts" unresolved. The dream's "navel," he called it—"the spot where it reaches down into the unknown."

This was Freud in his mystic mode, not the rigid rationalist of the stereotype. The thoughts from which the dream is born, he went on, can have no definite endings. Rather, "they are bound to branch out in every direction into the intricate network of our world of thought." Put mythic themes in place of dream-thoughts, understand "our world of thought" to be not just yours or mine but the total psychic life of our culture and species, and his words will apply to the collective dream we call the UFO.

And that dream does have a spot where it connects and draws nourishment from the unknown. We can't follow it or know what it is. We can only gaze on it, and marvel.

ACKNOWLEDGMENTS

I thank Jerry Clark, my fellow teen UFOlogist from the 1960s, for his lifelong friendship and his half a century of masterful writing on the UFO phenomenon, documenting and clarifying what's happened and what's been claimed to have happened, culminating now in the third edition of his indispensable *UFO Encyclopedia*.

I thank Marty Kottmeyer, UFO skeptic committed to understanding rather than debunking, for the boundless generosity with which he's shared with me his equally boundless knowledge of UFOlogy and popular culture and his thought-provoking judgments of the ways these have interacted in the course of our lifetimes.

I thank Jeff Kripal, J. Newton Rayzor Professor of Philosophy and Religious Thought at Rice University and the moving spirit behind the Archives of the Impossible collection at Rice's Fondren Library, for the inspiration given me by his brilliant work—the birthing of a new religious studies scholarship, nothing less—and for innumerable acts of encouragement, friendship, and assistance in the creation of this book.

I'm indebted to many others as well for their help, collegiality, and the wisdom they've shared: Marc Bregman, Thomas E. Bullard, Barna Donovan, Stephen C. Finley, the late Matthew J. Graeber, J. Albert Harrill, Rick Hilberg, David Houchin, Eric

Ouellet, Diana Pasulka, Tim Printy, Howard Schwartz, Eugene Steinberg, Jacques Vallee, Jesse Walker, and Bob Wilkinson.

Janice Dunnahoo of the Southeastern New Mexico Historical Society Archives and Elizabeth Van Tuyl of the Bridgeport History Center at the Bridgeport Public Library graciously responded to my queries and sent me important materials relating to the Roswell incident and Albert Bender's "silencing" by the men in black, respectively. Matthew J. Graeber, Jr., showed the greatest kindness in searching through his late father's files for a reproducible copy of the drawing that appears in this book as figure 2.

I'm grateful to Elizabeth Sheckler and the University of New Hampshire for their permission to reproduce Barney Hill's drawing of the alien head (figure 4); to Kathleen Lambert and Directed Media, Inc., for permission to reproduce Matthäus Merian's engraving of Ezekiel's vision (figure 7); to Rebecca Jewett, Matt Hill, and Orville Martin of the Ohio State University libraries for providing a reproducible image of the March 1945 *Amazing Stories* cover (figure 11); to Phyllis Galde, editor-in-chief of *Fate* magazine, for generously providing an image of the Spring 1948 cover (figure 13) and granting permission to use it; and to Sara Pezzoni and the University of Texas at Arlington Special Collections for doing the same for the 1947 photo of Major Jesse Marcel with the supposed Roswell debris (figure 14). Warm thanks also to Steve Davidson, editor and publisher of the newly revived *Amazing Stories*, for taking the time to clarify for me the copyright status of the magazine's 1940s artwork.

I'm blessed to have Susan Cohen of Writers House as my agent and, as my editorial and marketing team at Stanford University Press, Stephanie Adams, Barbara Armentrout, Emily-Jane Cohen, Jessica Ling, Faith Wilson Stein, and Kate Wahl. Rob Ehle designed a cover that in its beauty, mystery, and faithfulness to my conception of the book goes beyond anything I might have wished.

I am blessed also to be part of the wonderful writers' group led by novelist Laurel Goldman in Chapel Hill, North Carolina. For the past seven years, Laurel and my fellow writers have been my teachers, my guides, my cheerleaders, my inspiration. It's a pleasure to thank them by name: Chrys Bullard, Linda Finigan, Allison Freeman, Danny Johnson, Alice Kaplan, Kathleen O'Keeffe, Susan Payne, Martha Pentecost, and Lisa Rhodes.

The amazing Martin Brossman has been my coach, tireless and patient, in the often intimidating world of the social media. Novelist Beverly Swerling Martin guided me, as she has numberless other writers, through the equally daunting realm of agents and publishers. Alas, Beverly's no longer here to receive my thanks. She passed away, to my great sorrow, in December 2018.

My gratitude to Dr. Rose Shalom Halperin, my beloved life's companion of nearly forty years, knows no limits.

David J. Halperin
SEPTEMBER 2019

NOTES

ABBREVIATIONS

AS	*Amazing Stories* magazine
GBC	Gray Barker Collection, Clarksburg-Harrison Public Library, Clarksburg, WV
IUR	*International UFO Reporter*
JUFOS	*Journal of UFO Studies*
UFOE3	Jerome Clark, *The UFO Encyclopedia: The Phenomenon from the Beginning*, 3rd ed., 2 vols. (Detroit: Omnigraphics, 2018)

INTRODUCTION

Most such books: The literature is vast and has increased exponentially with the internet. A full enumeration of the "believer" literature, or even of its authors, would require more space than this book has available. The major books in the "debunking" stream are those of Donald H. Menzel, Philip Klass, and Robert Sheaffer. Plentiful debunking materials may be found at websites like http://www.csicop.org/, http://www.astronomyufo.com/UFO/UFO.htm, http://www.reall.org/. The authoritative reference on UFOlogy, written from a believer perspective but critical and balanced throughout is Jerome Clark, *The UFO Encyclopedia*, 3rd ed., 2 vols. (Detroit: Omnigraphics, 2018), henceforth *UFOE3*. **Donald Menzel . . . Carl Jung:** Donald H. Menzel, *The World of Flying Saucers: A Scientific Examination of a Major Myth of the Space Age*, with Lyle G. Boyd (New York: Doubleday, 1963); C.G. Jung, *Flying Saucers: A Modern Myth of Things Seen in the Skies* (New York: Harcourt, Brace, 1959), trans. R.F.C. Hull, *Ein moderner Mythus von Dingen, die am Himmel gesehen werden* (Zurich: Rascher & Cie., 1958). **twenty-first century cognitive psychologists:** e.g., Justin L. Barrett, *Why Would Anyone Believe in God?* (Walnut Creek, CA: AltaMira Press, 2004); Justin L. Barrett, *Born Believers: The Science of Children's Religious Belief* (New York: Free Press, 2012); Bruce M. Hood, *Supersense:*

Why We Believe in the Unbelievable (New York: Harper One, 2009); Jesse Bering, *The God Instinct: The Psychology of Souls, Destiny, and the Meaning of Life* (London: Nicholas Brealey, 2011). **Freudian dictum:** *Moses and Monotheism* (New York: Vintage Books, 1939), 107. **recent book on UFOs:** David Clarke, *How UFOs Conquered the World: The History of a Modern Myth* (London: Aurum Press, 2015). **Simon and Garfunkel:** Paul Simon and Art Garfunkel, "The Sound of Silence," recorded June 15, 1965, Columbia Records. **Area 51:** Annie Jacobsen, *Area 51: An Uncensored History of America's Top Secret Military Base* (New York: Little, Brown, 2011). **Barack Obama:** Paige Lavender, "I Think I Just Became the First President to Ever Mention Area 51," *Huffington Post*, December 9, 2013, http://www.huffingtonpost.com/2013/12/09/obama-area-51_n_4412310.html. **Hillary Clinton:** Lee Spiegel, "Hillary Clinton Vows to Investigate UFOs and Area 51," *Huffington Post*, January 4, 2016, http://www.huffingtonpost.com/entry/hillary-clinton-vows-to-investigate-ufos_us_5687073ce4b014efe0da95db. **"courting the UFO believer vote":** Mike Albo, "Hillary Courts UFO Believer Vote," *Good*, January 7, 2016, https://magazine.good.is/articles/hilary-ufo-politics. Clinton's remarks were made on December 29, 2015. **ABC News:** Alon Harish, "UFOs Exist, Say 36 Percent in *National Geographic* Survey," *ABC News*, June 27, 2012, https://abcnews.go.com/Technology/ufos-exist-americans-national-geographic-survey/story?id=16661311. **earlier surveys:** Thomas E. Bullard, *The Myth and Mystery of UFOs* (Lawrence: University Press of Kansas, 2010), 84–85; Roper Poll, "UFOs & Extraterrestrial Life: Americans' Beliefs and Personal Experiences," prepared for Sci Fi Channel, September 2002, https://web.archive.org/web/20071210164517/http://www.scifi.com/ufo/roper. **Why . . . want of public interest?** George P. Hansen, "James W. Moseley as Trickster," in *The Astounding UFO Secrets of James W. Moseley*, ed. Timothy Green Beckley (New Brunswick, NJ: Global Communications, 2013), 18–23. **folklorist Thomas Bullard:** Bullard, *Myth and Mystery*, 4; cf. George P. Hansen, *The Trickster and the Paranormal* (Bloomington, IN: Xlibris Corporation, 2001), 210–71. **squirmed away from the challenge:** Philip J. Klass, *UFOs Explained* (New York: Random House, 1974), 354–60. **George Orwell:** Orwell, "As I Please," April 14, 1944, in *The Collected Essays, Journalism and Letters of George Orwell*, ed. Sonia Orwell and Ian Angus, vol. 3, *As I Please: 1943–1945* (New York and London: Harcourt Brace Jovanovich, 1968), 122, referring to the belief in Hell professed by G.K. Chesterton. **betray an emotional engagement:** Allan Hendry, *The UFO Handbook: A Guide to Investigating, Evaluating and Reporting UFO Sightings* (Garden City, NY: Doubleday, 1979), 106–7. **symposium on UFOs:** Carl Sagan and Thornton Page eds., *UFOs—A Scientific Debate* (New York: Barnes & Noble Books, with Cornell University Press, 1972). **force its cancellation:** Sagan and Page, 301–2. **two psychiatrists:** Lester Grinspoon and Alan D. Persky, "Psychiatry and UFO Reports," in Sagan and Page, 245–46. **"feel the emotional tug of such things":** George Orwell, "Antisemitism in Britain," in Orwell and Angus, *Collected Essays*, vol. 3, 341. **Kenneth Arnold sighting . . . Socorro, New Mexico:** "Arnold Sighting," *UFOE3* 1:169–72; Don Ecsedy, "The Flying Saucer as I Saw It, Kenneth Arnold," *Foreshadower*, n.d., http://www.foreshadower.net/The%20Flying%20Saucer%20As%20I%20Saw%20It.php; "The Wraith of Arnold," *Foreshadower*, March 21, 2013, http://www.foreshadower.net/The%20Wraith%20of%20Arnold.php.; J.

Allen Hynek, *The UFO Experience: A Scientific Inquiry* (Chicago: Henry Regnery, 1972), 144–45; Matt Graeber, "21st Century UFOlogy, Part IV—Socorro Revisited," *SUNlite* 2, no. 2 (March-April 2010), 15–21, http://www.astronomyufo.com/UFO/SUNlite2_2.pdf; "Socorro CE2/CE3," *UFOE3* 2:1083–93. **"the best UFO case ever?"** Patrick Huyghe, "The Best UFO Case Ever?," in *Swamp Gas Times: My Two Decades on the UFO Beat* (New York: Paraview Press, 2001), 309–33. **A few other cases:** "Delphos CE2," *UFOE3* 1:400–402 (November 2, 1971); "Trans-en-Provence CE2," *UFOE3* 2:1131–32 (January 8, 1981). **10 percent were unsolved:** Estimates of the percentage of "unknowns" among total UFO reports range from 20 percent down to the single digits: Hendry, *UFO Handbook*, 22, 264; Cheryl Costa and Linda Miller Costa, *UFO Sightings Desk Reference: United States of America 2001–2015* (Syracuse, NY: Dragon Lady Media, 2017), 9–11; "Identification Studies of UFOs," Wikipedia, https://en.wikipedia.org/wiki/Identification_studies_of_UFOs. **photos taken by an Oregon farmer:** "McMinnville Photos," *UFOE3* 1:702–4. ***Footnote 1*: Ralph Blumenthal:** Helene Cooper, Ralph Blumenthal, and Leslie Kean, "Glowing Auras and 'Black Money': The Pentagon's Mysterious U.F.O. Program," *New York Times*, December 16, 2017, https://www.nytimes.com/2017/12/16/us/politics/pentagon-program-ufo-harry-reid.html. **Interviewed on MSNBC:** "Interview with Ralph Blumenthal: The Pentagon UFO Study," MSNBC, December 17, 2017, https://youtu.be/T-Dp1FzKods. **D.W. Pasulka:** D.W. Pasulka, *American Cosmic: UFOs, Religion, Technology* (New York: Oxford University Press, 2019), 17–24, 47–50, 73–77, 240–44.

CHAPTER 1: CONFESSIONS OF A TEENAGE UFOLOGIST

Kenneth Arnold: "Arnold Sighting," *UFOE3* 1:169–72; Don Ecsedy, "The Flying Saucer as I Saw It, Kenneth Arnold," *Foreshadower*, n.d., http://www.foreshadower.net/The%20Flying%20Saucer%20As%20I%20Saw%20It.php; "The Wraith of Arnold," *Foreshadower*, March 21, 2013, http://www.foreshadower.net/The%20Wraith%20of%20Arnold.php. **Roswell, New Mexico:** Karl T. Pflock, *Roswell: Inconvenient Facts and the Will to Believe* (Amherst, NY: Prometheus Books, 2001), 26. Additional references can be found in chapter 8 notes. **seven-foot monster:** Gray Barker, *They Knew Too Much About Flying Saucers* (New York: University Books, 1956), 11–35; five articles in *Goldenseal: West Virginia Traditional Life* 28, no. 3 (Fall 2002), http://www.wvculture.org/goldenseal/fall02/fall02.html. **"Shaver Mystery":** Barker, 59–67. **"Three men in black suits":** Barker, 92–93. **"invisible college":** Frances A. Yates, *The Rosicrucian Enlightenment* (London and Boston: Routledge & Kegan Paul, 1972); "J. Allen Hynek Center for UFO Studies," *UFOE3* 1:627. **"I have always felt":** Barker, *They Knew Too Much*, 129. **"My readers":** Barker, 140. **"died of a peculiar disease":** Barker, 62–63. **"Whoever or whatever":** Barker, 139. **"last great public investigative enterprise":** Brenda Denzler, *The Lure of the Edge: Scientific Passions, Religious Beliefs, and the Pursuit of UFOs* (Berkeley: University of California Press, 2001), 69, quoting David and Therese Marie Barclay, eds., *UFOs: The Final Answer?* (London: Blandford Press, 1993). **mimeographed *NJAAP Bulletin*:** *The NJAAP Bulletin*, November 27, 1963, David Halperin: Journal of a UFO Investigator, 2019, http://www.davidhalperin.net/wp-content/uploads/2012/08/NJAAP-Bulletin1.

pdf. **On April 24 . . . Lonnie Zamora:** J. Allen Hynek, *The UFO Experience: A Scientific Inquiry* (Chicago: Henry Regnery, 1972), 144–45; Patrick Huyghe, *Swamp Gas Times: My Two Decades on the UFO Beat* (New York: Paraview Press, 2001), 309–33; Matt Graeber, "21st Century UFOlogy, Part IV—Socorro Revisited," *SUNlite* 2, no. 2 (March-April 2010), 15–21, http://www.astronomyufo.com/UFO/SUNlite2_2.pdf; "Socorro CE2/CE3," *UFOE3* 2:1083–93; see Frederik Pohl, "The Fanciful World of Flying Saucers," in *The* NEW *Report on Flying Saucers: By the Publishers of* TRUE, ed. Frank Bowers (New York: Fawcett, 1967), 48–49, 73–76. **Glassboro, New Jersey:** David Halperin, "UFO Landing in Glassboro, NJ—Fifty Years Ago," *David Halperin* (blog), September 12, 2014, http://www.davidhalperin.net/ufo-landing-in-glassboro-nj-fifty-years-ago/. **the publisher will recall:** Ed Conroy, *Report on* Communion*: An Independent Investigation of and Commentary on Whitley Strieber's* Communion (New York: William Morrow, 1989), 38, quoting publisher James Landis. ***New York Times* bestseller list:** "Adult New York Times Adult Hardcover Best Seller Listings," September 20, 1987, Hawes Publications, http://www.hawes.com/pastlist.htm.

CHAPTER 2: SCENES FROM MAGONIA

Charles Lindbergh . . . Carl Jung: A. Scott Berg, *Lindbergh* (New York: Putnam's, 1998), 511–12; Deirdre Bair, *Jung: A Biography* (Boston: Little, Brown, 2003), 572–73; Arthur I. Miller, *Deciphering the Cosmic Number: The Strange Friendship of Wolfgang Pauli and Carl Jung* (New York: W.W. Norton, 2009), 244–46. The source for the encounter is an unpublished letter written by Lindbergh on December 11, 1968. **a mantra for Jung's old teacher, Sigmund Freud:** Ernest Jones, *The Life and Work of Sigmund Freud*, vol. 3 (New York: Basic Books, 1957), 381. **"UFOs Considered in a Non-Psychological Light":** C.G. Jung, *Flying Saucers: A Modern Myth of Things Seen in the Skies* (New York: Harcourt, Brace, 1959), 146–53. **"repressed uterus":** Jung, 30. **Jacques Vallee . . . Claude Lacombe:** Jeffrey J. Kripal, *Authors of the Impossible: The Paranormal and the Sacred* (Chicago: University of Chicago Press, 2010), 144; Mark O'Connell, *The Close Encounters Man: How One Man Made the World Believe in UFOs* (New York: HarperCollins, 2017), 320, who quotes J. Allen Hynek as proposing French space scientist Claude Poher as the model for the Lacombe character. Kripal's view seems the more solidly grounded. ***Passport to Magonia*:** Jacques Vallee, *Passport to Magonia: From Folklore to Flying Saucers* (Chicago: Henry Regnery, 1969). **Thomas Jefferson:** Anna Berkes, "Who Is the Liar Now?," *Monticello* (blog and community), November 14, 2008, http://www.monticello.org/site/blog-and-community/posts/who-liar-now. **Magonia, "land of the magicians":** Miceal Ross, "Anchors in a Three-Decker World," *Folklore* 109 (1998): 63–75; David Halperin, "The Magonia Problem," posted November 19, 2011, on *Magonia*, currently accessible at *More Magonia* (blog), http://moremagonia.blogspot.co.uk/2017/07/the-magonia-problem.html. **"psychosocial" theory:** Jerome Clark, "The Extraterrestrial Hypothesis in the Early UFO Age," in *UFOs and Abductions: Challenging the Borders of Knowledge*, ed. David M. Jacobs (Lawrence: University Press of Kansas, 2000), 139; Clark, "Psychosocial Hypothesis," *UFOE3* 2:938–48; Thomas E. Bullard, *The Myth and Mystery of UFOs* (Lawrence: University Press of Kansas, 2010), 252–85; David Clarke, *How*

UFOs Conquered the World: The History of a Modern Myth (London: Aurum Press, 2015). The outstanding organ of the "psychosocial" theory until 2008 was John Rimmer's *Magonia*, which maintains a web presence at *Magonia* Archive, http://magoniamagazine.blogspot.com/. **classic W.C. Fields movie:** *The Fatal Glass of Beer*, prod. Mack Sennett (Paramount Pictures, 1933). **UFOlogist Matt Graeber's phone:** The account that follows is taken from Matt Graeber, "The Cat and Mice Game," *SUNlite* 1, no. 4 (November-December 2009): 20–24, http://www.astronomyufo.com/UFO/SUNlite1_4.pdf. The drawing, reproduced here from an original provided through the kindness of the late UFOlogist's son, Matt Graeber, Jr., was made by Graeber from the witness's sketch. **Saturn-like ring:** Richard H. Hall, "Dyad 'Scout Craft,'" *IUR* 25, no. 4 (Winter 2000–01): 23–25; David Halperin, "A Case from the 'International UFO Reporter'—Scout Craft or Psychic Entities?," *David Halperin* (blog), November 17, 2015, http://www.davidhalperin.net/a-case-from-the-international-ufo-reporter-scout-craft-or-psychic-entities/. **my Facebook Fan Page:** David Halperin, January 13, 2013, Facebook, https://www.facebook.com/JournalofaUFOInvestigator; "Austin Powers (part 2) Giant Johnson," YouTube, https://youtu.be/EkdOAgQMQvA. ***Footnote* 7: Soviet moon probe Zond IV:** Thomas Bullard, *The Myth and Mystery of UFOs* (Lawrence: University Press of Kansas, 2010), 30–31. **Cedar Rapids, Iowa:** Kevin D. Randle, "UFOs on Memory Lane," *IUR* 26, no. 1 (Spring 2001): 9–11, 30; David Halperin, "A Case from the 'International UFO Reporter'—Scout Craft or Psychic Entities?," *David Halperin* (blog), November 17, 2015, http://www.davidhalperin.net/a-case-from-the-international-ufo-reporter-scout-craft-or-psychic-entities/. **the skies of Belgium . . . were filled with them:** Eric Ouellet, *Illuminations: The UFO Experience as a Parapsychological Event* (San Antonio and Charlottesville: Anomalist Books, 2015), 67–89, based largely on the two-volume report published by SOBEPS (Société belge d'étude des phénomènes spatiaux): *Vague d'OVNI sur la Belgique: Un dossier exceptionnel* (1991) and *Vague d'OVNI sur la Belgique, tome 2: Une énigme non résolue* (1994). For other accounts of the Belgian wave, see Richard M. Dolan, *UFOs and the National Security State: The Cover-Up Exposed, 1973–1991* (Rochester, NY: Keyhole Publishing, 2009), 500–502, 519–26; Leslie Kean, *UFOs: Generals, Pilots, and Government Officials Go on the Record* (New York: Harmony Books, 2010), 17–40. **The systematic history of the triangular UFO:** David Marler, *Triangular UFOs: An Estimate of the Situation* (CreateSpace Independent Publishing Platform, 2013; I owe this reference to Warren Naujalis); see also the index to Dolan, *UFOs and the National Security State*, s.v. "triangle-shaped aerial objects." **"signs and wonders" in the skies:** Jacques Vallee and Chris Aubeck, *Wonders in the Sky: Unexplained Aerial Objects from Antiquity to Modern Times* (New York: Jeremy P. Tarcher/Penguin, 2009); Vallee and Aubeck, *Wonders in the Sky*, deluxe ed., rev. (San Francisco: Documatica Research, 2016). **Yet radar is not infallible:** Kenneth R. Hardy, "Unusual Radar Echoes," in Carl Sagan and Thornton Page, eds., *UFO's—A Scientific Debate* (New York: Barnes & Noble Books, 1972), 183–89; Allan Hendry, *The UFO Handbook: A Guide to Investigating, Evaluating and Reporting UFO Sightings* (Garden City, NY: Doubleday, 1979), 70–71, 223–36. **without benefit of drink or drugs or sensory deprivation:** cf. Oliver Sacks, *Hallucinations* (New York: Alfred A. Knopf, 2012). **Morton Schatzman . . . "Ruth":** Morton

Schatzman, *The Story of Ruth* (New York: Putnam's, 1980). **Historian Ronald Hutton:** Ronald Hutton, *The Triumph of the Moon: A History of Modern Pagan Witchcraft* (Oxford: Oxford University Press, 1999), 269–71. ***Footnote 10:*** **A single mother in her thirties:** Russ Estes, in Kevin P. Randle, Russ Estes, and William P. Cone, *The Abduction Enigma* (New York: Forge Books, 1999), 72–79. **"Miracle of the Sun":** Jeffrey J. Kripal, *Authors of the Impossible: The Paranormal and the Sacred* (Chicago: University of Chicago Press, 2010), 275–82. **"Flying Saucers of Other Days":** Harold T. Wilkins, *Flying Saucers on the Attack* (New York: Citadel Press, 1954), 157–203. **suggestions of Jacques Vallee:** Jacques Vallee, *The Invisible College: What a Group of Scientists Has Discovered About UFO Influence on the Human Race* (New York: E.P. Dutton, 1975), summarized in D.W. Pasulka, *American Cosmic: UFOs, Religion, Technology* (New York: Oxford University Press, 2019), 162–71. **archival research by Portuguese UFOlogists:** translated from the Portuguese and published by Anomalist Books in its Fátima Trilogy: Joaquim Fernandes and Fina d'Armada, *Heavenly Lights: The Apparitions of Fátima and the UFO Phenomenon* (San Antonio and New York: Anomalist Books, 2005); Joaquim Fernandes and Fina d'Armada, *Celestial Secrets: The Hidden History of the Fátima Incident* (2006); Fernando Fernandes, Joaquim Fernandes, and Raul Berenguel, *Fátima Revisited: The Apparition Phenomenon in Ufology, Psychology, and Science* (2008). ***Footnote 11:*** **Truman Bethurum:** Truman Bethurum, *Aboard a Flying Saucer* (Los Angeles: DeVorss, 1954); "Bethurum Contact Claims," *UFOE3* 1:192–93. **Abraham Cardozo:** David J. Halperin, *Abraham Miguel Cardozo: Selected Writings*, Classics of Western Spirituality (Mahwah, NJ: Paulist Press, 2001), 84–86, 285–88. **Fifty thousand . . . Johannes Kepler:** Edward Rosen, trans., *Somnium: The Dream, or Posthumous Work on Lunar Astronomy* (Madison: University of Wisconsin Press, 1967), 15. **science-fiction bestseller of 1638:** Francis Godwin, *Man in the Moone; or A Discourse of a Voyage Thither by Domingo Gonsales*, summarized in Marjorie Hope Nicolson, *Voyages to the Moon* (New York: Macmillan, 1948), 71–85. **"all dressed in black":** Halperin, *Cardozo*, 389n37. The variant makes clear that all three entities were clad in black. **Virgin of the Immaculate Conception:** David Halperin, "Abraham Miguel Cardozo and the Woman on the Moon," *Kabbalah: Journal for the Study of Jewish Mystical Texts* 8 (2003): 51–64. **the *quaternity*:** C.G. Jung, "A Psychological Approach to the Dogma of the Trinity," in *Psychology and Religion: West and East*, vol. 11 of Jung, *Collected Works* (Princeton, NJ: University Press, 1958), 109–200. **ancient rabbinic literature:** David J. Halperin, *The Faces of the Chariot: Early Jewish Responses to Ezekiel's Vision* (Tübingen, Ger.: J.C.B. Mohr, 1988), 190–91. **A cigar, Freud . . . cigar:** Ralph Keyes, *The Quote Verifier: Who Said What, Where, and When* (New York: St. Martin's Griffin, 2006), 29–30. **Four Messiahs:** Halperin, *Cardozo*, 249–51, 264–66. **"Gill sighting":** in addition to the VFSRS report cited in note 8 in the chapter text, see J. Allen Hynek, *The UFO Experience* (Chicago: Henry Regnery, 1972), 145–50, 241–42; Donald H. Menzel, "UFO's—The Modern Myth," Appendix 1, in *UFO's—A Scientific Debate*, ed. Carl Sagan and Thornton Page (Ithaca, NY: Cornell University Press, 1972), 146–53; Philip J. Klass, *UFOs Explained* (New York: Random House, 1974), 234–44; "Gill CE3," *UFOE3* 1:533–36; and a series of important articles by Martin Kottmeyer: "Gill Again: The Father Gill Case Reconsidered," *Magonia* 54 (November 1995) and *Magonia* 55 (March 1996), http://

magoniamagazine.blogspot.com/2013/12/gill-again-father-gill-case-reconsidered.html; Kottmeyer, "The Astronomical Solution to Father William Gill's Position Sketches of 5 UFOs Seen over Papua, New Guinea on the evening of June 26, 1959," *The REALL News* 15, no. 5 (May 2007): 1, 4–9; Kottmeyer, "Gill's Sketch of 8 UFOs—A Solution," *Mrherr Zaar* Facebook page, May 16, 2017, https://www.facebook.com/la.wan.3538/posts/1895276350714620?__tn__=K-R. **twenty-five of them:** The names—twenty-five, including Gill, and including six teachers and two medical assistants—are listed on p. 12 of the VFSRS report. The introduction to Gill's report by the VFSRS speaks of twenty-seven people having signed "the original statement examined by VFSRS investigators." Had two people requested their names be deleted? **"they were angels":** attributed to Gill, not by name but by clear allusion, in Gary Bates, *Alien Intrusion: UFOs and the Evolution Connection* (Green Forest, AR: Master Books, 2004), 221. Bates claims to have heard Gill say this "at a conference I attended" (no date given). I thank Martin Kottmeyer for supplying me with this reference. **Gill offered a string of rejoinders:** quoted in "Gill CE3," *UFOE3* 1:535. **Nearly twenty years:** *UFOE3* 1:535. **Gill . . . scoffed at both ideas:** *UFOE3* 1:535. **We humans . . . subtle ways:** Bruce M. Hood, *Supersense: Why We Believe in the Unbelievable* (New York: Harper One, 2009), 25. **An indigenous belief:** Bill Gammage, *The Sky Travellers: Journeys in New Guinea 1938–39* (Melbourne: Miegunyah Press of Melbourne University Press, 1998), 1. **the land of the cargo cults:** Peter Lawrence, *Road Belong Cargo: A Study of the Cargo Movement in the Southern Madang District, New Guinea* (Manchester, UK: Manchester University Press, 1964); Peter Worsley, *The Trumpet Shall Sound: A Study of "Cargo" Cults in Melanesia*, 2nd ed. (New York: Schocken Books, 1968); G.W. Trompf, ed., *Cargo Cults and Millenarian Movements: Transoceanic Comparisons of New Religious Movements* (Berlin: De Gruyter Mouton, 1990); Trompf, "UFO Religions and Cargo Cults," in *UFO Religions*, ed. Christopher Partridge (London and New York: Routledge, 2003), 221–38. The possibility of a "cargo" connection in the Gill sighting is discussed but deemed improbable in Kottmeyer, "Gill Again" (November 1995). **Papuan university student:** G.W. Trompf, *Melanesian Religion* (Cambridge, UK: Cambridge University Press, 1991), 123–26. **"That 'great white leader' business":** *UFOE3* 1:535. The information that Gill left Boianai in September 1959 is on p. 534. **"totality . . . the archetype of self":** Jung, *Flying Saucers*, 20–21. **"if we got them to land":** *UFOE3* 1:535.

CHAPTER 3: THE ABDUCTIONS BEGIN

Betty and Barney Hill . . . Benjamin Simon: John G. Fuller, *The Interrupted Journey: Two Lost Hours "Aboard a Flying Saucer"*, with introduction by Benjamin Simon, MD (New York: Dial Press, 1966). The presenting symptoms (other than Barney's high blood pressure) are listed by Simon on p. 278, the blood pressure and the warts on p. 53. **"in analysing a dream":** Sigmund Freud, *The Interpretation of Dreams*, trans. and ed. James Strachey (New York: Avon Books, 1965), 555. **Betty wrote a week later to Major Donald E. Keyhoe:** letter to Donald Keyhoe, September 26, 1961, in Fuller, *Interrupted Journey*, 29–30. **Transcripts of the tape-recorded hypnotic sessions:** February 22 transcript in Fuller, ch. 5. **"This is *not* a flying saucer":** Fuller, 78. **"I want to wake**

up": Fuller, 82–83. **"showed very marked emotional discharge":** Fuller, 103. **UFO debunker Philip Klass:** *UFOs—Identified* (New York: Random House, 1968), 229–30. **Walter Webb . . . reported:** quoted in Stanton T. Friedman and Kathleen Marden, *Captured! The Betty and Barney Hill UFO Experience* (Franklin Lakes, NJ: New Page Books, 2007), 52. **"Dr. Simon had become sort of a close friend":** Fuller, *Interrupted Journey*, 132. **"I was hunting for rabbits":** Fuller, 88–89. **a past even more distant:** suggestion anticipated by C.B. Scott Jones, "Push My Buttons: Color and Sex," in *Phoenix in the Labyrinth* (Falls Church, VA: Human Potential Foundation, 1995), 52–75, cited by Brenda Denzler, *The Lure of the Edge: Scientific Passions, Religious Beliefs, and the Pursuit of UFOs* (Berkeley: University of California Press, 2001), 238. I have not seen Jones's book. **The year: 1763:** Marcus Rediker, *The Slave Ship: A Human History* (New York: Viking, 2007), 88–90. **You were abducted:** Rediker, *The Slave Ship*, 102. **"dark faces, framed by small holes":** Rediker, 2. **slave ships . . . altogether fantastic:** Rediker, 104–5, 147. **reaching into her mouth:** Fuller, *Interrupted Journey*, 175–76. **attention to their potential purchases' teeth:** Eric Robert Taylor, *If We Must Die: Shipboard Insurrections in the Era of the Atlantic Slave Trade* (Baton Rouge: Louisiana State University Press, 2006), 22–23; contemporary accounts of slave auctions at "Slave Auction, 1859," Eyewitness to History, 2005, http://www.eyewitnesstohistory.com/slaveauction.htm; "Slave Auctions: Selections from 19th-Century Narratives of Formerly Enslaved African Americans," *The Making of African American Identity,* vol 1., *1500–1865*, National Humanities Center Resource Toolbox, 2007, http://nationalhumanitiescenter.org/pds/maai/enslavement/text2/slaveauctions.pdf. ***Footnote 16:* one slave-trade historian's description:** Taylor, *If We Must Die*, 22-23. ***Footnote 17:* "My mouth was opened":** Fuller, *Interrupted Journey*, 187. **"two dreams, really":** Fuller, *Interrupted Journey*, 238. No such "body of water" is mentioned in the appendix to Fuller's book (295–302), which purports to be an account of Betty's dreams that she wrote down shortly after the experience (and well before the hypnosis). I have my doubts whether this narrative is what it claims to be. It feels much too fluent and coherent, not at all dreamlike, and it presupposes that the UFO pilots are a different species from us—whereas throughout most of the hypnotic sessions they're treated as essentially human. **his neck is left bruised:** Fuller, 254–55. **"coffles" . . . neck:** Taylor, *If We Must Die*, 15; *Narrative of the Life and Adventures of Charles Ball, a Black Man* (Pittsburg, 1854), in Ulrich B. Phillips, *Plantation and Frontier, 1649–1863* (Cleveland: A.H. Clark, 1909), 59; David and Charles Livingstone, *Narrative of an Expedition to the Zambesi and Its Tributaries . . .* (New York: Harper & Brothers, 1866), 374–79, from which figure 3 is taken; this and other illustrations in "Capture of Slaves and Coffles in Africa," *Slavery Images: A Visual Record of the African Slave Trade and Slave Life in the Early African Diaspora*, http://www.slaveryimages.org/s/slaveryimages/item-set/38. **children and grandchildren of Holocaust survivors:** Dina Wardi, quoted in Daan van Kampenhout, *The Tears of the Ancestors: Victims and Perpetrators in the Tribal Soul* (Phoenix, AZ: Zeig, Tucker & Theisen, 2008), 70; M. Gerard Fromm, ed., *Lost in Transmission: Studies of Trauma Across Generations* (London: Karnac Books, 2011). ***Footnote 18:* "Ghost in Your Genes":** "The Ghost in Your Genes" (transcript), *NOVA*, PBS, October 16, 2007, https://www.pbs.org/wgbh/nova/transcripts/3413_genes.html; cf. the more skeptical treatment in Nessa Carey, *The Epigenetics Revolution: How Modern Biology Is Rewriting Our Understanding of Genetics, Disease, and Inheritance* (New York: Columbia University Press, 2012), 97–114. **"I would look over at Betty":** Fuller, *Interrupted Journey*, 255. **Philip Klass:** Klass, *UFOs—Identified*, 230. **another New Hampshire family:** Jim Macdonald, "Alien Abduction: Betty & Barney Hill," *Making Light* (blog), posted September 19, 2007, http://nielsenhayden.com/makinglight/archives/009378.html. **the observation tower had been torn down:** "Details for Benchmark: PF0988," royswkr, "Fire tower . . . now removed," 9/24/2008 post, Geocaching, http://www.geocaching.com/mark/details.aspx?PID=PF0988. An earlier note, dated 8/3/2007, "confirmed that the tower is still there." **It was apparently replaced:** Tim Printy, "Taking the Betty and Barney Hill Drive," *SUNlite* 4, no. 2 (March-April 2012), 6–9, http://www.astronomyufo.com/UFO/SUNlite4_2.pdf. **"slanted . . . but not like a Chinese":** Fuller, *Interrupted Journey*, 88. **a sketch he made:** Fuller, 143; reproduced as figure 4. **Barney later told John Fuller:** Fuller, 260. **UFO skeptic and pop-culture expert Martin Kottmeyer:** Martin Kottmeyer, "The Eyes that Spoke," *Skeptical Inquirer* 4, no. 3 (September 1994), http://www.csicop.org/sb/show/eyes_that_spoke/. **"the eyes don't have a body":** Fuller, *Interrupted Journey*, 95. **"white men with horrible looks":** Taylor, *If We Must Die*, 26; Rediker, *The Slave Ship*, 108; both quoting *The Interesting Narrative of the Life of Olaudah Equiano*, published in 1789, describing events of 1754, during the former slave's childhood, http://www.gutenberg.org/ebooks/15399. **pushing a long needle:** Fuller, *Interrupted Journey*, 164–65. **"My groin feels cold . . . cup around my groin":** Fuller, 117, 123. **historical highway marker:** Lee Speigel, "Betty and Barney Hill UFO Abduction Story Commemorated On Official N.H. Highway Plaque," *Huffington Post*, July 25, 2011, http://www.huffingtonpost.com/2011/07/25/betty-and-barney-hill-ufo-experience_n_907770.html.

CHAPTER 4: THE LURE OF THE UNREMEMBERED

Dr. Rima Laibow: Dr. Rima Laibow, interview by Patrick Huyghe, in *Swamp Gas Times: My Two Decades on the UFO Beat* (New York: Paraview Press, 2001), 144–46; originally published in OMNI, September 1993. **stellar sales:** "Adult New York Times Adult Hardcover Best Seller Listings," Hawes Publications, http://www.hawes.com/pastlist.htm. **no critical acclaim whatsoever:** Gregory Benford, "They're Only Humanoids," *New York Times Book Review*, March 15, 1987; David Brooks, "Summertime Best Sellers: Irrationality Pays," *Wall Street Journal*, June 2, 1987. **a master artist named Ted Jacobs:** "About/Faculty," Studio Escalier: Contemporary Classical Art Center, n.d., https://studioescalier.com/students/faculty/; "Classical Realism," Wikipedia, https://en.wikipedia.org/wiki/Classical_Realism. An extensive website showcasing Jacobs's work, which I saw a few years ago, appears to have been removed. **nearly two hundred thousand such letters:** Whitley and Anne Strieber, *The* Communion *Letters* (London: Simon & Schuster, 1998; originally published 1997), 3, and dedication page; different numbers in Whitley Strieber and Jeffrey J. Kripal, *The Super Natural: A New Vision of the Unexplained* (New York: Jeremy P. Tarcher/Random House, 2016), 32. The archive of surviving letters, numbering in the thousands, is now available to researchers in the Anne and Whitley

Strieber Collection, Woodson Research Center, Fondren Library, Rice University, Houston. A selection of about one hundred is published in *The* Communion *Letters*. **"Sitting right there on the kitchen stove":** *The* Communion *Letters*, 27–29. **One man recalled:** John Mack, *Abduction: Human Encounters with Aliens* (New York: Scribner's, 1994), 271. **biochemist Kary Mullis:** *Dancing Naked in the Mind Field* (New York: Pantheon Books, 1998), 130–36. **Easy to make fun:** Thomas M. Disch's reviews in *The Nation* of *Communion* (March 14, 1987) and its sequel *Transformation* (November 14, 1988) provide repellent examples. The anal rape described by Strieber (see next section of this chapter) was cruelly parodied in Trey Parker and Matt Stone, "Cartman Gets an Anal Probe," *South Park* (pilot), August 1997, Comedy Central Network. **temporal lobe epilepsy:** Philip J. Klass, *UFO Abductions: A Dangerous Game* (Buffalo, NY: Prometheus Books, 1989), 135–36; cf. the exchange of letters between Ed Conroy and Dr. Donald F. Klein in Ed Conroy, *Report on* Communion*: An Independent Investigation of and Commentary on Whitley Strieber's* Communion (New York: William Morrow, 1989), 43–51. **the night of December 26, 1985:** Whitley Strieber, *Communion: A True Story* (New York: Avon Books, 1987), 11–21. **"the most essentially and powerfully feminine presence":** Strieber and Kripal, *The Super Natural*, 130. **Klein hypnotized Strieber:** transcripts in Strieber, *Communion*, 52–66 (March 1), 69–84 (March 6), 144–51 (March 10), 152–60 (March 14). **Klein would author a statement:** Strieber, 303; cf. Conroy, *Report on* Communion, 48. **Strieber speaks of being sodomized**: Strieber, *Communion*, 77–79 (March 6). **he could not tell what he remembered from what he imagined:** University of Texas episode discussed in Conroy, 91–96. Two further examples of the fluidity of Strieber's memories at David Halperin, "Alien Abduction, 'Erotic Mysticism'—The Strieber and Kripal Challenge (Part 2), *David Halperin* (blog), November 18, 2016, https://www.davidhalperin.net/alien-abduction-erotic-mysticism-the-strieber-and-kripal-challenge-part-2. **a short story called "Pain":** Whitley Strieber, "Pain," in Dennis Etchison, ed., *Cutting Edge* (Garden City, NY: Doubleday, 1986), https://www.scribd.com/document/194411862/Pain-by-Whitley-Strieber. Disch's review of *Communion* in *The Nation* stresses the importance of this story for understanding *Communion*. Cf. Strieber and Kripal, *The Super Natural*, 131–33. **she and the "powerfully feminine presence" . . . were one and the same:** cf. Strieber and Kripal, 133. **"anima" . . . "unconscious":** Strieber, *Communion*, 100. **"little green men":** Martin S. Kottmeyer, "Little Green Men," *The Anomalist* 10 (2002), 189–218. **said to have crashed in 1948:** Frank Scully, *Behind the Flying Saucers* (New York: Henry Holt, 1950). For this and the incidents described in the following paragraphs, see "Scully Hoax," *UFOE3* 2:1044–47; "Kelly-Hopkinsville CE3," *UFOE3* 1:642–43; "Close Encounters of the Third Kind," *UFOE3* 1:269–70; "Villas-Boas CE3," *UFOE3* 2:1226–29. ***Footnote 22:*** **"terrifying round object":** Whitley Strieber, *Communion: A True Story* (New York: Avon Books, 1987), 131. ***Footnote 23:*** **Coral and Jim Lorenzen:** Coral Lorenzen and Jim Lorenzen, *Flying Saucer Occupants* (New York: New American Library, 1967), 42–72. **shifted the blood-red hair:** Coral Lorenzen, interview with Kevin D. Randle (1972) in Kevin D. Randle, Russ Estes, and William P. Cone, *The Abduction Enigma* (New York: Forge Books, 1999), 33. ***Footnote 24:*** **J. Allen Hynek:** *The UFO Experience: A Scientific Inquiry*

(Chicago: Henry Regnery, 1972). **abducting aliens come in different shapes and sizes:** Thomas E. Bullard, *UFO Abductions: The Measure of a Mystery*, vol. 1 (Bloomington, IN: Fund for UFO Research, 1987), 238–80. **"The large, compelling eyes":** Bullard, vol. 1, 243–45. **the much-publicized abduction at Pascagoula:** "Pascagoula Abduction Case," *UFOE3* 2:893–98. The illustrations in Patrick Huyghe, *The Field Guide to Extraterrestrials* (New York: Avon Books, 1996) convey how little the eyes were characteristic of UFO aliens prior to the growth of the abduction tradition, and particularly prior to 1987. **sometimes proposed as a model:** e.g., Curtis Peebles, *Watch the Skies! A Chronicle of the Flying Saucer Myth* (Washington, DC: Smithsonian Institution Press, 1994), 234. **"Wells of darkness" . . . "old gods":** Strieber, *Communion*, 166, 89, 100. **sitting with Ted Jacobs:** Strieber, 165–66. **the ever-helpful Budd Hopkins:** Jacobs had worked with Hopkins at least since 1980, when he provided a painting of the alien abductors of "Steven Kilburn" (pseudonym) for Budd Hopkins, *Missing Time: A Documented Study of UFO Abductions* (New York: Richard Marek Publishers, 1981). **Abductions' Heyday: The 1990s:** David M. Jacobs, *Secret Life: Firsthand Documented Accounts of UFO Abductions* (New York: Simon & Schuster, 1992); John E. Mack, *Abduction: Human Encounters with Aliens* (New York: Charles Scribner's Sons, 1994); C. D. B. Bryan, *Close Encounters of the Fourth Kind: Alien Abduction, UFOs, and the Conference at MIT* (New York: Alfred A. Knopf, 1995); Thomas E. Bullard, "Abduction Phenomenon," *UFOE3* 1:1–38. **A story circulated:** not quite an urban legend, since the witness—Bruce Lee, a senior editor for *Communion*'s publisher William Morrow—was not only identified but stood by his story. First reported by Tracy Cochran, "Invasion of the Strieber Snatchers," *New York*, March 30, 1987, 26 (citing an unnamed "senior editor"); Whitley Strieber, afterword, *Transformation: The Breakthrough* (New York: Avon Books, 1988), 235–37; and Conroy, *Report on Communion*, 39–42. **that number had leaped into the thousands:** In the summer of 1992, Thomas E. Bullard sent a survey questionnaire to thirty-one abduction investigators; thirteen sent back usable responses. Those thirteen claimed to have dealt with a total of 1,700 cases of abduction: Bullard, "The Influence of Investigators on UFO Abduction Reports: Results of a Survey," in Andrea Pritchard et al., *Alien Discussions: Proceedings of the Abduction Study Conference Held at MIT, Cambridge, MA* (Cambridge, MA: North Cambridge Press, 1994), 571–619; more fully in *The Sympathetic Ear: Investigators as Variables in UFO Abduction Reports* (Mt. Rainier, MD: Fund for UFO Research, 1995). Extrapolate these figures to all thirty-one individuals queried, and the number of reported abductions rises above four thousand. **Roper poll of doubtful methodology:** *Unusual Personal Experiences: An Analysis of the Data from Three National Surveys Conducted by the Roper Organization* (Las Vegas: Bigelow Holding Corporation, 1992); Robert L. Hall, Mark Rodeghier, and Donald A. Johnson, "The Prevalence of Abductions: A Closer Look," *JUFOS* n.s. 4 (1992): 131–35; Peter Brookesmith, "Roper's Latest Knot: The 1998 Abduction Survey," *The Anomalist* 8 (2000): 32–38; Huyghe, *Swamp Gas Times*, 235–39. ***Footnote 28:* the comic strip *Guy Stuff*:** *Denver Post*, July 28, July 30, August 1, 1992. **the vanished children:** Bullard, *The Myth and Mystery of UFOs* (Lawrence: University Press of Kansas, 2010), 178–79; "Abduction Phenomenon," *UFOE3* 1:17. Bullard traces the popularity of the missing-children motif to the story of

"Kathie Davis," made famous through Budd Hopkins, *Intruders: The Incredible Visitations at Copley Woods* (New York: Random House, 1987). **alien eyes . . . their sexual overtones sometimes very blatant:** Jacobs, *Secret Life*, 96–99, 198, 202. **A male abductee:** Mack, *Abduction*, 177–200. **"Screen memories":** Sigmund Freud, "Screen Memories," in *The Standard Edition of the Complete Psychological Works of Sigmund Freud*, vol. 3 (London: Hogarth Press, 1953–1974), 301–22 (originally published in German in 1899). For the concept in the abduction literature, see Jacobs, *Secret Life*, 50; Geoff Olson, "The Eyes Have It," *IUR* 19, no. 6 (November-December 1994): 10–12; Strieber in Strieber and Kripal, *The Super Natural*, 214. **The friendship soured:** Klass, *UFO Abductions*, 141–49; cf. "Strieber, Louis Whitley," *UFOE3* 2:1112–14; Strieber, *Transformation*, 274–76. ***The UFO Controversy in America*:** David M. Jacobs, *The UFO Controversy in America* (Bloomington: Indiana University Press, 1975). **"We now know the alarming dimensions":** David M. Jacobs, *The Threat: Revealing the Secret Alien Agenda* (New York: Simon & Schuster, 1998), 258. **biography of T.E. Lawrence:** John E. Mack, *A Prince of Our Disorder: The Life of T.E. Lawrence* (Cambridge, MA: Harvard University Press, 1976). **raised in a secular Jewish household:** Ralph Blumenthal, "Alien Nation: Have Humans Been Abducted by Extraterrestrials?" posted May 10, 2013, *Vanity Fair*, https://www.vanityfair.com/culture/2013/05/americans-alien-abduction-science, published as "Alien Invasion" in the June 2013 print issue. **The thread running through Mack's endeavors:** Stephen Rae, "John Mack," *New York Times Magazine*, March 20, 1994, 30–33. **his hands-down favorite was an Israeli woman:** Mack, *Abduction*, 241–62. **In Beirut in 1980:** John E. Mack, "Trying to Make a Difference," in Ellen L. Bassuk and Rebecca W. Carman, eds., *The Doctor-Activist: Physicians Fighting for Social Change* (New York: Springer Science+Business Media, 1996), 224–25. **Lawrence . . . was also a pro-Zionist:** Mack, *Prince of Our Disorder*, 252–53, 259–61, 268–69; cf. David Fromkin, *A Peace to End All Peace: The Fall of the Ottoman Empire and the Creation of the Modern Middle East* (New York: Avon Books, 1989), 345; Andrew Lawler, "Alien Concepts: An Interview with Dr. John Mack," John Mack Institute, 2001, originally published in *New Age Journal*, July 2001, http://johnemackinstitute.org/2001/07/alien-concepts-an-interview-with-dr-john-mack/. **Bassett proclaimed her coup:** James Willwerth, "The Man From Outer Space," *Time*, April 25, 1994, 74–75, http://content.time.com/time/magazine/article/0,9171,164273,00.html; Thomas G. Genoni, Jr., "Exploring Mind, Memory, and the Psychology of Belief," *Skeptical Inquirer* 19, no. 1 (January/February 1995), https://www.csicop.org/si/show/exploring_mind_memory_and_the_psychology_of_belief. **Philip Klass wondered rhetorically:** *UFO Abductions: A Dangerous Game* (Buffalo, NY: Prometheus Books, 1989), 168–69. **Hopkins . . . using the words "I bet":** Bryan, *Close Encounters of the Fourth Kind*, 370, 386. **"Underground!"** Bryan, 375. **The friend who'd shared:** Bryan, 392. **The psychiatrist James S. Gordon:** "The UFO Experience," *Atlantic Monthly* 268, no. 2 (August 1991), 82–92. **Carl Sagan:** Budd Hopkins, "Carl Sagan and Me," *IUR* 22, no. 2 (Summer 1997): 11–12, 28–30. **A second Roper poll:** Brookesmith, "Roper's Latest Knot." **The "implants":** Keith Basterfield, "The Implant Motif in UFO Abduction Literature," *JUFOS* n.s. 8 (2003): 49–83. **not the era's only expedition back into the mists of the unremembered:** cf. Thomas Bullard, "False

Memories and UFO Abductions," *JUFOS* n.s. 8: 85–160. **"You may have no conscious memory of being abused":** Ellen Bass and Laura Davis, *The Courage to Heal: A Guide for Women Survivors of Child Sexual Abuse* (New York: Perennial Library, 1988), 22. **The backlash . . . was ferocious:** Bass and Davis, "Honoring the Truth: A Response to the Backlash," in *The Courage to Heal*, 3rd ed. (New York: HarperPerennial, 1994), http://fsa-cc.org/wp-content/uploads/2012/07/HONORING-THE-TRUTH.pdf. The literature on the controversy is extensive and often vehement. The case for the essential reliability of recovered memories is stated eloquently, and in my view persuasively, by Ross E. Cheit, "Consider This, Skeptics of Recovered Memory," *Ethics & Behavior* 8 (1998), 141–60; Ross E. Cheit, "Junk Skepticism and Recovered Memory: A Reply to Piper," *Ethics & Behavior* 9 (1999), 295–318; Ross E. Cheit, *The Witch-Hunt Narrative: Politics, Psychology, and the Sexual Abuse of Children* (New York: Oxford University Press, 2014). Cf. Bessel A. van der Kolk, *The Body Keeps the Score: Brain, Mind, and Body in the Healing of Trauma* (New York: Penguin Books, 2014), 173–201. **Bessel van der Kolk:** van der Kolk, 191. **"part of a pattern so shocking":** Strieber and Kripal, *The Super Natural*, 208–9. **"the prevalence of childhood sexual abuse":** Susan Marie Powers, "Thematic Contact Analyses of the Reports of UFO Abductees and Close Encounter Witnesses: Indications of Repressed Sexual Abuse," *JUFOS* n.s. 5 (1994): 52. **"One possible explanation":** Susan Marie Powers, "Dissociation in Alleged Extraterrestrial Abductees," *Dissociation* 7 (1994): 49. Cf. Susan Marie Powers, "Fantasy Proneness, Amnesia, and the UFO Abduction Phenomenon," *Dissociation* 4 (1991): 46–54; George K. Ganaway, "Historical versus Narrative Truth: Clarifying the Role of Exogenous Trauma in the Etiology of MPD and Its Variants," *Dissociation* 2 (1989): 205–20, UFO abductions discussed on 213–14. **David Jacobs wrote in 1992:** Jacobs, *Secret Life*, 286. **Hopkins did a hypnotic regression:** Bryan, *Close Encounters of the Fourth Kind*, 224, 353–57, 383. **His family pleaded for clemency:** Will Bueche, "Driver in Dr. John Mack Accident Sentenced," UFO UpDates (mailing list), October 8, 2005, http://ufoupdateslist.com/2005/oct/m08-012.shtml, drawing on a notice that had appeared on http://www.johnemack-institute.org. **David Jacobs soldiered on:** Jack Brewer, "The Bizarre World of Doctor David Jacobs: An Interview and Review," The UFO Trail, April 26, April 29, and May 3, 2012, http://ufotrail.blogspot.com/2012/04/bizarre-world-of-doctor-david-jacobs.html. **Abductions were still reported and remembered:** Bullard, "Abduction Phenomenon," *UFOE3* 1:10–13. Martin Kottmeyer, "Abduction Mythos Master Chronology" (which he was kind enough to share with me) lists 464 abduction reports from 2000 through 2014 (though often referring to incidents that allegedly happened years earlier). The notorious cases of "Emma Woods" (pseudonym for one of Jacobs's abductees) and James Mortellaro (one of Hopkins's) belong to the first half of this period: Jeremy Vaeni, "Aliens vs. Predator: The Incredible Visitations at Emma Woods," *UFO Magazine* 24, no. 1, issue 154 (December 2010): 34–45, https://cropcirclefilms.com/wp-content/uploads/2014/10/UFO-Magazone-online-102010.pdf; Carol Rainey, "The Priests of High Strangeness: Co-creation of the 'Alien Abduction Phenomenon,'" *Paratopia* 1, no. 1 (January 2011), http://www.carolrainey.com/pdf/ParatopiaMag_vol1_1-15-11.pdf; Jack Brewer, *The Grays Have Been Framed: Exploitation in the UFO Community* (privately published, 2016), 43–106. **"huge staring eyes of the old gods":** Strieber, *Communion*, 100. **Predionica mask:** Marija Gimbutas, *The Gods and Goddesses of Old Europe 7000–3500 BC: Myths, Legends and Cult Images* (Berkeley: University of California Press, 1974), 57–66. **Michael Hesemann's *UFOs: The Secret History*:** Michael Hesemann, *UFOs: The Secret History* (New York: Marlowe & Company, 1998), 449. Kottmeyer also cites Lynne Kitei, *The Phoenix Lights: A Skeptic's Discovery That We Are Not Alone* (Charlottesville, VA: Hampton Roads Publishing, 2004), 220; I have not seen this book. **Random coincidences . . . are part of our daily lives:** David J. Hand, *The Improbability Principle: Why Coincidences, Miracles, and Rare Events Happen Every Day* (New York: Scientific American/Farrar, Strauss and Giroux, 2014). ***Footnote 33:* "doppelgängers" . . . posted to the Web:** Luke Darby, "This App Matches Your Face to a Museum Portrait and the Results May Vary," GQ, January 14, 2018, https://www.gq.com/story/app-face-museum-portrait; Steve Dent, "Google's Museum App Finds Your Fine Art Doppelgänger," Engadget, January 15, 2018, https://www.engadget.com/2018/01/15/googles-museum-app-finds-your-fine-art-doppelganger/. **"That book started to sell":** Conroy, *Report on* Communion, 38.

CHAPTER 5: ANCIENT ABDUCTEES

Footnote 34*: abducted . . . from the dock in the Pascagoula River:** Ralph and Judy Blum, *Beyond Earth: Man's Contact with UFOs* (New York: Bantam Books, 1974), 9–36; Philip J. Klass, *UFOs Explained* (New York: Random House, 1974), 293–311; Tony Nugent, "Quicksilver in Twilight: A Close Encounter with a Hermetic Eye," in *Cyberbiological Studies of the Imaginal Component in the UFO Contact Experience*, ed. Dennis Stillings (St. Paul, MN: Archaeus Project, vol. 5, 1989), 109–24; audio and transcription of the two men's conversation in the documentary film *UFO's Invade the US* (date uncertain, possibly 2009), on disc 1 of *Aliens, Abductions and Extraordinary Sightings* (Golden Valley, MN: Mill Creek Entertainment, 2011), approximately 21'50" – 26'04", courtesy Wendy Conners, Fadeddiscs.com (I thank Martin Kottmeyer for calling my attention to this resource); "Pascagoula Abduction Case," *UFOE3* 2:893–98. **Michael Lieb and Stephen C. Finley:** Michael Lieb, *Children of Ezekiel: Aliens, UFOs, the Crisis of Race, and the Advent of End Time* (Durham: Duke University Press, 1998). Stephen C. Finley, "The Meaning of *Mother* in Louis Farrakhan's 'Mother Wheel': Race, Gender, and Sexuality in the Cosmology of the Nation of Islam's UFO," *Journal of the American Academy of Religion* 80 (2012): 434–65; "Hidden Away: Esotericism and Gnosticism in Elijah Muhammad's Nation of Islam," in *Histories of the Hidden God: Concealment and Revelation in Western Gnostic, Esoteric, and Mystical Traditions*, ed. April DeConick and Grant Adamson (Sheffield, UK: Equinox, 2013), 259–80; "Mathematical Theology: Numerology in the Religious Thought of Tynnetta Muhammad and Louis Farrakhan," in *Esotericism in African American Religious Experience: "There Is a Mystery,"* ed. Stephen C. Finley, Margarita S. Guillory, and Hugh R. Page (Leiden: E.J. Brill, 2015), 123–37; "The Supernatural in the African American Experience," in *Religion: Super Religion*, ed. Jeffrey J. Kripal (Farmington, MI: Macmillan, 2017), 231–46. Cf. also Ilia Rashad Muhammad, *UFOs and the Nation of Islam: The Source, Proof, and Reality of the Wheels* (Memphis, TN: Nation Brothers, 2013), uncritical but valuable for its insider perspective; David Halperin, "An African American UFOlogy?," *David Halperin* (blog), September 26, 2014, https://www.davidhalperin.net/an-african-american-ufology; Edward E. Curtis IV, "Science and Technology in Elijah Muhammad's Nation of Islam: Astrophysical Disaster, Genetic Engineering, UFOs, White Apocalypse, and Black Resurrection," *Nova Religio: The Journal of Alternative and Emergent Religions* 20 (2016): 5–31; and the touching memoir of the twin sisters Shurlene B. Wallace and Earlene V. Carr, *From the MotherLand to the MotherShip* (Dallas, TX: Crystal City Publications, 2001). **"Ezekiel saw the wheel":** R.N. Dett, *Religious Folk-Songs of the Negro as Sung at Hampton Institute* (Hampton, VA: Hampton Institute Press, 1927), 60–61; "Ezekiel Saw the Wheel," variations on lyrics, Mudcat Café (mailing list), various dates, https://mudcat.org/thread.cfm?threadid=42235. **"The Four-Faced Visitors of Ezekiel":** *Analog Science Fact-Fiction* 67, no. 2 (March 1961): 99–115 (reprinted as *The Four-Faced Visitors of Ezekiel: Ezekiel and the Ancient Spacemen: Extreme UFOs in the Bible*, CreateSpace Independent Publishing Platform, 2015, http://www.gutenberg.org/files/30252/30252-h/30252-h.htm). Similarly, M.K. Jessup, *UFO and the Bible* (New York: Citadel Press, 1956; repr. 1970 (Clarksburg, WV: Saucerian Books, 1970), 55–59; Y.N. ibn A'haron [Yonah Fortner], "Extraterrestrialism as an Historical Doctrine: Part 4: K'vod Y'hova; the Glory of the Lord," *Saucer News* 6, no. 4 (September 1959), 11–12; Erich von Däniken, *Chariots of the Gods? Unsolved Mysteries of the Past* (New York: Bantam Books, 1969), 37–39; Josef F. Blumrich, *The Spaceships of Ezekiel* (London: Corgi Books, 1974); "Ancient Astronauts in the UFO Literature," *UFOE3* 1:103–14; "Extraterrestrialism," *UFOE3* 1:472–73. Cf. Donald H. Menzel, *Flying Saucers* (Cambridge, MA: Harvard University Press, 1953), 124–34, who interprets the vision (very implausibly) as an atmospheric phenomenon akin to contemporary flying saucers; and the extraordinary Ezekiel-UFO drawings found in 2008 in a wooden box abandoned by a North Carolina roadside (David Halperin, "The 'Box of Crazy,' UFOs, and Ezekiel's Vision (Part 1)," *David Halperin* (blog), November 21, 2013, https://www.davidhalperin.net/the-box-of-crazy-ufos-and-ezekiels-vision-part-1/). **mythic iconography:** Othmar Keel, *Jahwe-Visionen und Siegelkunst: Eine neue Deutung der Majestätsschilderungen in Jes 6, Ez 1 und 10 und Sach 4* (Stuttgart: Verlag Kathologisches Bibelwerk, 1977), 125–273. **Ezekiel's wheels:** on the late fourth-century BCE Gaza coin, showing a bearded deity on a chariot-throne with prominent wheels, see Keel, *Jahwe-Visionen*, 273; Baruch Kanael, "Ancient Jewish Coins and Their Historical Importance," *Biblical Archaeologist* 26 (1963): 40–41. ***Footnote 36: **some early transmitter:** David J. Halperin, "The Exegetical Character of Ezek. x 9–17," *Vetus Testamentum* 26 (1976): 129–41, and the sources cited on 129. **human-faced monsters called "cherubim":** W.F. Albright, "What Were the Cherubim?" *Biblical Archaeologist* 1 (1938): 1–3; Keel, *Jahwe-Visionen*, 15–45. **bear only a distant resemblance:** Keel, 253. **Jung had a handle on it:** *Answer to Job* (London: Ark Paperbacks, 1984; first published in German in 1952, first published in English in 1954), 32, 33, 95–96; *Flying Saucers: A Modern Myth of Things Seen in the Skies* (New York: Harcourt, Brace, 1959), 114. **"Symbols that have an archetypal foundation":** C.G. Jung, "A Psychological Approach to the Dogma of the Trinity," in *Psychology and Religion: West and East*, vol. 11 of Jung, *Collected Works* (Princeton, NJ: University Press, 1958), 111.

Scriptures to be kept away from the young: Origen, "Prologue to the Commentary on the Song of Songs," in R.P. Lawson, trans., *Origen: The Song of Songs, Commentaries and Homilies* (New York: Newman Press, 1956), 23. **"unless he is wise":** Mishnah, Hagigah 2:1. **fire might leap out from them:** Babylonian Talmud, Hagigah 13a. **Some researchers place them:** The classic studies (favoring an early dating) are Gershom G. Scholem, *Major Trends in Jewish Mysticism* (New York: Schocken Books, 1954), 40–79; Gershom G. Scholem, *Jewish Gnosticism, Merkabah Mysticism, and Talmudic Tradition* (New York: Jewish Theological Seminary of America, 1960). My own views are expressed in David J. Halperin, *The Merkabah in Rabbinic Literature* (New Haven, CT: American Oriental Society, 1980); and David J. Halperin, *The Faces of the Chariot: Early Jewish Responses to Ezekiel's Vision* (Tübingen, Ger.: J.C.B. Mohr, 1988). Important recent studies include James R. Davila, *Descenders to the Chariot: The People behind the Hekhalot Literature* (Leiden: Brill, 2001); Ra'anan S. Boustan, *From Martyr to Mystic: Rabbinic Martyrology and the Making of Merkavah Mysticism* (Tübingen, Ger.: Mohr Siebeck, 2005); and Peter Schäfer, *The Origins of Jewish Mysticism* (Princeton, NJ: Princeton University Press, 2009). The introduction to James R. Davila, *Hekhalot Literature in Translation: Major Texts of Merkavah Mysticism* (Leiden: Brill, 2013) gives a good summary of the current state of research. **a peculiar Hebrew literature called *Hekhalot*:** published most fully by Peter Schäfer, *Synopse zur Hekhalot-Literatur* (Tübingen, Ger.: Mohr, 1981); normally cited by paragraph numbers in the *Synopse*, which Davila also uses for *Hekhalot Literature in Translation*. **"Rabbi Ishmael said":** *Synopse*, no. 81. **In one episode:** *Synopse*, nos. 201–3. **"taller than mountains" . . . "eat glowing coals out of their mangers":** *Synopse*, nos. 213–14. **They do it to each other:** Schäfer, *Geniza-Fragmente zur Hekhalot-Literatur* (Tübingen, Ger.: Mohr-Siebeck, 1984), no. 8, 2b, 27–32; cf. *Synopse*, nos. 186, 536, 796, 816. **they do it to the human visitor:** *Synopse*, no. 407. **a human being can do the same to an angel:** *Synopse*, no. 636; cf. Michael D. Swartz, *Scholastic Magic: Ritual and Revelation in Early Jewish Mysticism* (Princeton, NJ: Princeton University Press, 1996), 140. **"bring him back . . . from the vision":** *Synopse*, nos. 224–28, describing Nehunyah's recall from his trance-journey, is universally regarded as an insertion into the extended story of Nehunyah's lecture; Peter Schäfer, "Ein neues *Hekhalot Rabbati*-Fragment," in *Hekhalot-Studien* (Tübingen, Ger.: J.C.B. Mohr, 1988), 96–103. This does not affect the likelihood of its reflecting something that was actually practiced. **Gershom Scholem:** Scholem, *Jewish Gnosticism*, 10. **The shaman journeys in spirit:** Daniel Merkur, *Becoming Half Hidden: Shamanism and Initiation among the Inuit* (Stockholm: Almqvist & Wiksell, 1985), 95–101, quoting Knud Rasmussen. On "*merkavah* mysticism" and shamanism, see Davila, *Descenders to the Chariot*. **a quarter of abduction stories:** Bullard, *UFO Abductions: The Measure of a Mystery*, vol. 1, 112–17; "Abduction Phenomenon," *UFOE3* 1:16–17. **Betty Andreasson:** Raymond E. Fowler, *The Andreasson Affair: The Documented Investigation of a Woman's Abduction Aboard a UFO* (Newberg, OR: Wild Flower Press, 1979), 86. **"a very curious . . . change of phraseology":** Scholem, *Jewish Gnosticism*, 20; Annelies Kuyt, *The "Descent" to the Chariot: Towards a Description of the Terminology, Place, Function and Nature of the Yeridah in Hekhalot Literature* (Tübingen: J.C.B. Mohr, 1995, reviewed by David J. Halperin, *Journal of Jewish Studies* 47 [1996], 386–88); Guy G.

Stroumsa, "Mystical Descents," in *Death, Ecstasy, and Other Worldly Journeys*, ed. John J. Collins and Michael Fishbane (Albany: State University of New York Press, 1995), 139–54. **"A Sexual Image in *Hekhalot Rabbati* and Its Implications":** David J. Halperin, "A Sexual Image in *Hekhalot Rabbati* and Its Implications," in *Proceedings of the First International Conference on the History of Jewish Mysticism: Early Jewish Mysticism*, ed. Joseph Dan (Jerusalem: Hebrew University, 1987; *Jerusalem Studies in Jewish Thought* 6, 1–2), English section, 117–32. The passage is in *Synopse*, nos. 244–50. **"Ophannim" . . . a class of angel:** Babylonian Talmud, Hagigah 13b. **winnowers' sieve:** reading *menappim*, "winnowers"; all the manuscripts are corrupt at this point. **the clue in another passage:** *Synopse*, no. 189 (also from *Hekhalot Rabbati*). **a patient of Freud's:** Sigmund Freud, *The Interpretation of Dreams*, trans. and ed. James Strachey (New York: Avon Books, 1965), 234–35. ***Footnote 39:* multiplication process:** Based ultimately on the Targum to Ezekiel 1:6, developed in *Hekhalot Zutarti* ("The Lesser Treatise of the Palaces"), *Synopse*, no. 354. **Sheela-na-gig:** Jørgen Andersen, *The Witch on the Wall: Medieval Erotic Sculpture in the British Isles* (Copenhagen: Rosenkilde and Bagger, 1977); Anthony Weir and James Jerman, *Images of Lust: Sexual Carvings on Medieval Churches* (London: B.T. Batsford, 1986); Barbara Freitag, *Sheela-na-gigs: Unravelling an Enigma* (London & New York: Routledge, 2004); Georgia Rhoades, "Decoding the *Sheela-na-gig*," *Feminist Formations* 22 (2010): 167–94. ***Footnote 40: The Astounding She Monster*:** Tim Lucas, "Close Encounters With the Astounding She Monster," *Video WatcHDog*, no. 158 (September/October 2010), 16–19. ***Footnote 41:* another Hekhalot passage:** *Synopse*, no. 102; Elliot R. Wolfson, *Through a Speculum That Shines: Vision and Imagination in Medieval Jewish Mysticism* (Princeton, NJ: Princeton University Press, 1994), 92. **More than one researcher . . . shamanic trance journeys:** Alvin H. Lawson, "Perinatal Imagery in UFO Abduction Reports," *Journal of Psychohistory* 12 (1984), 211–39, especially 227; Peter M. Rojcewicz, "The Extraordinary Encounter Hypothesis and Its Implications for the Study of Belief Materials," *Folklore Forum* 19 (1986): 131–52; Thomas E. Bullard, "UFO Abduction Reports: The Supernatural Kidnap Narrative Returns in Technological Guise," *Journal of American Folklore* 102 (1989), 147–70; Kenneth Ring, "Near-Death and UFO Encounters as Shamanic Initiations: Some Conceptual and Evolutionary Implications," *ReVISION* 11 (1989): 14–22; Kenneth Ring, *The Omega Project: Near-Death Experiences, UFO Encounters, and Mind at Large* (New York: William Morrow, 1992); John Mack, *Abduction: Human Encounters with Aliens* (New York: Charles Scribner's Sons, 1994), index s.v. "shamans." **humiliating and sometimes painful ordeals:** Bullard, "UFO Abduction Reports," 162–63. **Mircea Eliade's account:** *Shamanism: Archaic Techniques of Ecstasy* (Princeton, NJ: Princeton University Press, 1964), 34; cf. J.R. Porter, "Muhammad's Journey to Heaven," *Numen* 21 (1974), 64–80. **helping spirits . . . "crow, etc.)":** Eliade, *Shamanism*, 89; cf. Mack, *Abduction*, 32, 408. **"a love affair with a goddess":** Strieber, in Whitley Strieber and Jeffrey J. Kripal, *The Super Natural: A New Vision of the Unexplained* (New York: Jeremy P. Tarcher/Random House, 2016), 97. **"in the form of a beautiful woman":** Davila, *Descenders to the Chariot*, 55, from Joan Halifax, *Shamanic Voices: A Survey of Visionary Narratives* (New York and London: Arkana/Penguin, 1979), 120–23. **"On that night in December 1985":** Strieber, in Strieber and Kripal, *The Super Natural*,

130. **kidnapped or enticed into fairyland:** Bullard, "UFO Abduction Reports," 159–61; Thomas E. Bullard, *The Myth and Mystery of UFOs* (Lawrence: University Press of Kansas, 2010), index, s.v. "fairies," and, with particular attention to the motif of stolen children and alien "hybrids," 176–200. **Georgia Rhoades:** Rhoades, "Decoding the *Sheela-na-gig*," 167. **thinkable that this was the point:** Weir and Jerman, *Images of Lust*, 11. **coins deposited . . . worn away by caressing fingers:** Rhoades, "Decoding the *Sheela-na-gig*," 175, 191–92. **"vulgarly called the Idol":** Andersen, *Witch on the Wall*, 10. **ethnographic data:** Andersen, 131–37, followed by Rhoades, "Decoding the *Sheela-na-gig*," 173–75. **Rhoades writes:** Rhoades, 175. **borderline between the living and the dead:** cf. Freitag, *Sheela-na-gigs*, 68–118. **one Bible scholar:** Samuel Sandmel, "Parallelomania," *Journal of Biblical Literature* 81 (1962): 1–13, https://www.scribd.com/document/220553887/Parallelomania-by-Samuel-Sandmel. **Jerome Clark:** "Psychosocial Hypothesis," *UFOE3* 2:938–48, quote on 946. **masks a myth much like that of the Babylonians:** Wilhelm Bousset, *The Antichrist Legend: A Chapter in Jewish and Christian Folklore* (London: Hutchinson, 1896); Umberto Cassuto, *The Goddess Anath: Canaanite Epics of the Patriarchal Age* (Jerusalem: Magnes Press, 1971); Arvid S. Kapelrud, "The Mythological Features in Genesis Chapter I and the Author's Intentions," *Vetus Testamentum* 24 (1974), 178–86. **Strieber's now deceased wife, Anne:** Strieber, in Strieber and Kripal, *The Super Natural*, 37, 73–74. Cf. Kripal's comments, Strieber and Kripal, 52–53; Whitley and Anne Strieber, *The Communion Letters* (London: Pocket Books, 1997), 259–81. **Gershom Scholem thought so:** Gershom Scholem, *Jewish Gnosticism*, 14–19. **an important difference:** Martha Himmelfarb, "The Practice of Ascent in the Ancient Mediterranean World," in *Death, Ecstasy, and Other Worldly Journeys*, ed. John J. Collins and Michael Fishbane (Albany: State University of New York Press, 1995), 123–37. **a Greek verb:** Henry George Liddell and Robert Scott, *A Greek-English Lexicon*, 9th ed. (Oxford: Clarendon Press, 1940), s.v. "*harpazo*." ***Footnote 45:* 2 Corinthians 12:1–5:** James D. Tabor, *Things Unutterable: Paul's Ascent to Paradise in Its Greco-Roman, Judaic, and Early Christian Contexts* (Lanham, MD: University Press of America, 1986); C.R.A. Morray-Jones, "Paradise Revisited (2 Cor 12:1–12): The Jewish Mystical Background of Paul's Apostolate," *Harvard Theological Review* 86 (1993): 177–217, 265–92; cf. Margaret M. Mitchell, *Paul, the Corinthians, and the Birth of Christian Hermeneutics* (Cambridge, UK: Cambridge University Press, 2010), 79–94. **the composite text . . . 55 CE:** J. Albert Harrill, *Paul the Apostle: His Life and Legacy in Their Roman Context* (Cambridge, UK: Cambridge University Press, 2012), 169–70, following Mitchell's analysis. **not, apparently, to be equated:** Morray-Jones, "Paradise Revisited," 284–92. Morray-Jones's own proposal, that 2 Corinthians 12:1–5 alludes to the experience in the Jerusalem Temple described in Acts 22:17–21, seems to me unconvincing. **Jeffrey Kripal:** Jeffrey J. Kripal, *Comparing Religions: Coming to Terms* (Chichester, UK: Wiley Blackwell, 2014), 82–83, 273–78, cf. 346, 385. **turned sour and nasty:** J. Albert Harrill, *Paul the Apostle: His Life and Legacy in Their Roman Context* (Cambridge, UK: Cambridge University Press, 2012), 61–67. ***Footnote 46:* multiple heavens:** *Testament of Levi*, chapters 2–3; *Book of the Secrets of Enoch (2 Enoch)*, chapters 8–9; Babylonian Talmud, Hagigah 12b. **Betty Hill was shown a book:** Fuller, *Interrupted Journey*, 173–78. **"epilepsy . . . malady":** Margaret

M. Mitchell, *Paul, the Corinthians, and the Birth of Christian Hermeneutics* (Cambridge, UK: Cambridge University Press, 2010), 11; cf. C.R.A. Morray-Jones, "Paradise Revisited (2 Cor 12:1–12): The Jewish Mystical Background of Paul's Apostolate," *Harvard Theological Review* 86 (1993): 281–83. **"Implants":** Keith Basterfield, "The Implant Motif in UFO Abduction Literature," *JUFOS* n.s. 8 (2003): 49–83, listing 84 cases, including Strieber's. **Whitley Strieber was among them:** in Strieber and Kripal, *The Super Natural*, 174–88. **thornlike in their appearance:** Roger K. Leir, *The Aliens and the Scalpel: Scientific Proof of Extraterrestrial Implants in Humans* (Columbus, NC: Granite Publishing, 1998), plate 15; color photos at J.J.P. Robinson, "Alien Implants: Proof of Physical Contact?," May 13, 2017, https://www.jp-robinson.com/single-post/Alien-Implants-Proof-of-Physical-Contact.

CHAPTER 6: THREE MEN IN BLACK

although he was both: John C. Sherwood, "Gray Barker: My Friend, the Myth-Maker," *Skeptical Inquirer* 22, no. 3 (May-June 1998), https://www.csicop.org/si/show/gray_barker_my_friend_the_myth-maker. He uses *mythmaker* in precisely the way I do not. **Barker described Bender:** Gray Barker, *They Knew Too Much About Flying Saucers* (New York: University Books, 1956), 69. **chief timekeeper:** Max Krengel, "We Want You to Meet," *Space Review* 1, no. 1 (October 1952): 12. **Others . . . portrayed him differently:** e.g., Robert Sheaffer, *UFO Sightings: The Evidence* (Amherst, NY: Prometheus Books, 1998), 196–97, based on the self-description in Albert K. Bender, *Flying Saucers and the Three Men* (Clarksburg, WV: Saucerian Books, 1962), 15–18. **Two documentary films:** Ralph Coon, *Whispers from Space* (1995); Bob Wilkinson, *Shades of Gray* (2009). Wilkinson's is the masterpiece. **"I am neither a scientist nor a scholar":** Barker, *They Knew Too Much*, 14–15. **a seven-foot monster . . . near Flatwoods:** Barker, 11–35. **barn owl:** Joe Nickell, "The Flatwoods UFO Monster," *Skeptical Inquirer* 24, no. 6 (November-December 2000), https://www.csicop.org/si/show/flatwoods_ufo_monster. **quarterly called *The Saucerian*:** Barker, *They Knew Too Much*, 42. **Barker . . . had written to him:** Barker, 66–67. **The IFSB . . . *Space Review*:** "Bender Mystery," *UFOE3* 1:189–92. The complete file of *Space Review*, October 1952–October 1953, was republished (under Bender's name) by Saucerian Books, Clarksburg, WV, 1962. **On Sunday, September 27:** described in a "talking letter"—a letter spoken into a tape recorder—from Lucchesi to Barker, made on September 29 and quoted in full in Barker, *They Knew Too Much*, 111–22. I see no reason to question the letter's authenticity. **The following Sunday, October 4:** The transcript of the interview (Barker, 129–35) is supposedly based on Roberts's notes. Though doubtless edited by Barker for greater effect, they seem to me essentially genuine. As we'll see in a moment, Bender's description of the clothing of his three visitors doesn't quite suit what Barker would have wanted him to have said; in spite of that, Barker didn't tamper with his testimony. **James Moseley . . . recalled:** James W. Moseley and Karl T. Pflock, *Shockingly Close to the Truth: Confessions of a Grave-Robbing Ufologist* (Amherst, NY: Prometheus Books, 2002), 120. **Correspondence in the Barker Collection:** Barker to Jessup, December 17, 1954; Jessup to Barker, December 20, 1954; Barker to Jessup, December 27, 1954; Jessup to Barker,

December 28, 1954, file Jessup, Morris K. Correspondence w/ Gray Barker, 1954–57, Gray Barker Collection, Clarksburg-Harrison Public Library, Clarksburg, WV (hereafter GBC). **one of Barker's . . . cards:** Barker, *They Knew Too Much*, 95–98; referenced in Bender to Roberts, September 9, 1953, Bender Correspondence—August Roberts File, GBC. **a panel of scientists:** Brad Sparks, "Robertson Panel," *UFOE3* 2:1012–18. **Bender needed to be paid a visit:** possibly preceded by an exchange of letters, in which Bender responded to an inquiry with an outline of his beliefs about flying saucers. This will explain Bender's cryptic allusion to having sent his theory to a "friend" prior to the three men's visit (Barker, *They Knew Too Much*, 132); cf. Lem M'Collum, "Mystery Visitors Halt Research: Saucerers Here Ordered to Quit," Bridgeport *Sunday Herald*, November 29, 1953, which speaks of Bender's having "submitted the report of the saucer conclusions of the IFSB" to an unnamed "higher authority." I'm immensely grateful to the Bridgeport Public Library and to Elizabeth Van Tuyl for providing me with a scan of this article. **a "nonsensical" business:** Bender to Roberts, August 4, 1954, GBC. **wooing Betty Rose:** Bender, *Flying Saucers and the Three Men*, 159–61; "Albert Bender to Wed Betty Rose Saturday," Bridgeport *Telegram*, October 13, 1954. ***Footnote 48:* Michael D. Swords:** "Tales from the Barker Zone: Three Days at the Gray Barker Manuscript Depository," *IUR* 17, no. 6 (November-December 1992): 4–10. ***Footnote 49:* "suspected Red activity" . . . "fantastic rumor":** Bender, *Flying Saucers and the Three Men*, 141–42. **"UFO is a bucket of shit":** Greg Bishop, "Interview: James Moseley, 1994," *In Honor of Jim Moseley*, February 5, 2014, https://www.jimmoseley.com/2014/02/interview-james-moseley-1994-by-greg-bishop/, originally published in *The Excluded Middle* magazine, 1994; recited by Moseley in both *Whispers from Space* and *Shades of Gray*. The poem's date is uncertain. John C. Sherwood, "Gray Barker's Book of Bunk: Mothman, Saucers, and MIB," *Skeptical Inquirer* 26, no. 3 (May-June 2002), http://www.csicop.org/si/show/gray_barkers_book_of_bunk_mothman_saucers_and_mib), says that Moseley told him Barker had written it in the late 1950s. This is impossible: the poem's "Shushed by the three men / Or masturbated by space men" is a clear allusion to the "three women in white" of Bender's 1962 book (with *women* replaced by *men*; make of that what you will). On the other hand, the absence of any figure who came to UFOlogical prominence after 1960 suggests it can't have been written too many years afterward. **squalid pranks:** Sherwood, "Gray Barker's Book of Bunk"; Moseley and Pflock, *Shockingly Close to the Truth!*, 124–27 (the "Straith letter" of 1957), 199–201 (the "Lost Creek saucer film" of 1966). *Whispers from Space* has a long, excruciating segment on the faking of the "Lost Creek" movie and the shaming of those who were taken in by it. **"Gray turned into a total hoaxer":** quoted in Jim Keith, *Casebook on the Men in Black* (Lilburn, GA: IllumiNet Press, 1997), 157–58. **"for God's sake be careful" . . . "I hope not":** Barker, *They Knew Too Much*, 244, 246, 238. **common knowledge . . . among UFOlogy's cognoscenti:** Moseley and Pflock, *Shockingly Close to the Truth!*, 121. **autobiographical accounts . . . underage boys:** interviews with Houchin and with Barker's niece in Bob Wilkinson, *Shades of Gray*; Gabriel McKee, "A Contactee Canon: Gray Barker's Saucerian Books" (paper, Sacred Literature, Secular Religion, LeMoyne College, October 2, 2015), 3–4, https://www.academia.edu/17008532/A_Contactee_Canon_Gray_Barkers

_Saucerian_Books. Precisely what happened in 1962 remains obscure. Barker's lover, interviewed in *Whispers from Space*, makes chilling reference to "evil children" on whom he blames the whole affair. **"world . . . come to an end?"** Barker, *They Knew Too Much*, 133. **recurrent theme:** e.g., 35, 166–76. **Maury Island incident:** "Maury Island Hoax," *UFOE3* 1:720–23. The main primary sources are Kenneth Arnold's reminiscences (nearly five years after the event) in Kenneth Arnold and Ray Palmer, *The Coming of the Saucers* (Amherst, WI: Legend Press, 1952), 9–84; and Jack Wilcox (FBI agent) to J. Edgar Hoover, memorandum, August 19, 1947, reproduced in Steven Edmiston and Scott Schaefer, *The Maury Island Incident*, press release (?), August 19, 2014, http://www.southkingmedia.com/wp-content/Maury%20Island%20Incident/AgentWilcoxMemo081947.pdf. Cf. Edward J. Ruppelt, *The Report on Unidentified Flying Objects* (Garden City, NY: Doubleday, 1956), 24–27. **when the Man in Black first entered the story:** Arnold (in Arnold and Palmer, *Coming of the Saucers*, 34–35) represents Dahl as having told him about the Man in Black in Arnold's hotel room on the evening of July 29. A variant appears in the Wilcox memo of August 19 (9), contradicting Arnold as to both the date and the place of Dahl's conversation with the stranger and saying nothing of the man's black clothing or preternatural knowledge of Dahl's experience. I assume Dahl told multiple versions of the mystery-man story in the days following the plane crash on August 1 and that in retrospect Arnold conflated one of these with Dahl's original account of his UFO encounter, which he indeed heard in his hotel room on the evening of July 29. **confessions of seventeenth-century witches:** Margaret Alice Murray, *The Witch-Cult in Western Europe* (Oxford: Oxford University Press, 1921), 31–43; Keith, *Casebook on the Men in Black*, 15–26. ***Footnote 51:*** **Talmudic legend:** Babylonian Talmud, Yoma 39b; parallel in the Palestinian Talmud, Yoma 27a, which admittedly has the old man dressed in white on the final occasion as in his earlier encounters with the high priest, the evil omen lying solely in his entering with the priest but not going out with him. **Scotland in 1670:** Murray, *Witch-Cult in Western Europe*, 43. **England in 1682:** Montague Summers, *The Geography of Witchcraft* (Evanston & New York: University Books, 1958), 152. **Tituba, the slave woman:** Marion L. Starkey, *The Devil in Massachusetts: A Modern Enquiry into the Salem Witch Trials* (Garden City, NY: Dolphin Books, 1949), 59; Stacy Schiff, *The Witches: Salem, 1692* (New York: Little, Brown, 2015), 53. **Norway in 1730:** "Men in Black," *UFOE3* 1:726, drawing from Rossell Hope Robbins, *The Encyclopedia of Witchcraft and Demonology* (New York: Crown, 1959), 288–89. **small metal disk . . . "Kazik":** Bender, *Flying Saucers and the Three Men*, 91. **implanted in him an "impulse":** Bender, 156–57. **the disk vanished:** Bender, 175. **Barker . . . expressed reservations:** Bender, 191–94. **Moseley has plausibly suggested:** Moseley and Pflock, *Shockingly Close to the Truth!* 121. **they regularly abducted humans:** Bender, *Flying Saucers and the Three Men*, 91, 118. ***Footnote 53:*** **"Suppose there was another world . . . people were black":** Barker, *They Knew Too Much*, 133. **"a strange-looking table" . . . "Three beautiful women":** Bender, 153–55. **a physical implant:** Bender, 177. **A casebook published in 1997:** Keith, *Casebook on the Men in Black*; Jenny Randles, *The Truth behind Men in Black* (New York: St. Martin's Paperbacks, 1997), covers much the same ground. See also "Men in Black," *UFOE3* 1:726–37. **carrying a sickle:**

Keith, 183. **MIB-themed pranks:** Keith, 171–74; Randles, *The Truth behind Men in Black*, 158–60. **Herbert Hopkins:** "Oxford Abduction Case," *UFOE3* 2:861–65. Clark bases his account largely on a series of *Flying Saucer Review* articles from 1976 and 1978 by Brent M. Raynes, Shirley C. Fickett, and Berthold Eric Schwarz, reprinted in Berthold Eric Schwarz, *UFO Dynamics: Psychiatric and Psychic Aspects of The UFO Syndrome* (Moore Haven, FL: Rainbow Books, 1983), 214–72. The first-person narrative in Schwarz, 241–45, is a synthesis of several versions related by Hopkins in a series of interviews; an audio recording of one of these is at Wendy Connors, "High Strangeness 03: Dr. Herbert Hopkins, MD," *Faded Discs*, September 11, 1976, https://archive.org/details/HighStrangeness-Guide/03.mp3, and it is the source of most of my quotes. For Howard Hopkins's recollections of his uncle Herbert, his cousin John, and John's wife, Maureen, see Howard Hopkins, "The Truth About a Man in Black," *Dark Bits* (blog), January 13, 2008, https://web.archive.org/web/20080524015603/http://howardhopkins.blogspot.com/2008/01/truth-about-man-in-black.html; and Howard Hopkins, "More MIB Weirdery," *Dark Bits* (blog), January 23, 2008, https://web.archive.org/web/20080723185406/http://howard-hopkins.blogspot.com/2008/01/more-mib-weirdery.html; cf. "The Sad Truth behind an MIB Story," *Magonia*, February 27, 2009, http://pelicanist.blogspot.com/2009/02/sad-truth-behind-mib-story.html. **obsolete cars that seem brand new:** UFOlogist Rick Hilberg, interviewed in *Shades of Gray* (2009). ***Footnote 55:* one bizarre case from 1968:** Keith, *Casebook on the Men in Black*, 162–70; Randles, *The Truth behind the Men in Black*, 154–56. **The witness is flawed:** Even without his nephew's testimony to his drinking, Hopkins's bizarre insistence at the beginning of the *Faded Discs* interview that he had no prior interest in UFOs is enough to discredit his reliability; it's clear from the interview that he was deeply involved in abduction research. **fantastic details:** Apart from those mentioned in the text, the man arrives at Hopkins's door instantaneously after telephoning him (in an age before cell phones); he has no eyebrows or eyelashes; his speech and movements run down at the end of his visit as though he's a machine whose battery is dying; after leaving Hopkins's house, he vanishes, walking in a direction by which he'd have no way out of the property; once he's gone, Hopkins finds in the driveway an inexplicable "series of marks that looked like a small caterpillar tractor tread," which disappear overnight. ***Footnote 56:* photographed wearing what appears to be lipstick:** Wilkinson, *Shades of Gray*, 1 hr. 6' 23"; cf. Moseley and Pflock, *Shockingly Close to the Truth!* 121. **"Have you heard of men in black?"** Robbie Graham, *Silver Screen Saucers: Sorting Fact from Fantasy in Hollywood's UFO Movies* (Hove, UK: White Crow Books, 2015), 12–13. **opening . . . second-highest grossing:** "1997 Domestic Grosses," *Box Office Mojo*, IMDb, http://www.boxofficemojo.com/yearly/chart/?yr=1997&p=.htm. ***Men in Black 3* surpassed it:** Pamela McClintock, "Box Office Report: 'Men in Black 3' Becomes Highest-Grossing Title in Franchise," *Hollywood Reporter*, July 1, 2012, https://www.hollywoodreporter.com/news/box-office-report-men-black-mib3–will-smith-tommy-lee-jones-josh-brolin-sony-343957. ***Footnote 58:* a visit . . . from a bizarre couple:** Schwarz, *UFO Dynamics*, 245–50; Hopkins, "More MIB Weirdery." **"Here Come the Men in Black":** Will Smith, "Here Come the Men in Black," *Big Willie Style*, 1997, Will Smith Lyrics, AZ Lyrics, https://www.azlyrics.com/lyrics

/willsmith/meninblack.html. **a nod . . . toward Frank Scully:** stated as fact in Jack Womack, *Flying Saucers Are Real! The UFO Library of Jack Womack* (New York: Anthology Editions, 2016), 39; vs. Brian Lowry, *The Truth Is Out There: The Official Guide to* The X-Files (New York: HarperPrism, 1995), 11. **MIBs . . . remain marginal to *The X-Files*:** Two of them appear as semicomic figures in the highly atypical episode "Jose Chung's *From Outer Space*," April 12, 1996, a pastiche and parody of multiple features of UFO lore. The exception clarifies the rule: it's only when we (temporarily) stop taking *The X-Files* plotline seriously that the Men in Black have any place in it. **baroque counterhistory:** Michael Barkun, *A Culture of Conspiracy: Apocalyptic Visions in Contemporary America* (Berkeley: University of California Press, 2003), 79–97; "Dark Side," *UFOE3* 1:357–74. **"Surely," he wrote . . . "on your honor as an American":** Barker, *They Knew Too Much*, 132, 152. **three out of four Americans trusted the government:** Pew Research Center, "Public Trust in Government: 1958–2017," December 14, 2017, http://www.people-press.org/2017/12/14/public-trust-in-government-1958-2017/?mod=article_inline. **Barna Donovan:** Barna Donovan, *Conspiracy Films: A Tour of Dark Places in the American Conscious* (Jefferson, NC: McFarland, 2011), 179.

CHAPTER 7: SHAVER MYSTERY

what . . . made it a mystery: cf. Richard Toronto, *War over Lemuria: Richard Shaver, Ray Palmer and the Strangest Chapter of 1940s Science Fiction* (Jefferson, NC: McFarland, 2013), 119. Palmer seems to have been conscious of the oddity of the usage and to have made occasional attempts to explain it; e.g., The Observatory . . . by the Editor, *AS* 21, no. 4 (April 1947): 9. **They were an odd couple:** Toronto's *War over Lemuria* is the best account of the pair and their synergy. Fred Nadis, *The Man From Mars: Ray Palmer's Amazing Pulp Journey* (New York: Jeremy P. Tarcher/Penguin, 2013), which focuses on Palmer, is also very much worth reading. The discussion in Jeffrey J. Kripal, *Mutants and Mystics: Science Fiction, Superhero Comics, and the Paranormal* (Chicago: University of Chicago Press, 2011), 92–111, is brief but very insightful. **"Deliberate Manipulator":** Ray Palmer, foreword to *The Secret World*, vol. 1, *1975* (Amherst, WI: Amherst Press, 1975), 8. **in September 1943:** date supplied by Palmer, The Observatory, *AS* 21, no. 6 (June 1947): 8. Toronto, *War over Lemuria*, 58, gives the date as October but provides no source. **This, at any rate, is the legend:** questioned in Jim Pobst, *Shaver Resharpened* (privately published, 1982), 4–6. **"tero see a dero":** The published text, "troc see a dero," is evidently a misprint. **Mantong:** Ray Palmer, "Mantong: The Language of Lemuria," appendix to "I Remember Lemuria!," *AS* 19, no. 1 (March 1945): 71, 206. ***Miracle on 34th Street* . . . fifty thousand:** Toronto, *War over Lemuria*, 118. **ultimate autodidact . . . "inner hiding place of the human mind":** Ray Palmer, "Martian Diary—Book I," in *The Secret World*, 29–30. **The two men struck up a correspondence:** Pobst, *Shaver Resharpened*, 8–16, gives the following dates: December 25, 1943, Shaver mails Palmer the manuscript of "Warning to Future Man"; January 14, 1944, Palmer writes that he's "giving serious consideration" to the manuscript; January 1944, Shaver sends Palmer an itinerary of the travels of Mutan Mion; February 1944, Shaver sends Palmer the manuscript of the story "Cavern Called Hel," later retitled "Cave City of Hel"; early March 1944, Palmer begins the rewrite of "Warning to Future Man," under the working title of "The True Story of Lemuria," and Shaver writes to Palmer with an account of his voices, travails, wanderings; March 1944, the first notice hyping the forthcoming story appears in the issue of *AS* with the cover date of May 1944; September 1944, fuller notice hyping the story appears in the December 1944 issue; December 8, 1944, the March 1945 issue, containing "I Remember Lemuria!," hits the stands. **attributed to Shaver in a "foreword":** "I Remember Lemuria!," *AS* 19, no. 1 (March 1945): 14. **memories that stretched back to infancy and beyond:** Palmer, "Martian Diary," 13–17. **prepublication hype:** The Observatory, *AS* 18, no. 3 (May 1944): 6, 193. **"I Remember Lemuria!":** "I Remember Lemuria!," *AS* 19, no. 1: 11–70. ***Footnote 64:* He was soon to backtrack:** in an editorial footnote to Richard S. Shaver, "Thought Records of Lemuria," *AS* 19, no. 2 (June 1945): 52. **malformed dwarfs:** "I Remember Lemuria!," 56. **our lives are brief and sorry affairs:** "I Remember Lemuria!," 46, 51, 64, 70. ***Footnote 65:* "abandoned caves and cities":** "I Remember Lemuria!," *AS* 19, no. 1: 56–57. ***Dero* . . . "detrimental robot":** "Thought Records of Lemuria," *AS* 19, no. 2: 22n. **"detrimental energy robotism":** "I Remember Lemuria!," *AS* 19, no. 1: 28–29. **torment people on the surface . . . responsible for belief in religion:** Richard Shaver, quoted in the editorial note to "I Remember Lemuria!," 57; Ray Palmer, The Observatory, *AS* 21, no. 6 (June 1947): 8. **"you trip him and laugh":** Ray Palmer, editorial note to Richard S. Shaver, "Thought Records of Lemuria," *AS* 19, no. 2 (June 1945): 30. **"Thought Records of Lemuria":** Shaver, "Thought Records of Lemuria," *AS* 19, no. 2: 12–52. **"This is our enemy's pleasure palace":** Shaver, "Thought Records of Lemuria," *AS* 19, no. 2: 29–30. **Shaver wrote the story in January 1945:** inferred from the date January 18, 1945, of "Open Letter to the World" with which he prefaces it ("Thought Records of Lemuria," *AS* 19, no. 2: 12–15). **First in Detroit:** Toronto, *War over Lemuria*, 88–113. ***Footnote 67:* Shaver himself noted the parallel:** author's footnote to "Thought Records of Lemuria," *AS* 19, no. 2: 47. **In an interview given in 1973:** Eugene Steinberg, "The Caveat Emptor Interview: Richard S. Shaver," *Caveat Emptor* 10 (November-December 1973): 5–10; issues of *Caveat Emptor* at http://files.afu.se/Downloads/Magazines/United%20States/Caveat%20Emptor/. **Book of Job:** 1:15–19. **an interview twenty years later:** Steinberg, "The Caveat Emptor Interview: Ray Palmer," *Caveat Emptor* 1 (Fall 1971): 9–12, 26. The interview was conducted in October 1965, first published six years afterward. ***Footnote 71:* Palmer . . . imagined:** Toronto, *War over Lemuria*, 105. **In one of his . . . footnotes:** Palmer, "Thought Records of Lemuria," *AS* 19, no. 2: 33. In a note on p. 34, Palmer calls Mu "an abbreviation for Lemuria." In the regular column Report From the Forgotten Past? in the same issue, however, Palmer distinguishes the two: the continent Mu "is not to be confused with Mr. Shaver's Lemuria which is the Earth itself" (p. 189). **Lemuria was originally a scientific hypothesis:** L. Sprague de Camp, *Lost Continents: The Atlantis Theme* (New York: Ballantine Books, 1970), 53–56. **spinoffs of *Atlantis* or *Atlantean*:** Palmer, "I Remember Lemuria!" *AS* 19, no. 1: 16; the home city of the Atlan narrator, Mutan Mion, is Sub Atlan, located just below "Surface Atlan" or Atlantis. The metropolis at the center of "Mother Mu" toward which Mutan Mion journeys is Tean City, probably a shortened form of "Atlantean." **"olden rite, the nocturnal**

Lemuria": Ovid, *Fasti*, book 5, lines 419–92; Sir James George Frazer, trans., *Publii Ovidii Nasonis Fastorum Libri Sex: The* Fasti *of Ovid*, vol. 1 (London: Macmillan, 1929), 275–81. This translation was published too late for Palmer to have seen it as a child. There were earlier translations, however, and one of these, or a book quoting one of these, is likely to have been among the holdings of the Milwaukee Public Library ca. 1920. **the cover of the June 1947 *Amazing Stories*:** All *AS* covers from this period at Pulps.Retro-Scans.com, http://pulps.retro-scans.com/Pulps-A/Amazing-Stories-1940-1953/Amazing-Stories.php. **"That's how it looks!"** The Observatory, *AS* 21, no. 4 (April 1947): 8. ***Footnote 72: Lemuria* . . . hardly occurs in the stories:** The only mention of the name in "I Remember Lemuria!" after the foreword is on 52, where we present-day surface-dwellers are called "Lemurians unborn." **identifies her as the princess Vanue:** Compare the cover of the March 1945 *AS* with the full-page illustration at the beginning of "I Remember Lemuria!" depicting "Glorious Vanue, Elder God." **"a Martian . . . abandoned":** Nadis, *The Man from Mars*, 206–10. **the cover of the July 1943 issue:** Nadis, 44–45. Cf. the September 1944 cover, where a bald, repellent, mostly naked dwarf brandishing a pistol tugs at the wrist of a lovely uniformed WAC with flaming red hair, who draws back in revulsion. Palmer with his auburn-haired beauty of a mother? Also the February 1942 cover, which parallels that of March 1945 but with perspective and power relations reversed: it's the stooped dwarf in little boy's clothing, not the obviously terrified young woman, who's at the controls of what turns out to be a time machine. **all but one included a story by Richard Shaver:** Jim Pobst, *A Checklist of the Fiction of Richard S. Shaver* (Maple Ridge, BC: Spayderine Press, 1982). **an extra 50,000; all 185,000 copies sold:** Pobst, *Shaver Resharpened*, 13–15; Palmer, "Martian Diary," 38–39; cf. Nadis, *The Man from Mars*, 75. **sold 261,611 copies:** Toronto, *War over Lemuria*, 152. **trimmed back drastically:** Bill Hamling's recollection confirms Palmer: "*Astounding Science Fiction* . . . had 80,000 [readers]. Ziff-Davis had three or four times that through Palmer and the Shaver Mystery" (quoted in Toronto, 151). But Hamling and Palmer were good friends, and it's possible Hamling was repeating the figures Palmer had fed him. Chester S. Geier estimates that *AS* "was selling some 90,000 copies" per month, "where a SF magazine was doing well to sell 50,000 copies and very well to sell 70,000 per month" (quoted in Toronto, 154). But in 1990, Curtis Fuller (who became Palmer's partner in publishing *Fate* magazine) told Jerome Clark that "an audit indicated no significant change in circulation figures" with the advent of the Shaver Mystery (Clark, "Shaver Mystery," *The UFO Encyclopedia*, 2nd ed. [Detroit: Omnigraphics, 1998] 2:845; omitted from "Shaver Mystery," *UFOE3*). **telepathic messages . . . from their recently deceased pet turtle:** Wesley and Bruce Herschensohn (letter), Report From the Forgotten Past?, *AS* 19, no. 2 (June 1945): 189–90. **a letter from a certain "A.C.":** Discussions, *AS* 20, no. 3 (June 1946): 178. **seventy-eight stories authored or coauthored:** Pobst, *Checklist*. **Not all . . . revolved around the central mythos:** There's no allusion to it, as far as I can see, in Richard S. Shaver, "The Mind Rovers," *AS* 21, no. 1 (January 1947). **"Calling All Crackpots" and "Crackpot Heaven":** Thomas S. Gardner, in *Fantasy Commentator*, spring and summer issues, 1945; quoted in William S. Baring-Gould, "Little Superman, What Now?" *Harper's Magazine* 193 (September 1, 1946), 285–86; Toronto, *War over*

Lemuria, 140–41. **They passed resolutions:** "A Rocketeer's Credo," quoted in Pobst, *Shaver Resharpened*, 17, from a resolution brought forward at the Fifth "World" Science Fiction Convention, Philadelphia, September 1947. **In his editor's column:** The Observatory, *AS* 20, no. 4 (July 1946): 6. **"Cult of the Witch Queen":** Richard S. Shaver and Bob McKenna, "Cult of the Witch Queen," *AS* 20, no. 4 (July 1946): 10–38, 109–45. ***Footnote 73:* whose four books:** *The Book of the Damned* (1919), *New Lands* (1923), *Lo!* (1931), *Wild Talents* (1932); reprinted in Charles Fort, *The Books of Charles Fort* (New York: Henry Holt, 1941). ***Footnote 74:* front cover . . . of *Science Wonder Stories*:** "First Instance of the Flying Saucer as a Space Craft?," Science Fiction & Fantasy Stack Exchange (Q&A community), September 2015, https://scifi.stackexchange.com/questions/103526/first-instance-of-the-flying-saucer-as-a-space-craft. **proclaimed creator:** Armando Simon, "Pulp Fiction UFOs: How the Origin of the Idea of UFOs Developed from the Extraterrestrial Spacecraft Depicted in Pulp Magazines," *Skeptic*, Summer 2011, https://www.questia.com/read/1G1-268309705/pulp-fiction-ufos-how-the-origin-of-the-idea-of-ufos. **Paul's oeuvre:** "The Official Frank R. Paul Gallery," Room 1, n.d., *Science Fiction and Fantasy Art by Frank Wu*, http://www.frankwu.com/paul1.html. **accompanying commentary:** Alexander Blade, "Stories of the Stars," *AS* 20, no. 5 (August 1946): 177. **"Let's make a few predictions":** The Observatory, *AS* 21, no. 4 (April 1947): 9. **went to press on March 13:** date given in The Observatory, *AS* 21, no. 6 (June 1947): 6. **Palmer quoted Shaver:** The Observatory, *AS* 21, no. 6: 8. **One of the four Shaver stories:** Richard S. Shaver, "Witch's Daughter," *AS* 21, no. 6: 62–88; quotes from 69, 77. **"A portion . . . has now been proved!":** The Observatory, *AS* 21, no. 10 (October 1947): 6. **shortly before July 4:** date clear from Palmer, The Editor Interrupts, *AS* 21, no. 10: 172. **"flying pie-pans":** The Editor Interrupts, *AS* 21, no. 10: 172. **"underground hideouts of an unknown race":** The Observatory, *AS* 21, no. 10: 6. **Shaver was less enthusiastic:** Richard S. Shaver, "There's Pie in the Sky" (letter to the editor), *AS* 21, no. 10: 178. **beginning its long decline:** Toronto, *War over Lemuria*, 152–72. **first tentative feelers:** Kenneth Arnold and Ray Palmer, *The Coming of the Saucers* (Amherst, WI: Legend Press, 1952), 20–24. **he founded a new magazine, *Fate*:** Nadis, *The Man from Mars*, 115–20. **Gray Barker:** Barker, *They Knew Too Much*, 147–48. **evolved . . . into . . . *Flying Saucers*:** Nadis, *The Man from Mars*, 164–66. **"rock books" . . . "rokfogos":** Toronto, *War over Lemuria*, 218–22, 232–34. ***Footnote 76:* recognized and exhibited as "outsider art":** "Richard Sharpe Shaver," Wikipedia, https://en.wikipedia.org/wiki/Richard_Sharpe_Shaver; Michael Smith, "Drawings and Videos from Storage," April 13–May 12, 2007, Christine Burgin Gallery, https://www.christineburgin.com/exhibitions/. **"He believed in only one God":** Toronto, 235. **Shaver admitted to Eugene Steinberg:** Steinberg, "The Caveat Emptor Interview: Richard S. Shaver," 6. **never had much impact beyond them:** I'm aware of two descriptions of the Shaver Mystery in mainstream publications, both disparaging, both in the context of broader articles on science fiction: William S. Baring-Gould, "Little Superman, What Now?" *Harper's Magazine* 193 (September 1, 1946): 283–88; Winthrop Sergeant, "Through the Interstellar Looking Glass," *Life* 30, no. 21 (May 21, 1951): 127–40. "The Super Race," the cover story of *Blackhawk* comic book no. 103 (August 1956), http://comicbookplus.com/?dlid=14359, is plainly inspired by the Shaver Mystery, perhaps mediated through Barker's *They Knew Too Much About Flying Saucers* (released on May 10, 1956; Barker to Jessup, March 29, 1956, GBC). **The real money was in soft-core porn:** Toronto, *War over Lemuria*, 180–83. **he opened himself to interviewer Steinberg:** "The Caveat Emptor Interview: Ray Palmer," 11–12. **told . . . a UFO conference:** Toronto, *War over Lemuria*, 119. ***Footnote* 77: John Keel:** John Keel, "The Man Who Invented Flying Saucers," *Fortean Times* 41 (Winter 1983): 52–57, http://greyfalcon.us/The%20Man%20Who%20Invented%20Flying%20Saucers.htm. **parroted Keel's designation:** Curtis Peebles, *Watch the Skies! A Chronicle of the Flying Saucer Myth* (Washington, DC: Smithsonian Institution Press, 1994), 3–4; Nadis, *The Man from Mars*, 115–37. Both Peebles and Nadis use the catchy phrase as the title for a section or a chapter. **"black and silent expanse of water":** Richard S. Shaver and Bob McKenna, "Cult of the Witch Queen," *AS* 20, no. 4 (July 1946): 35. **"War has come to a horrible pass":** Ray Palmer, editorial comment on R.L. Tanner, "Stay Out of the Caves!" Report from the Forgotten Past, *AS* 19, no. 4 (December 1945): 169.

CHAPTER 8: ROSWELL, NEW MEXICO

UFO crash at Roswell: The two most valuable book-length studies are Karl T. Pflock, *Roswell: Inconvenient Facts and the Will to Believe* (Amherst, NY: Prometheus Books, 2001); and Kevin D. Randle, *Roswell in the 21st Century: The Evidence as It Exists Today* (Naples, FL: Speaking Volumes, 2016); many excellent articles have appeared in the periodical *International UFO Reporter* (hereafter *IUR*). The only academic monograph devoted to the subject—Benson Saler, Charles A. Ziegler, and Charles B. Moore, *UFO Crash at Roswell: The Genesis of a Modern Myth* (Washington, DC: Smithsonian Institution Press, 1997)—has some useful insights but is handicapped by the authors' patronizing contempt for the UFOlogists, referred to more than once as "true believers." **issued the following announcement:** quoted in Pflock, *Roswell*, 26–27. **He took pictures:** close analysis of the circumstances in Randle, *Roswell in the 21st Century*, 11–23. **actress Demi Moore:** Bruce Handy, "Roswell or Bust: A Town Discovers Manna Crashing from Heaven and Becomes the Capital of America's Alien Nation," *Time*, June 23, 1997, 62. **Stanton Friedman . . . ought to get in touch with Jesse Marcel:** Don Berliner and Stanton T. Friedman, *Crash at Corona: The U.S. Military Retrieval and Cover-Up of a UFO* (New York: Paraview Special Editions, 2004; originally published 1992), 8–11. **Jesse Marcel Jr. . . . awakened one July night:** Pflock, *Roswell*, 26, Marcel's affidavit (dated May 6, 1991) on 268; Robert J. Durant, "C.B. Moore's Mogul Tape," *IUR* 23, no. 2 (Summer 1998): 7–9, 32. **Interviewed . . . for a Roswell daily newspaper and the Associated Press:** "Harassed Rancher Who Located 'Saucer' Sorry He Told About It," Roswell *Daily Record*, July 9, 1947, 1 https://www.reddit.com/r/UFOs/comments/4h7qzv/roswell_daily_record_july_9_1947_harassed_rancher/. The AP story appeared, e.g., in the Las Cruces (NM) *Sun News*, July 10, 1947, 2; I'm grateful to Janice Dunnahoo of the Southeastern New Mexico Historical Society Archives for providing a scan of this article. Quotes in the following paragraphs are from the Roswell *Daily Record*. **what would have induced him . . . indigestible stuff:** Kevin D. Randle, "Bessie Brazel's Story," *IUR* 20, no. 3 (May-June 1995): 3–5, 25; Thomas J. Carey and Donald R. Schmitt, "Flight to Fort Worth: From

Complicity to Cover-up," *IUR* 25, no. 2 (Summer 2000): 30. **In an affidavit forty-six years later:** dated September 22, 1993; in Pflock, *Roswell*, 277–78. Bessie Brazel's reliability as a witness is questioned in Randle, "Bessie Brazel's Story," and defended in a letter published by Pflock in *IUR* 20, no. 5 (Winter 1995). In *Roswell in the 21st Century* (45, 54), Randle seems to accept Pflock's correction. **its indestructibility:** e.g., Jesse Marcel, interviewed in 1979 by William L. Moore and Stanton Friedman, quoted in Charles Berlitz and William L. Moore, *The Roswell Incident* (New York: Grosset & Dunlap, 1980), 66. **On Monday, July 7:** on the date, see Pflock, *Roswell*, 89–92. **"He brought some of the material into the house":** Pflock, 268. **or possibly even without it:** so Marcel told Moore and Friedman in 1979: "I heard he wasn't authorized to do this, and I believe he was severely reprimanded for it" (Berlitz and Moore, *The Roswell Incident*, 68). Haut himself always insisted he acted with Blanchard's approval: Randle, *Roswell in the 21st Century*, 205–28. **"RAAF Captures Flying Saucer" . . . "Empties Roswell Saucer":** Scans of the newspaper articles may be found on the web by doing an image search for "roswell daily record." **Charles Moore . . . had a memory of flowered tape:** Charles B. Moore, "The Early New York University Balloon Flights," in Saler, Ziegler, and Moore, *UFO Crash at Roswell*, 82, 112–13, cited in Pflock, *Roswell*, 161–62. My description of Project Mogul follows those of Charles Moore and Pflock. ***Report of Air Force Research*:** Colonel Richard L. Weaver, *Report of Air Force Research Regarding the "Roswell Incident,"* July 1994, www.nsa.gov/Portals/70/documents/news-features/declassified-documents/ufo/report_af_roswell.pdf, which was released on September 8 and reissued the following year as part of a massive document, Richard L. Weaver and James McAndrew, *The Roswell Report: Fact versus Fiction in the New Mexico Desert* (Washington, DC: Headquarters United States Air Force, 1995), https://apps.dtic.mil/dtic/tr/fulltext/u2/a326148.pdf. ***Footnote 84:* 'Roswell UFO Encounter 1995':** proclamation signed by New Mexico Secretary of State Stephanie Gonzales, on display in Roswell's International UFO Museum. **columnist Molly Ivins:** Molly Ivins, "We're Odd, but Hey, We're 221," Raleigh *News & Observer*, July 4, 1997, from Fort Worth *Star-Telegram*. **its problems:** In addition to those mentioned in the text, engineer Robert A. Galganski has argued in a series of *IUR* articles that a Mogul balloon train could not have produced the quantity of materials discovered by Brazel: Robert Galganski, "The Roswell Debris: A Quantitative Evaluation of the Project Mogul Hypothesis," *IUR* 20, no. 2 (March-April 1995): 3–6, 23–24; Robert Galganski, "An Engineer Looks at the Project Mogul Hypothesis," *IUR* 23, no. 2 (Summer 1998): 3–6, 32; Robert Galganski, "The Roswell Debris Field: Size Doesn't Matter," *IUR* 25, no. 4 (Winter 2000–2001): 14–19, 30. **a contemporary diary entry:** journal of Dr. Albert P. Crary, published as Appendix 17 in the Air Force's 1995 *Roswell Report*, entry for June 4, 1947. Randle's analysis of the diary and its implications (*Roswell in the 21st Century*, 354–71) is convincing. **UFOlogists have pointed out:** e.g., Robert J. Durant, "Project Mogul Still a Flight of Fancy," *IUR* 26, no. 1 (Spring 2001): 17–28. **the recollection of Colonel Blanchard's wife:** Pflock, *Roswell*, 96, quoting William Moore. Cf. Thomas J. Carey, "The Continuing Search for the Roswell Archaeologists: Closing the Circle," *IUR* 19, no. 1 (January-February 1994): 10, which cites a secondhand report of a crashed UFO that "everyone at first thought . . . was a Russian device, but it wasn't." **sometimes called hieroglyphics:** e.g., Jesse Marcel, quoted in Berlitz and Moore, *The Roswell Incident*, 66; Jesse Marcel, Jr., affidavit in Pflock, *Roswell*, 268; Glenn Dennis, affidavit in Pflock, *Roswell*, 254 (quoted below). Cf. Durant, "C.B. Moore's Mogul Tape." **apparently decorative flower patterns:** Moore's statements about the tape are oddly inconsistent: David Halperin, "Roswell and Mogul: The Memories of Charles B. Moore, Part 2," *David Halperin* (blog), May 19, 2017, https://www.davidhalperin.net/roswell-and-mogul-the-memories-of-charles-b-moore-part-2/. **Vern and Jean Maltais . . . told a strange story:** Berliner and Friedman, *Crash at Corona*, 13–14. **reported in his book *The Roswell Incident*:** Berlitz and Moore, *The Roswell Incident*, 53–62. **Harold Baca:** Berliner and Friedman, *Crash at Corona*, 88; Randle, *Roswell in the 21st Century*, 323–24. **No archaeologists . . . can be found:** Thomas J. Carey, "The Search for the Roswell Archaeologists: Casting the Net," *IUR* 18, no. 6 (November-December 1993): 3–8, 23–24; Thomas J. Carey, "The Continuing Search for the Roswell Archaeologists: Closing the Circle," *IUR* 19, no. 1 (January-February 1994): 4–12; cf. Thomas J. Carey, "The Strange Saga of 'Cactus Jack,'" *IUR* 22, no. 1 (Spring 1997): 3–11. Carey's argument that the archaeological team did exist, that its leader was Texas Tech history professor W. Curry Holden, and that Holden and his students did encounter a crashed UFO—not on the Plains of San Agustin but at the "real" impact site thirty miles north-northwest of Roswell—is unconvincing. Kevin Randle, who initially accepted it (*The Truth About the UFO Crash at Roswell* [New York: Avon Books, 1994], 7–8, 131), seems to have had second thoughts, for in Randle, *Roswell in the 21st Century* there's no mention of Holden. **Jim Ragsdale:** Affidavit (dated January 27, 1993) in Pflock, *Roswell*, 272; Pflock's index, s.v. "Ragsdale" and "Truelove"; Kevin D. Randle, "The Truth About the Jim Ragsdale Story," *IUR* 21, no. 3 (Fall 1996): 13–16, 29–30. **Glenn Dennis:** extensively discussed in Pflock, *Roswell*, 127–42; Randle, *Roswell in the 21st Century*, 211–14. The affidavit (August 7, 1991) from which the following quotes are taken is in Pflock, 254–56. **"Dennis had told them":** Randle, *Roswell in the 21st Century*, 141, quoting Thomas J. Carey and Donald R. Schmitt, *Witness to Roswell Revised and Expanded* (Pompton Plains, NJ: New Page Books, 2009), 145. **Dennis's own account:** Leon Jaroff, "Did Aliens Really Land?" *Time*, June 23, 1997, 70. **Stanton Friedman . . . interviewed Dennis in August 1989:** Berliner and Friedman, *Crash at Corona*, 114–20. **Friedman asked Dennis for the name:** reported, not in Friedman's account of the interview, but by Pflock, *Roswell*, 128–34, from which the information in this paragraph is taken. **Gerald Anderson . . . a liar and a hoaxer:** Randle, *Roswell in the 21st Century*, 325–51. ***Footnote 89:* Fanton . . . served as Dennis's inspiration:** McAndrew, *Roswell Report*, 82–83; followed by Pflock, *Roswell*, 138–39. **"Dr. Buskirk":** Randle, 338–41. **Anderson told Kevin Randle in February 1990:** Randle, 326–27. **by September 1990:** interviewed by Friedman, see Berliner and Friedman, *Crash at Corona*, 105–8. **by March 1991:** interviewed by Bob Oeschler, see Randle, *Roswell in the 21st Century*, 334–35. **Dennis's story was featured:** pointed out by Pflock, *Roswell*, 119. Charles A. Ziegler, in Saler, Ziegler, and Moore, *UFO Crash at Roswell*, 45–46, suggests, less plausibly, that the influence went the other way. **as one interpreter has pointed out:** Ziegler, 45–46. **Judas Iscariot . . . Jews have been stereotyped:** Ruth Mellinkoff, "Judas' Red

Hair and the Jews," *Journal of Jewish Art* 9 (1982): 31–46. **children's taunt song:** Richard Wright, *Black Boy (American Hunger): A Record of Childhood and Youth* (New York: HarperCollins, 1998; originally published 1945), 61 (chapter 2). **demon-god Set or Seth:** Plutarch, *Isis and Osiris*, especially chs. 22 (359E), 30 (362E), 31 (363A), 33 (364A-B), 44 (368F), 55 (373D), with the commentary of J. Gwyn Griffiths, *Plutarch's De Iside et Osiride* (Cambridge, UK: University of Wales Press, 1970); H. te Velde, *Seth, God of Confusion: A Study of His Role in Egyptian Mythology and Religion* (Leiden: E.J. Brill, 1977); te Velde, "Seth," in Donald B. Redford, *The Ancient Gods Speak: A Guide to Egyptian Religion* (New York: Oxford University Press, 2002), 331–34; Gay Robins, "Color Symbolism," in Redford, 57–61; J. Hill, "Set," Ancient Egypt Online, 2008, https://www.ancientegyptonline.co.uk/set.html. **red-haired or ruddy-skinned:** Frank Cole Babbitt picks the former option in his translation of *Isis and Osiris* 30 (362E) (*Plutarch's Moralia V*, Loeb Classical Library [Cambridge, MA: Harvard University Press, and London: William Heinemann, 1936]). Griffiths chooses the latter. **as a medieval devil is black:** Jeffrey Burton Russell, *Lucifer: The Devil in the Middle Ages* (Ithaca, NY: Cornell University Press, 1984), 68–69. **he "made all the threats":** James McAndrew, *The Roswell Report: Case Closed* (Washington, DC: Headquarters, United States Air Force, 1997), 194, quoting the transcript of an interview used for the video *Recollections of Roswell: Part 2* (Washington, DC: Fund for UFO Research, 1993). McAndrew gives no date for the interview; it seems to represent an intermediate stage between the Friedman interview of September 1990 and the Oeschler interview of March 1991. **"All of a sudden":** McAndrew, *Roswell Report*, 191. **Anderson told a reporter:** Mike O'Brien, "Fact or Fantasy?" Springfield (MO) *News-Leader*, December 9, 1990, 5–7, quoted in Randle, *Roswell in the 21st Century*, 335. ***The Roswell Report: Case Closed*:** McAndrew, *Roswell Report: Case Closed*. Ignored for the most part by his fellow skeptics, mocked by the crashed-spaceship advocates, McAndrew is given his due by Pflock, *Roswell*, 140: "on key issue after key issue, his evidence and analysis are compellingly persuasive." **"dummies" . . . "plastic dolls":** McAndrew, *Roswell Report*, 56, 60, 191, 218. **an eerie chill:** McAndrew, 64, 190. **I posted to my blog:** David Halperin, "UFO Landing in Glassboro, NJ, Fifty Years Ago," *David Halperin* (blog), September 12, 2014, https://www.davidhalperin.net/ufo-landing-in-glassboro-nj-fifty-years-ago/ (12 September 2014); discussion and analysis at David Halperin, "Glassboro to Roswell: The Telescoping of Memory," *David Halperin* (blog), April 7, 2017, https://www.davidhalperin.net/glassboro-to-roswell-the-telescoping-of-memory/. The woman's comment on my blog post was lost during an updating of my website; I have her subsequent emails on file. **McAndrew tells the story:** McAndrew, *Roswell Report*, 94–99; followed by Pflock, *Roswell*, 140–41. ***Footnote 92:*** **Aldeburgh flying platform:** "The Aldeburgh Platform," Part 1, n.d., http://aldeburghplatform.blogspot.com/ (John Harney's website); Chris Aubeck and Martin Shough, *Return to Magonia: Investigating UFOs in History* (San Antonio and Charlottesville: Anomalist Books, 2015), 299–314. The December 1915 issue of the American magazine *The Electrical Experimenter* featured flying platforms, imaginatively situated on Mars, on its cover: http://www.magazineart.org/main.php/v/technical/electricalexperimenter/ElectricalExperimenter1915-12.jpg.html. Did this or some similar picture influence the woman's recollections? ***Footnote 93:***

Norio Hayakawa . . . Robert Lazar's stories: Annie Jacobsen, *Area 51: An Uncensored History of America's Top Secret Military Base* (New York: Little, Brown, 2011), 13–15. **Kodachrome slides:** David Halperin, "The Roswell Slides and Neil DeGrasse Tyson," *David Halperin* (blog), June 18, 2015, https://www.davidhalperin.net/the-roswell-slides-and-neil-degrasse-tyson/. **Charles Ziegler:** in Saler, Ziegler, and Moore, *UFO Crash at Roswell*, 71–72. **"an essential item . . . is impounded or hoarded":** Saler, Ziegler, and Moore, 51, cf. 67. **Near Eastern vegetation deities:** Thorkild Jacobsen, *The Treasures of Darkness: A History of Mesopotamian Religion* (New Haven: Yale University Press, 1976), 25–73. **Norse gods:** Carolynne Larrington, *The Norse Myths: A Guide to the Gods and Heroes* (London: Thames & Hudson, 2017), 179–200. **the Greek Icarus:** following Ovid, *Metamorphoses*, Book 8, lines 183–235, trans. A.S. Kline (2000), http://ovid.lib.virginia.edu/trans/Metamorph8.htm#482327661. **Canaanite deity:** David J. Halperin, "Ascension or Invasion: Implications of the Heavenly Journey in Ancient Judaism," *Religion* 18 (1988): 47–49, and the sources cited there. **vibrant gaiety of the "Roswell UFO Festival":** Warmly and beautifully depicted by National Geographic Explorer Asher Jay in a 2017 Airbnb video, https://youtu.be/JVDAAsqdySw. **Mexican Day of the Dead festivities:** Stanley Brandes, *Skulls to the Living, Bread to the Dead: The Day of the Dead in Mexico and Beyond* (Malden, MA: Blackwell, 2006). **"the seminal event" . . . World UFO day (July 2):** "World UFO Day," Days of the Year, https://www.daysoftheyear.com/days/ufo-day/. The website worldufoday.com, which would have provided first-hand information on the event, seems no longer to be functional; cf. "World UFO Day," Wikipedia, last edited June 6, 2018, https://en.wikipedia.org/wiki/World_UFO_Day, and the sources cited there. ***Footnote 96:*** **Proposed . . . as the date of the crash:** Pflock, *Roswell*, 22–23; Kevin D. Randle and Donald R. Schmitt, *UFO Crash at Roswell* (New York: Avon Books, 1991), 199 (versus the same authors' timeline in their 1994 *Truth About the UFO Crash at Roswell*, where the date is shifted to July 4); Kevin Randle and Donald Schmitt, "When and Where Did the Roswell Object Crash?" *IUR* 19, no. 1 (January-February 1994): 13–16. **a modern reworking of an old Epicurean slogan:** quoted on the web, e.g., at "Epicurus>Quotes>Quotable Quotes," Goodreads, https://www.goodreads.com/quotes/662599-why-should-i-fear-death-if-i-am-then-death; based on Epicurus's letter to Menoeceus in R.D. Hicks, *Stoic and Epicurean* (New York: Charles Scribner's Sons, 1910), 169, http://www.epicurus.net/en/menoeceus.html). **The 509th Bomb Group:** "509th Composite Group," Atomic Heritage Foundations, June 4, 2014, https://www.atomicheritage.org/history/509th-composite-group.

EPILOGUE: JOHN LENNON IN MAGONIA

"On the 23rd Aug. 1974" . . . sketch Lennon did at about the same time: Alejandro Rojas, "John Lennon's UFO Doodle Auctioned Off," Open Minds, March 25, 2014, http://www.openminds.tv/john-lennons-ufo-doodle-auctioned/26659 (March 25, 2014); Lee Speigel, "John Lennon's UFO-Inspired Art Fetches Big Bucks," *Huffington Post*, March 29, 2014, https://www.huffingtonpost.com/entry/john-lennon-1974-ufo-drawing-auction_n_5038538.html; Jared Sauceda, "John Lennon Album Sleeve Art Recalls Alleged 1974 UFO Sighting," Inquistr, April 21, 2014, https://www.inquisitr.

com/1221048/john-lennon-album-sleeve-art-recalls-alleged-1974-ufo-sighting/. **"Nobody Told Me":** John Lennon, "Nobody Told Me," *Milk and Honey*, 1984, John Lennon Lyrics, AZ Lyrics, https://www.azlyrics.com/lyrics/johnlennon/nobodytoldme.html. **Lennon . . . was living with Pang:** Bill Harry, *The John Lennon Encyclopedia* (London: Virgin Books, 2001), s.v. "Pang, May," 698–701. **as she told an interviewer:** Larry Warren, "There's UFOs Over New York and John Lennon Wasn't Too Surprised or Why I Hate December," *The Researcher*, the magazine of the Merseyside Anomalies Research Association (MARA), quoted in David Halperin, "John Lennon, May Pang, and the UFO (1)—Their Story," *David Halperin* (blog), February 11, 2016, https://www.davidhalperin.net/john-lennon-may-pang-and-the-ufo-1–their-story/. **"I drop the clothes":** Halperin, "John Lennon, May Pang." (I took the quote from a post on the now-defunct Examiner.com website: www.examiner.com/article/john-lennon-said-there-s-ufo-s-over-new-york-remembering-his-ufo-experience-on-august-23-1974.) **"I was standing, naked":** quoted in Ray Coleman, *Lennon* (New York: McGraw Hill, 1985), 507–8. Cf. the 1997 interview with May Pang, "The John Lennon UFO Encounter New York 1974 August 23rd," at https://youtu.be/Jdw4cibPh-U, 2' 5". **hit it with a brick:** radio interview quoted in Sauceda, "John Lennon Album Sleeve Art." **The photos turned out blank:** Warren, "There's UFOs Over New York." **"imagine" an ideal world:** John Lennon, "Imagine," *Imagine*, 1971, John Lennon Lyrics, AZ Lyrics, https://www.azlyrics.com/lyrics/johnlennon/imagine.html. **Lennon has denied he was on any drug:** Coleman, *Lennon*, 507–8. **Unitarian minister Forrest Church:** as quoted in Joe Holley, "F. Forrester Church, 61; Influential N.Y. Unitarian Minister," *Washington Post*, September 29, 2009, http://www.washingtonpost.com/wp-dyn/content/article/2009/09/28/AR2009092803831.html. **Freud once wrote:** *The Interpretation of Dreams*, trans. and ed. James Strachey (New York: Avon Books, 1965), 564.

INDEX

Page numbers in italics indicate illustrations.

www.ingramcontent.com/pod-product-compliance
Ingram Content Group UK Ltd.
Pitfield, Milton Keynes, MK11 3LW, UK
UKHW042055240225
455503UK00005B/102/J

9 781503 607088